The History and Theory of Fetishism

Marx, Engels, and Marxisms

The collapse of ("communism") as a geopolitical force has liberated Marx, Engels, and all the variants of Marxism from ideologically motivated and intellectually stultifying presumptions. Running contrary to nineteenth and twentieth century practices of conflation and simplification, this innovative series revitalizes major figures and intellectual traditions, and its authors and editors present recent scholarly discoveries in imaginative ways, challenging twenty first century readers with unfamiliar perspectives.

Terrell Carver and Marcello Musto, Series Editors

A Political History of the Editions of Marx and Engels's "German ideology Manuscripts"
Terrell Carver and Daniel Blank

Marx and Engels's "German ideology" Manuscripts: Presentation and Analysis of the "Feuerbach chapter"
Terrell Carver and Daniel Blank

The History and Theory of Fetishism
AlfonsoM aurizioI acono

The History and Theory of Fetishism

Alfonso Maurizio Iacono

Translated by
Viktoria Tchernichova and Monica Boria,
with the collaboration of
Elizabeth MacDonald

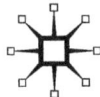

THE HISTORY AND THEORY OF FETISHISM
Copyright © Alfonso Maurizio Iacono 2016

All rights reserved. No reproduction, copy or transmission of this publication may be made without written permission. No portion of this publication may be reproduced, copied or transmitted save with written permission. In accordance with the provisions of the Copyright, Designs and Patents Act 1988, or under the terms of any licence permitting limited copying issued by the Copyright Licensing Agency, Saffron House, 6-10 Kirby Street, London EC1N 8TS.

Any person who does any unauthorized act in relation to this publication may be liable to criminal prosecution and civil claims for damages.

First published 2016 by
PALGRAVE MACMILLAN

The author has asserted their right to be identified as the author of this work in accordance with the Copyright, Designs and Patents Act 1988.

Palgrave Macmillan in the UK is an imprint of Macmillan Publishers Limited, registered in England, company number 785998, of Houndmills, Basingstoke, Hampshire, RG21 6XS.

Palgrave Macmillan in the US is a division of Nature America, Inc., One New York Plaza, Suite 4500, New York, NY 10004-1562.

Palgrave Macmillan is the global academic imprint of the above companies and has companies and representatives throughout the world.

Hardback ISBN: 978-1-137-54114-7
E-PUB ISBN: 978-1-137-54116-1
E-PDF ISBN: 978-1-137-54115-4
DOI: 10.1057/9781137541154

Distribution in the UK, Europe and the rest of the world is by Palgrave Macmillan®, a division of Macmillan Publishers Limited, registered in England, company number 785998, of Houndmills, Basingstoke, Hampshire RG21 6XS.

Library of Congress Cataloging-in-Publication Data

Iacono, Alfonso M., 1949–
    Theories of fetishism : the philosophical and historical problem of an "immense misunderstanding" / Alfonso Maurizio Iacono.
      pages cm
    Includes bibliographical references and index.

    ISBN 978-1-137-54114-7

      1. Fetishism—History. 2. Fetishism—Philosophy. I. Title.

GN472.I24 2015
202'.109—dc23   2015010790

A catalogue record for the book is available from the British Library.

"'My dear child, bless your fetishes, worship them as long as you live, and they will ensure that you live happily; you have the honor to be a slave to our lords the whites, and thereby you have made your father and your mother wealthy'. Alas! I don't know if I made them wealthy, but they certainly didn't make me happy."
Voltaire, Candide, Chapter XIX

Contents

Acknowledgments		ix
Introduction		1
One	The Theoretical and Historical Assumptions Underpinning the Concept of Fetishism	11
Two	Charles de Brosses's Theory of Fetishism	55
Three	The Concept of Fetishism as a Theoretical and Historical Problem	75
Four	Marx's Theory of Fetishism	101
Five	History, Nature, and System: Marx's Anthropological Conception	131
Notes		151
Bibliography		183
Index		197

Acknowledgments

I would like to thank Marcello Musto, Viktoria Tchernichova, Giacomo Brucciani, Gianni Paoletti and Luca Mori for their help and belief in the project. I owe a debt of gratitude to Carla Masolino for her encouragement, assistance and support. I would also like to thank my daughters Arianna and Elena Iacono and my son Giorgio Iacono for always being there for me.

Introduction

0. What import can the presentation of research carried out into fetishism have? To answer this question we must stop and look around us. We are literally surrounded by fetishes, that is to say, by objects endowed with qualities pertaining to human relationships. Despite their familiar appearance, it is precisely by virtue of these qualities that they take on a different aura. In this process, lifeless things come to life and, at the same time, they beguile and fascinate people. Any discussion of these mechanisms necessitates a reflection on cognitive processes, focusing attention not only on the relations between the self and others or the self and the world, but also on the relation of the self with the self. It is also a means to keep one's critical awareness alive when entering places that are unrelated to the real world and are outside of time: those Platonic caves where fiction loses its frame and where the boundaries between the real and virtual world collide. Shopping centers—places where the consumer is free to look at fetish commodities without necessarily having to buy them—are an example of this.

The topic of religious, socioeconomic, and psychoanalytical fetishism concerns the concept of objects that stand in the place of a god, things that stand in the place of men, parts that stand in the place of the whole: that is to say, objects whose origin and sense of substitution have been lost or concealed. Standing in the place of someone else is a feature of representative and symbolical forms. It is extremely important, from an educational point of view, to be critically aware of these forms, because they help in the exploration of cognitive distance. The observer has to be aware that his position is not an easy one, since he tends to veer between immersing himself in the subject and wandering too far away from it.

This is not a question of recovering the pureness of the object as opposed to its alleged representative or symbolic distortion. Neither is it a question of asserting the truth of the thing as opposed to its appearance. The issue lies in managing to critically grasp the gap that inevitably opens up as soon as representation takes the place of the object being represented. Every trace of the object is lost the moment this substitution is concealed or forgotten. The gap becomes invisible. This, precisely, is the nucleus that generated the multifaceted notion of *fetishism* in eighteenth-century philosophical discourse.

1. The aim of this book is to provide readers with the historical context necessary for understanding the concept of "fetishism" and, by following the historical development of the concept, to offer readers an overview of the ideologies, the prejudices and the critical sense that shaped the Western observer's view of otherness and of his own world. On the one hand, the book examines the moment when the Western observer turned his colonizing and evangelizing gaze to continents such as Africa and America, while, on the other, it discusses the observer's attempt to see his own world with different eyes and from a critical perspective.

What is intriguing about the history of the concept of fetishism and indeed the word itself is that its semantic metamorphosis provides us with historical and epistemological evidence of the ways in which the Western observer approached the problem of universality and attempted to integrate the Other. By means of a gradual mutation in his position, he has come to observe himself through the Other and—insofar as he has managed to become Other—formed an ability to observe himself from a critical perspective.

It is within this process of mutation that the concept of fetishism has developed. Initially related to the conjectural history of religion, the notion was later extended to include the issue of the relation between man and commodities. In the end, it grew into the chief theoretical protagonist of psychoanalysis: as a matter of fact, the notion of fetishism is already present in Freud's early writings and keeps recurring throughout his works, up until his last unfinished writing on the split of the Self.

2. The history of the notion of fetishism can be divided into two parts. The first concerns the history of the life and death of a concept that was initially regarded as a scientific notion bound to a specific and autonomous form of religious belief. In this sense it is the history of a colonial *misunderstanding*, which lasted approximately from 1760 to the turn of the twentieth century and transformed the Western observer's beliefs and prejudices into a *scientific* category. The second part mirrors the first and is closely related to it. Soon enough, fetishes and fetishism were perceived as concepts that that could facilitate the Western observer's critical self-reflection. Indeed, not only was he in a position to observe—from the outside—the world of *others, the primitives and savages*, but, despite remaining within the Western world, he also managed to simulate an outside gaze and, by assuming a different perspective, observe his own world as the *others* might have.

This issue implies a shift of the point of view. Let us consider an eloquent example drawn from Voltaire's *Candide*. While approaching the city of Suriname, Candide and Pangloss run into a Negro slave dressed in rags and missing both a hand and a leg:

"My God!" said Candide in Dutch, "what are you doing lying here, my friend, in this dreadful state?"

"I'm waiting for my master, Mr Van der Hartbargin, the well-known trader," replied the Negro.

"And is it Mr Van der Hartbargin," said Candide, "who has treated you like this?"

"Yes, sir," said the Negro, "it is the custom. We are given one pair of short denim breeches twice a year, and that's all we have to wear. When we're working at the sugar mill and catch our finger in the grinding-wheel, they cut off our hand. When we try to run away, they cut off a leg. I have been in both these situations. This is the price you pay for the sugar you eat in Europe. However, when my mother sold me for ten Patagonian crowns on the coast of Guinea, she said to me: 'My dear child, bless our fetishes, worship them always, they will bring you a happy life. You have the honour of being a slave to our lords and Masters the Whites and, by so being, you are making your father's and mother's fortune'. Alas! I don't know if I made their fortune, but they didn't make mine. Dogs, monkeys, parrots, they're all a thousand times less wretched than we are. The Dutch fetishes who converted me tell me every Sunday that we are all the sons of Adam, Whites and Blacks alike. I'm no genealogist, but if these preachers are right, we are all cousins born of first-cousins. Well, you will grant me that you can't treat a relative much worse than this."[1]

Voltaire's irony enables us to throw light upon what may indeed be called a shift in the point of view. Among the fetishes that were passed on to him by his parents, the slave from Suriname—a victim of colonialism who is exploited by his white master—also finds what he calls "Dutch fetishes." He finds himself in the midst of a bizarre symbolical and epistemological passage through which Suriname's "fetishes" set off for Holland and the West. Essentially, this amounts almost to a homeward journey for the fetishes: a journey that, even if not exactly a return to their nation of origin, is at least a return to the continent to which they owe their name. For, in point of fact, the word "fetish" was coined by the Portuguese, who are as European as the Dutch, and they used it to refer to the African cult objects they noticed along the West coast of Africa. This word, in turn, comes from the Latin "facticius," meaning artificial. As a noun, the word has also assumed the meaning of "witchcraft" and sorcery. Attributed to the religious practices of African peoples, the term "fetish" constitutes a symbol of colonial power. In referring to the religious practices of *others*, this word—which would soon find an equivalent in French, German, English, Italian, Spanish, and Dutch—acquired the power to represent "reality." The Western point of view becomes, by means of the Western word, not only the name of the thing, but the thing itself. Paradoxically, the word "fetish" became the expression of the process that Marx and Freud would subsequently individuate—although interpreting different phenomena—in the symbolic transmutation of the *thing*, the moment in which the thing takes the place of human and social relationships.

3. It is precisely irony that can help us to shift the point of view and lead us away from the fetishization of the fetish.

What does it mean to shift the point of view? When I say, for instance, "the Western point of view," I assume a shift in perspective. I have already placed myself outside (obviously, in a simulated way) the boundaries of this point of view and have already managed to imagine at least one non-Western point of view. In a way, this epistemological situation reminds us of the issue raised by Velázquez in *Las Meninas*, where he draws himself while drawing, thus simulating a point of view (outside the picture) which is external and which differs from the point of view represented by the place where he is in fact drawing. This capacity to disengage and detach enables the observer to observe his own point of view from the outside. It can assume a number of different forms that, in turn, are intertwined with the ways in which the observer handles his epistemological and philosophical relationships concerning the idea of universality. Nevertheless, one of these ways is quite peculiar, since it plays its game in a subtly ambiguous but fascinating manner: it places the observer at the edge of the point of view and invites him to go beyond it. I am referring to the brilliant use to which the philosophers of the Enlightenment frequently put the trope of *irony*. One need only mention Montesquieu's *Persian Letters* or Diderot's *Jacque the Fatalist*. Undoubtedly, Voltaire's *Candide* is one of the best-known and most accomplished examples where, as we have already seen, the mention of the "Dutch fetishes" contributes to foregrounding the ironic effect generated by the shift in perspective: the Negro slave from Suriname designates as "fetishes" cult objects belonging to the Christian religion, whose principles contradict the colonial practice of slavery.

Let us examine this more in detail. As far as this ironic writing is concerned, the ironic feature that concerns us most is precisely that centered on the fetishes. In the passage quoted above, this European word is pronounced by the Negro slave from Suriname who, finding himself caught between two religions—the religion of his fathers and that of his masters—designates as "fetishes" both the cult objects belonging to his country of origin and the cult objects belonging to the country of origin of his master, Mr. Van der Hartbargin. The act of designating Christian cult objects and Christian religious practices as "fetishes" represents a shift in perspective, which in turn is represented by another observer. It is not so much a shift as an inversion of the parts. The place previously held by the Western observer for looking upon savages' cult objects and calling them "fetishes" is now occupied by the Surinamese observer—enslaved by the whites—who looks at Christian cult objects, uses them in his practices, and calls them "fetishes." The parts are thus inverted and the point of view shifts: a Western experience—Christian religion—is seen from the outside: it is seen by an observer whose point of view is determined and delimited by his religious faith. The contradiction emerges precisely through this shift/inversion: "Dutch fetishes" preach brotherhood and equality, and yet the Negro from Suriname—who has been converted to these new fetishes—is enslaved and exploited.

4. Throughout these passages and semantic transmutations, the concept of *fetishism* has often, and quite problematically, been intertwined with the implicit notion of substitution. The battle that was fought, both individually and collectively, by David Hume and Charles de Brosses around the middle of the eighteenth century consisted in the attempt to interpret the origin of religion from an anthropological viewpoint. In this sense, it was a battle against the universalism of revealed religion, one of whose corollaries was the idea of degeneration, of the permanent deterioration of peoples devoted to idolatry. Idolatry was held to be the expression of a bad substitution, a replacement of the creator with the creature, of the original with the copy. As long as the copy represents the original, there will always be difference in similarity, as Giovanni Damasceno argued. But when the difference disappears, then one comes up against a case of bad substitution: the golden calf that replaces the one true and invisible God. Be that as it may, substitution nevertheless implies both the presence of the original and the copy that represents it.

However, the whole anthropological and psychological problem arises from an idea delineated by Hume in his *Treatise of Human Nature*: "In all cases we transfer our experience to instances, of which we have no experience, either *expressly* or *tacitly*, either *directly* or *indirectly*."[2] In *The Natural History of Religion* he makes an observation which, in a sense, constitutes a complement to what he had already written in the *Treatise*: Hume argues: "There is an universal tendency amongst mankind to conceive all beings like themselves, and to transfer to every object those qualities with which they are familiarly acquainted, and of which they are intimately conscious."[3] As in a *mise en abyme*, or in a painting within a painting, these words would be quoted by Edward Burnet Tylor and, through him, by Sigmund Freud,[4] down to the art historian David Freedberg.[5]

We can agree with the fact that people tend to transfer to objects the qualities they are more familiar with. Today we would say that people tend to project themselves onto objects and onto other human beings. But how does this transposition occur? What exactly happens when we assimilate into our experience cases and events we have no experience of?

The extraneousness, the irregularity, the unfamiliarity of objects, and events give rise to uncertainty, doubt, fear, curiosity, wonder, awe. Fear and awe, in particular, mark the boundary between the regular order in which human beings are immersed and the irregular phenomena that give rise to their questions on the world they live in.[6] The relationship between the idea of knowledge and emotions such as fear and awe has profoundly marked Western philosophy both in ancient times, through Democritus, Plato, and Aristotle, and in the modern world, through Hobbes, Spinoza, Vico, Hume, and Adam Smith. This very same nucleus would lead to the complex and tortuous elaboration of the Freudian notion of the Uncanny (*Das Unheimlich*).

When we speak about substitution, we obviously assume that something has been substituted by something else. Now, when this something else is seen as an improper substitution, as a bad substitution, then it directly follows that what has been substituted possesses—as far as its task and its role are concerned—greater ontological value. In this framework idolatry may therefore be seen as a bad substitution of monotheistic truth, which in turn should logically precede idolatry and polytheism: an assumption that consequently generates an ad hoc type of history capable of confirming this *truth*. The theoretical assumption surreptitiously seeks for confirmation in the hypothetical historical process and acquires a tangible form: starting from an originary monotheism one degenerates into polytheism and idolatry. Precisely for this reason, the transposition of specifically human characteristics into things serves the function of substitution. But the objects of substitution have changed: the characteristics of human beings mirror themselves in nature's phenomena and substitute themselves for the real causes that produced these phenomena. Indeed the process of their divinization brings forth, while at the same time concealing, this substitution. Therefore, the idea of substitution pertains to the observer and—as Wittgenstein would say—to his formal connections; not to the people that are observed.[7] The process of looking into the truth and conscience of these people is always influenced by the way one structures and carries out the observation, as well as by the way one introduces the observation into their world. Hume does this by adopting the criterion of assimilation to his own cultural world—a criterion that acknowledges the *others* and their diversity through the prism of time and progress.

5. Like many anthropological theories and ethnographical conceptions, eighteenth- and nineteenth-century theories of fetishism throw much more light upon Europe's cultural and colonial universe than that of African, Asian, and American peoples. The development of the concept of fetishism is characterized by a change in the positioning of the phenomenon: it is not elsewhere anymore; it lies, instead, within the Western system and its culture, within the world of commodities, within the world of the psyche, within places where it is strictly and directly intertwined with the problem of substitution.

When Marx spoke about *commodity fetishism*—a notion that would profoundly influence, among others, György Lukács, Walter Benjamin, Theodor Wiesengrund Adorno, and subsequently Baudrillard, and which would form the basis of Guy Debord's theory—he was referring precisely to a process of *substitution* according to which commodities are endowed with qualities deriving from human relations.[8] In the era of so-called globalization, this process of *substitution* has become so pronounced that it has assumed the perturbing and seductive features of a sublime omnipotence. Even if we stay within the confines of psychoanalysis, the notion of *substitution* remains of central importance when addressing the topic of *fetishism* from Freud to Lacan.[9] But there are further implications. Without the concept of *substitution*, it even becomes difficult to understand the meaning of phenomena such as the prohibition of incest or the process of transference that takes place when children feel anger toward Snow White's stepmother rather than toward their own mother.[10]

We live by substitutes. We create them. We build substitutes that do not substitute, because their *standing in place of something else* very often is not an act of replacement, but the production of a new world. Religions with only one invisible god fear substitutes because they lead to idolatry and fetishism. Conversely, societies where commodities are mass produced venerate the unique object—which is separated from its aim and exhibited in a museum—and view it as a fetish. Indeed, it is impossible to provide a substitute—unless improperly—for what is single and *unique* (a god, an object). The word *fetish* comes from "factitius," which means man-made, but it also resembles "fictitius," not genuine, false. All that is artificial, that is to say, all that is made deliberately, runs the risk of assuming the color of artifice, the features of deceit, the shadow of falseness. And yet, nothing of what is human can be held to be devoid of the artificial. Leopardi, Nietzsche, and Pirandello searched for the truth with the acute and bitter awareness of living in a world of illusion, whereas Shakespeare, Coleridge, and Baudelaire walked into this world and invited their audience and their readers to do same, so as to transform their critical awareness of a truth that frees one from deceit into the explicit game of substitution which contains in itself the truth of illusion. Does not art derive precisely from this game of illusion that assumes the contours of truth? And does not this game of illusion (a game that often turns into deceit, especially nowadays, in the era of well-defined reproduction) arise in turn from the way we cognitively structure the world, that is, the way we create presences so as to provide a substitute for what is absent? Maybe the point lies in the contradiction inherent in that game of mirrors which is the drama of *mimesis*: precisely when it instills a desire for resemblance, it makes us discover the sense of difference and, along with this, the autonomy Kant identified with enlightenment and thinking on one's own—an autonomy that can be truly achieved only in acknowledging the fact that we depend upon others and upon our relations with others.

6. The story of the concept of fetishism is the story of a misunderstanding. And misunderstandings are never innocent. Even less so was the one that arose from colonialism and that ascribed to the *savages* with a *primitive* mind the adoration of fetishes. What is more, it ascribed to them a religion marked by fetishism, which is assumed to mark the first stage in the evolution of religious belief and its social organization and representation.[11] Compared to Charles de Brosses and the philosophical and anthropological thought of the nineteenth century, and despite starting from different assumptions, Marx and Freud generated an epistemological shift by placing the observer's viewpoint within the context of observation. Nevertheless, this shift does not offer a return to the observer's lost innocence. The act of simulating an external perspective—when the observer is situated within the context of observation—is quite different from the pursuit of a "neutral" viewpoint. Directing the Western gaze away from the Other and toward oneself as an instance of Other permeates a substantial part of twentieth-century reflection on fetishism. However, instead of putting everything back in its right place after the initial misunderstanding had been cleared up, this process complicated things even further.

Many contemporary philosophers, historians, psychoanalysts, art historians, sociologists, and psychologists have employed the notion of *fetish* or *fetishism*, sometimes drawing on de Brosses, sometimes on Marx and other times on Freud. Still, one of the most substantial contributions to the history of this concept has been made by William Pietz,[12] who recently declared: "The continuous changes in the use of this word, the innumerable transmutations of its meaning, represent the most fascinating chapter in the history of theory; a history that keeps unfolding and whose semantics are constantly enriched. Ultimately, this is what happens to every fetish worthy of the name."[13]

In his work on fetishism Bruno Latour[14] argues that Marx and Freud are still entrenched behind the image of a social science which—in an illusory and deceptive way—claims to free everyone, not only Westerners, from the nebulosity of beliefs as such.[15] I am not sure about the extent to which Marx and Freud were under any illusions about the ways of the world. Undeniably, the epistemological shift they generated has stimulated many reflections that go beyond their personal beliefs and scientific ideologies. Whatever meaning we attach to *being* and whatever meaning we attach to *conscience*, it still remains impossible to judge a man on the basis of his level of self-awareness. Or at least, not exclusively so.

Chapter One
The Theoretical and Historical Assumptions Underpinning the Concept of Fetishism

From "Fetish" to "Fetishism"

The word "fetish" derives from the Portuguese "feitiço" and, since it refers to cult objects of the so-called savage peoples, it may already be found in sixteenth-century accounts of the Portuguese voyages to West Africa.[1] This word, in turn, comes from the Latin "facticius," meaning artificial. As a noun, the word has also assumed the meaning of "witchcraft" and sorcery.[2] Hence, it is a word with which Europeans originally indicated the indigenous cults of Guinea.

The notion of "fetishism" emerged as a key concept for a theory of primitive religion only in 1760, when Charles de Brosses anonymously published his *Du Culte des Dieux fétiches*.[3]

Throughout the intervening period a parallel was progressively being drawn between the notion of the fetish, a phenomenon pertaining to African religious behavior, in particular to the inhabitants of Guinea, and "primitive" religious practices in other parts of the world. At the same time, the religions of the "savages" were also being compared to the religions of ancient civilizations.

The theoretical generalization drawn by de Brosses—who was the first to systematically use the concept of fetishism to define what he considered to be humanity's primordial cult, practiced both by the so-called savage peoples and by the ancient Egyptians—can be seen as the large-scale outcome of theoretical and conceptual elaborations which progressively gained ground between the end of the seventeenth and the first half of the eighteenth century by means of the voyage accounts of travelers who had visited non-Western countries.

de Brosses's achievement therefore represents a final phase, even before becoming a starting point for the success of the concept of fetishism in the ethnographic field. When de Brosses wrote the book, he did nothing more than integrate two elements and place them within the concept of fetishism: on the one hand, he took into consideration the theoretical results of the comparative method which, owing to the contribution of many authors, was being forged and enriched by the idea that it was possible to draw a parallel between the religions, customs, and ways of life of the ancients and the savages; on the other, he adopted the methods used for reconstructing the origins and progress of human societies which, simultaneously and parallel to de Brosses's reflections, were building up to the much debated concept of "civilization."[4]

The Fetish and the Rise of the Comparative Method of Inquiry

When de Brosses's book appeared in 1760, the term "fetish" had already been circulating for some time, not only for designating West African religious practices, but also as a *comparative* point of reference for the investigations and conjectures concerning the religions of primitive people and those of "savages" living in different parts of the world.

For instance, in 1691 the Dutchman Balthazar Bekker published a book entitled *De Betooverte Weereld*, in which it is possible to trace a comparative analysis between ancient paganism and primitive religious practices. The book was soon translated into French and gained a wide circulation.[5] It offers wide-ranging comparisons and in-depth analyses of all ancient and "savage" peoples. Having introduced Guinea's "Fetisso" to this context, Bekker did not however extend the concept to all analyzed peoples, as de Brosses would do later, but drew a comparison between Guinea's practices and those pertaining to other "savage" African and American peoples in order to examine the traits they had in common.

Nonetheless, it is worth quoting his project of inquiry at length, because it immediately allows us to individuate the framework within which his comparative method was developing.

> In the First Book I run all over the World, to find whence this Opinion has its Original. And for this purpose I have omitted neither time nor place. I observe that the subject ought to be examined in two Respects; in respect of the Devil, to find what is his Knowledge and Power; and in respect of Men, to see what they learn and effect by his means. But because these things are preternatural, or are so thought to be, and that by consequence they are known only to God, I have judg'd it necessary, to know what are the Opinions of Men concerning the Divinity, and Spirits in general, either good or bad, and of human Souls separated from their Bodies by death, which are also Spirits: I make a search of all these things, First, in the Books of the Ancients, and afterwards in the Moderns of all Religions, and amongst all Nations, distinguishing them into *Pagans, Jews, Mahometans* and *Christians*, in reference to the present state of the World.[6]

The overview he gives of the ancient pagan and modern religions of Europe, Asia, Africa, and America allows Bekker to come to the conclusion that all these religions share the notion of an omnipotent superior divinity, which is, however, associated with a series of inferior gods, "that the Greeks have often called them Demons, and likewise Gods, as most of the Pagans do at this day."[7]

As far as these demons or inferior gods are concerned, he argues that they

> have every one their share in the Administration of the Universe, directing the affairs of Men under the name and Authority of the Sovereign God, and being as mediators between him and Men: They converse also with these last, who can, by their means, know and effect things above the power of Nature. This knowledge gives some the name of Diviners, and these Operations cause others to be called Magicians and Sorcerers; in consequence of which, all the effects we cannot give a Reason for, or find the cause of, are attributed to these Demons or inferior Gods.[8]

As may be seen, Bekker's first step is to delimit the field of inquiry: it is not possible to examine the devil or what people do by means of the devil. Instead, it is possible to analyze the feelings they have toward the divinity. Thus, what Bekker intends to explore are ideas and religious practices, or, rather, what people think and do in obedience to a belief in superior beings and existence outside the body. Insofar as this is a study of feelings and practices, Bekker's analysis is straightforwardly anthropological. Indeed, the premise he bases his inquiry on is a detachment from the field of theology. Bekker does not intend to take into consideration the devil's actions or the actions of the people who communicate with him, but only what they believe in. The object of analysis is not the devil's existence, but people's belief in him. Concerning demons, Bekker observes that pagans, both ancient and modern, attribute to them any effects they are otherwise unable to explain. We have thus reached the philosophical reflection of the late-seventeenth and eighteenth centuries, which attempted to omit forms of supernatural intervention when describing or explaining facts. From Hobbes to Spinoza,[9] an explanation for people's belief in supernatural and invisible beings was sought in the erroneous attribution to causes arising from natural phenomena, while at the same time the role of demons and their involvement in the practices of ancient and modern pagans was debated. Some years before the appearance of Bekker's work, another Dutchman, Antonius van Dale, showed—thus entering into debate with Catholics—that it was wrong to regard demons as the protagonists of oracles, just as it was wrong to affirm that the oracles had come to an end after the advent of Christianity.[10] Shortly afterwards, Fontenelle published his *Histoire des Oracles*—which was in part a readaptation of van Dale's work, as the author himself states in the Preface[11]—thus facilitating the vast dissemination of these influential ideas. Even though Fontenelle tried to delimitate van Dale's subject by leaving out the examination of magic supposedly produced by demons[12]—an aspect van Dale complained about[13]—his *Histoire des Oracles* nevertheless played a crucial role in the process that enabled a different conception of religious facts to gain ground. Leaving the Devil out of the account, out of the sphere of philosophical hypothesis and historical interpretation, meant freeing up the study of religious facts from the problem posed by theology; in this way it could be included in the field, as well as within the confines, of human behavior. From this point of view, the question concerning the cause of false beliefs had to be appropriately answered. But, consequently, this could no longer be done by referring to the intervention of elements external to human nature, such as demons;[14] the answer had to be found within the definition of human nature itself. One of the directions in which the comparative method would shortly afterwards develop was in fact marked by the issue of establishing the principles of human nature, in order that they could be used as a basis for comparing the beliefs and customs of peoples distant in space and time, as well as for explaining their origin.

Balthazar Bekker does not go as far as this. Although familiar with van Dale's writings,[15] which underline the fallaciousness inherent in attributing natural phenomena to the action of demons or demigods, he does not provide any philosophical generalization as to the possible causes of this fallacy. The comparison he makes between the ancient and modern pagans is merely phenomenological. Bekker was content simply with establishing and describing the analogy of the beliefs. In Chapter IX of his first book, where he describes African practices, Bekker mentions—by quoting Carolinus[16]—the "Fetissos" of the inhabitants of Guinea. A particularly noteworthy kind of *fétisso* concerns the Mountains. They are seen as fetishes because the inhabitants of Guinea believed them to be the cause of thunder and lightning.[17] We find here, albeit still only partially formulated, an element that would subsequently be used again and generalized, thus proceeding along the lines laid down by an ancient tradition: as a matter of fact, de Brosses will connect fetishism—intended as a general phenomenon affecting both ancient and modern peoples—to the already established idea of the deification of *nature's irregular phenomena*, whose causes those peoples were unable to understand. However, as far as fetishes are concerned, Bekker already compares what he sees as a typically Guinean phenomenon to other analogous pagan phenomena. Obviously, we do not find here a general theory of the comparative method capable of accounting for the analogies between the beliefs of such radically different peoples. And yet, the analysis of the general similarities between the beliefs and practices of both ancient and modern pagans, the methodologically grounded exclusion of demons from the explanation of these beliefs and practices, and the (albeit only marginal) introduction of the issue of thunder and lightning—namely of nature's irregular phenomena—randomly bring in some elements that would soon form the basis for a theoretical generalization. Essentially, Bekker's writings present some of the elements that will be formally correlated in the construction of the theory of fetishism.

Another Dutchman, Willem Bosman—one of de Brosses's openly acknowledged sources—narrated, in epistolary form, the account of a journey around Guinea.[18] In Letter X he speaks at length about the phenomenon of the fetishes.[19] An interesting aspect of Bosman's analysis is that he finds it very hard to distinguish between the originary beliefs of the inhabitants of Guinea and the beliefs introduced by Europeans and subsequently assimilated by the indigenous peoples. For instance, he affirms that the inhabitants of Guinea believe in one true god, but is unsure whether this belief was implanted in them by Europeans or not.[20] In any case, fetishes are seen as a characteristic feature. Not only do they coexist with the figure of the one true god, but—and this is the reason for suspecting that the acquisition of a single divinity is not a recent one—they continue to be the main object of worship and propitiation.[21]

In Bosman's writings there are, furthermore, two marginal yet significant passages, in which the author refers to practices performed outside Guinea as fetishes. As a matter of fact, Bosman compares the fetishes of the "negroes" with "Italian fetishes" (which concern the art of poisoning) and finds the latter to be far more dangerous than those used by the inhabitants of Guinea. He adds jokingly: "Though I must confess that I like that of the Italians so little, that I had rather walk over all that the Negroes can lay for me, than have any thing to do with theirs."[22] He discovers, in addition, a likeness between Guinea's fetish practices and those of Formosa Island.[23]

But the most surprising feature of Bosman's account is in actual fact the definition of fetishes. Even though fetishes are used for a variety of purposes and are essential for the actions and needs of men—thus fulfilling a religious role—and even though sacrifices are made for and cults are dedicated to them, it is still unclear to Bosman what exactly they represent for the inhabitants of Guinea.

> How their Gods are represented to them, or what idea they form of them, I never yet could learn, because indeed they do not know themselves: What we are able to observe is, that they have a great number of False Gods; that each Man, or at least each House-keeper, hath one; which they are persuaded narrowly inspects their Course of Life, and rewards Good, and Punishes

Wicked Men; but their Rewards consist in the Multiplicity of Wives and Slaves, and their Punishments in the want of them; though the most terrible Punishment they can imagine is Death; of which they are terribly afraid: And, indeed, 'tis this which enflames their Zeal in Religious Affairs, and occasions their Abstinence from forbidden Meats and Drinks, fearing they should dye if they but once tasted it. Murder, Adultery, Thievery, and all other such like Crimes, are here accounted no Sins, because they can expiate them with Money; which they cannot do in any other Mis-deeds, which still remain charged to their Account.[24]

Accordingly, fetishes have a powerful religious value, and yet Bosman still does not comprehend what they represent and how they are related to idols. What is more, he does not comprehend—and argues that the inhabitants of Guinea themselves do not know—how their idols are represented. We are thus faced with a series of problems concerning the misinterpretation of the fetishes' lack of symbolic function, although the symbolic function of Guinean religion is more than evident in the scenario described here. Bosman himself speaks about Guinean religious prohibitions—prohibitions that, since they are not related to transgressions and crimes such as murder, adultery, or theft, he does not fully comprehend—which in actual fact show a highly developed symbolic function in Guinean religion and relationships. He refers to the confusion about fetishes and idols as a confusion affecting the inhabitants of Guinea and the *representative* function that fetish objects might have had in relation to the divinities. But, above all, what Bosman's discourse—and that of others to come—implies is the idea of arbitrariness in the choice of fetish objects.

We are thus on the threshold of an important consideration with regard to de Brosses's invention of the concept of fetishism: fetishes do not possess any symbolic or representative power, and if they do, it is only at a primordial level. Potentially therefore, they can be placed on the first level of a scale according to which human beings—and collectively the various peoples—have developed their beliefs. de Brosses's grasp of the significance of fetishes marks the first step in a meaningful direction.

As far as the relationship between fetishes and idols is concerned, as early as the nineteenth century John Lubbock, while classifying religious beliefs in stages, argued that fetishism belonged to a phase characterized by the absence of idols,[25] whereas at the beginning of the twentieth century Wundt would speak about the arbitrary nature of fetishes.[26]

But Bosman says something more than that: even though the arbitrariness in the choice of the fetish object is implicit, it is nevertheless also true that—as he argues—each person, or at least each family, has their own particular fetish. In the nineteenth century McLennan would make a distinction between fetishism and totemism precisely on the basis of the latter's characteristic of social classification.[27] *Defining the fetish, therefore, has been a constant problem. Or, rather, we might argue that the problem of the fetish coincides with the problem of its definition.* What do all these objects grouped together under the name "fetish" mean? The concept of fetishism would gain ground precisely because of an inability to answer this question. Conversely, the decline in the concept of arbitrariness and the development of anthropological analysis within the field of the symbolic systems observable in the so-called savage or primitive religions entailed the reformulation, if not the disappearance, of the concept of the fetish.[28] This is the apparently paradoxical—but at the same time extremely significant—trait of the fetish, whose reality coincides with the reality of its description and observation—that is to say, the ways in which description and observation find a place in specific conceptual systems and specific formal connections.

But from this perspective the basic question is: how and in what way does the fetish transform into fetishism and thus acquire a generalized significance within a comparative method? How and in what way was fetishism formally connected to a conceptual system capable of accounting for the most disparate phenomena and assimilating them within the same framework?

The confusion between fetishes and idols and the poor capacity for representation observed by Bosman also contributed to the success of the fetish in European philosophical and anthropological thought. This confusion was later coupled with the notion of arbitrariness, which, when attributed to the Guineans' mode of reasoning—who were considered to be savages and primitives—in actual fact concealed the Europeans' incapacity to understand these same mental and symbolic processes. European philosophers held the beliefs of the "savages" to be false, to be errors produced by an inability to understand the real causes of natural phenomena, wrongly attributed instead to fetishes, idols, or divinities. Similarly, the same accusation can be made against the European philosophers, who attributed to arbitrariness the very features they did not understand, namely the characteristics of the worlds they were trying to get acquainted with, exploit, and take advantage of. But before specifically examining the epistemological problem of the comparative method, which would systematically gain ground in the eighteenth century and play an essential role in de Brosses's theorization of fetishism, it is worthwhile adding some further reflections on the way the notion of the fetish was gaining ground (although almost only in Guinea) as a tool for comparing different worlds and peoples. For some time the fetish was compared to supposedly analogous phenomena and practices observable in other countries and other peoples, but called by other names. Even though Bosman speaks about "Italian fetishes," a generalization providing a univocal and methodical definition of the fetish was still a long way off.

In his last work, entitled *Réponses aux questions d'un provincial*, in which he compares Greek and Roman paganism to the paganism of "savage" peoples with the aim of showing the analogies between them, Pierre Bayle discusses the Guinea fetish by quoting Bosman's work at length.[29] The author of *Various Thoughts on the Occasion of a Comet*, who had rationally explained the relationship that ought to pertain with the irregular phenomena of nature and had fought superstition by interpreting it as the attribution of unexplainable natural phenomena to divine intention, expresses himself as follows on Guinean religion:

> Do you see in this anything that might be related to good customs? Can't you see that what they teach about the reward for good deeds and the punishment for bad ones, both in this life and in the next, does not help to make them virtuous, since they say that, in order to earn the reward, it suffices to abstain from a particular kind of food, observe the feasts and keep one's oaths. This last notion would acquire some meaning if only it was not so easy to devise a means for breaking them.[30]

Bayle adds a substantial element to Bosman's theorizations: the practices associated with fetishes are *external*, and are thus instrumentally bound to interests and needs. Therefore, the exteriority of this religious practice is added to the absence of representation and to the notion of arbitrariness. It is interesting to note that in 1793 Kant would formulate a distinction between religion and fetishism by attributing to the latter the characteristic of exteriority.[31]

The works of the Jesuit Lafitau play an extremely significant role in this congeries of definitions and attributions. Considered to be one of the founding fathers of the comparative method, he is indisputably one of the most important theoretical sources for de Brosses (which is the reason why, specifically, we shall be examining his *Moeurs des sauvages*). Lafitau mentions the notion of the fetish in a footnote to the chapter on religion, where he makes a comparison between the practices of Guinea, those of the Island of Formosa, and the practices of North American Indians, with whom he is directly acquainted and who are, as is widely known, the object of his remarkable comparative analysis.

Lafitau observes:

> The fetish is a kind of talisman or something which corresponds to the *Manitou* of the Americans [Indians]. These idolatrous Negroes of Africa have, especially in things pertaining to religion, customs very like those which are seen widespread in America. One sees also an identical conformity

of mores with the Americans among some primitive peoples of East India. But I do not see any place where this conformity is more exact than among the primitives of the Island of Formosa near China and Japan.[32]

Fetishes and Manitou: The correspondences between the customs of American "savages" and African "Negroes"—already underlined by Bekker—are specified further in this case. And yet, the word fetish still designates Guinean practices analogous to the ones observed by other peoples and called by other names. The conditions for the generalization of the notion of the fetish were becoming more favorable, even though the comparative theories still confined themselves to comparing analogous practices designated with different names, without attempting to bring them under the same category.

And yet, despite the correspondences between the practices of the ancients and the savages, and the analogies between different kinds of savages, African cult objects, designated as fetishes and called by other names in other countries, were still arbitrarily chosen.

For instance, Lafitau himself uses the generic term "*sort*" to indicate objects used by American Indians when casting spells against ills. It is worth remembering that the term "fetish" means artificial and, as a noun, also indicates "witchcraft," "magical practice." It is also interesting to note that in the recent American edition of Lafitau's *Moeurs des savages*, "*sort*" is translated as "charm," whereas the section in which Lafitau lists the objects used as a "*sort*" is entitled "Fetishes or Charms."[33] All this confirms the fact that while words such as "*fétiche*," "*sort*," and "charm" tend to designate the same things, their precise meaning still remains unclear. Lafitau states:

> In his hands Father Garnier had several of these charms, which the Indians whom he had converted had given him. One day I begged him to examine them with me, arousing his curiosity for the first time. There was a great quantity of them; they were little bundles of twisted hair, bones of serpents or extraordinary animals, pieces of iron or bronze, figures of dough or corn husks and other similar objects which could not, in themselves, have any connection with what they were supposed to effect but could operate only by supernatural power in consequence of some formal or tacit agreement.[34]

We are dealing here with American Indian charms, objects capable of saving their owners from harm and guarding against ills thanks to their supernatural virtues, without which they would not otherwise have functioned. Lafitau remains at the level of description, as is the case with Bosman and the fetishes of Guinea. The significance behind the choice of these objects, randomly collected and described in his work, is lost on him. But, as Mauss will argue, these objects are not in actual fact chosen arbitrarily.

They depend on the code of magical and religious practices and on the symbolic value they assume through these codes.[35]

An analogous idea was expressed some years later by the Chevalier des Marchais—another of de Brosses's sources—in his travel account of Guinea quoted by Labat. This is what he writes about African religion:

> They worship only fetishes. They fear them and do not love them at all. They pray to them so as to avoid being harmed. Those who have more wit than others agree upon the fact that nothing good can come from fetishes. These fetishes are devoid of any specific form: they can be a chicken-bone, a desiccated monkey skull, a fish-bone, a stone, a date-stone, a bundle of peculiar little sticks with parrot feathers in it, a horn full of dirt and many other similar things.[36]

Once again, we find the idea of absence, the idea that fetishes have no representative value, that they are arbitrarily chosen, and the relationship with them is based on fear and mistrust. But, unlike in Bosman's work, fetishes are not used out of interest and need in this case. On the contrary, one tries to propitiate them so as to stay out of harm's way, as they preside over prohibitions.

The Chevalier des Marchais's description of the Guinean fetish cult does not stop here. He affirms that there are specific fetishes and generic ones, as well as large fetishes related to the chief or the village: "such as: a mountain, a large cliff, a big tree or a huge bird."[37] In this respect des Marchais is more specific than Bosman, since he distinguishes between fetishes concerning individuals and fetishes relating to the collectivity or to the person representing it, even though his remarks on the moral function of fetishes are analogous to the Dutchman's: "If, by mistake or for another reason, someone were to kill any of these birds, his life would be in extreme danger; yet if a person steals from somebody else's garden, it is seen as a sign of good fortune and that very same person does not fail to bring the bird something to eat."[38]

Along the same lines as Bosman, des Marchais goes on to describe the cult of the mountains:

> These people respect the highest mountains, where it is known that thunder has struck several times, and consider them to be the abode of their fetishes. Since the poor divinities may feel pressing needs in those wild and desert places, they are assiduous in bringing offerings to the feet of the mountains: some rice, millet, corn, bread, palm oil, wine, or, in other words, anything the divinities might need for drinking or eating.[39]

What is iterated here is the relationship between the religion of the "savages" and the irregular phenomena of nature. de Brosses would individuate in Hume the theoretical basis for this relationship, while des Marchais and Bosman would provide him with the descriptive basis of the field.

Finally, des Marchais compares the Guinean natives' fetishes with the practices of the ancients: "The fetish is for them almost the same as the mouth of truth was for the ancients."[40]

In this brief overview of explorers who witnessed African fetish cults—or similar cults in other countries—and of philosophers whose comparative assessments were grounded in the analogies existing between the customs and the religious practices of "savages" and "ancients," as far as the word fetish is concerned, the descriptive and the comparative moment are related in the following manner:

(a) The analogy between the practices of the savage peoples and the practices of the ancients has already been provided with a systematic basis.
(b) This systematic basis is correlated to the alleged primitiveness and uncouthness of the beliefs held by the ancients and by the savages.
(c) On the one hand, this primitiveness and uncouthness fit into traditional discourse on pagan religions, while, on the other, they feature in rationalistic debate on the need to exclude the active intervention of the supernatural from human affairs (van Dale, Fontenelle, Bekker) and, thus, from historical and sociological analysis. Pagan cults, such as oracles, are not the fruit of the Devil's actions or his mimetic abilities. By disregarding this aspect, it becomes possible to promote the possibility of a new type of historical analysis based on the behavior of human nature and its ability to improve and progress, as shown by the development of the Western world. There is no need for the observer to turn to the supernatural anymore to explain the "Other." On the contrary, the "Other" provides a mirror through time, a means of looking back. The observer's high ground, consisting of the superiority of his developed world, becomes his viewpoint.
(d) The fetish is still within the confines of Africa: the cult is similar to those followed by the American "savages," the natives of Formosa Island, and the ancients. It is an uncouth and primordial cult, devoid of representational strength and thus of the systematicity characterizing the cults of idols. Basically, it is a form of idolatry in its primitive stage.
(e) The fetish is arbitrary: fetish objects can be of the most disparate types. They can be natural or artificial objects without any *apparent* relation to the function they are supposed to carry out. They impose prohibitions and offer remedies.

(f) The fetish concerns an external cult: the fetish is feared rather than loved. The relationship with it is instrumental, based on interest andn eeds.

(g) There are specific fetishes for each individual and general fetishes for the family, the chief, or the village.

This outline is functional to the formulation of some observations on the relationship between description and observer. We see that in those cases where the description is given in an apparently pure form, that is, without explanatory statements, it is in actual fact merely assumed and depends on the conceptual prejudices of the observer. For instance, if the arbitrariness of the fetish objects or the variety of the specific and general fetishes is taken into consideration, it will be seen that the accounts provide records and case studies of these phenomena without any further meaningful explanations. In actual fact, instead of being imputed to the explorers' descriptive inadequacy, the apparent confusion caused by the variety of the fetish objects becomes a confirmation of the cult's primeval status. The descriptions are such not because it was impossible to provide an explanation, but because the primitiveness of Guinean life is itself a sufficient explanation for what appears to be confused and arbitrary in the description. But surely this trait does not in itself exclude accuracy in the description. It enables us to understand the process according to which the notion of the arbitrariness of the fetish objects was for a long time seen not as an object of doubt and inquiry, but as confirmation of the primitive status of a cult followed by people whose minds were "simple" and undeveloped and, therefore, ready to accept whatever explanation they were offered for the phenomena and events they had to cope with. In this regard, it was actually the European observer who tended to accept whatever the most superficial explanation was, inasmuch as his observation was based on a comparative assumption that, while recognizing the similarities between "savages" and "savages" and between "savages" and ancients, also drew an important conclusion based on two premises: the first concerned the superiority of his culture; the second was related to the fact that this very same culture was phylogenetically bound to the primitive ones. It originated from them. This fundamental conviction universalized Western culture and civilization over history and time and played a homogenizing role. Phylogeny—the conceptualization of the role played by historical continuity in the progress of civilization, a prerequisite for the genesis of civilization and its human origin—provided an opportunity to recognize the "Other" by acknowledging common ancestors and lines of descent. At the same time, this process paved the way for a comparison related to the notion of historical scale and the idea of progress. Through this comparison, the diversity of the "Other" was projected into the past and turned once again into inferiority, even though it was the inferiority of an ancestor.

Even in those cases where no common origin for all human races was posited (as, for instance, in Voltaire),[41] the notion of conformity between "savages" and ancients produced the same result, at least from this point of view, since—assuming that civilized Europeans descended from ancients and that the ancients themselves had once been savages—the substitution of the notion of monogenism with the notion of polygenism nonetheless entailed the classification of peoples according to a European idea of progress.[42] As my analysis of Fontenelle's work will attempt to show, the savage stage of non-Western peoples probably depended on the fact that they were still young and, therefore, behaved like the ancients did in their early history. If, in any case, "savages" could be compared with ancient peoples and analogies be drawn between their customs and ways of life, the originary savage stage of the ancients implied the idea that both could be juxtaposed with the superiority of civilized Europeans. When we call attention to Fontenelle's idea that admiration for the ancients was one of the chief obstacles to progress, it is essential to consider this fundamental aspect of the problem, which implicated non-Western peoples such as American Indians and African Negroes in a declaration of Western civilization's alleged superiority. This decisive point turned the idea of progress (set against the ancient traditions from which the Europeans descended) into a universal value and transformed the attainments of Western civilization into the results achieved by Civilization. It is essential to take all this into consideration if we wish to avoid taking an over-sentimental and rhetorical view of the major issues raised in Western culture in the modern era.

In any case, the acknowledgment that the ancients had also once been savages became a fundamental acquisition in the process that led to the assertion of the universality of modern Western civilization, and had a considerable influence on the ways in which this assertion was theorized. In this respect, the contribution of the Jesuit Lafitau was crucial. As we shall see, he reversed the axis of the comparison between "savages" and ancient peoples and made the relationship bilateral by affirming that not only had the study of ancient people been useful to him in order to understand the customs of the Hurons and the Iroquois, but also the customs of the Hurons and the Iroquois had been useful to him in order to throw some light upon the originary customs of the ancients. The twentieth-century rediscovery of this idea by anthropologists and scholars of classical antiquity was accompanied by theoretical and historical considerations that aimed at questioning the centrality of Greek culture in studies of antiquity. Conversely, in the eighteenth century it contributed to the secularization[43] of the notion of universality in the Western world. Descending from savages meant building an ad hoc history: far from limiting the universal scope of Western history, the fact that the ancients had also been savages made it stronger by transforming it. The break with ancient traditions made at the turn of the eighteenth century was considered a way of affirming the superiority of the Moderns not only compared to the past, but also compared to the surrounding world. In this sense, the category of the *modern* was elaborated not only in relation to antiquity, but also in relation to the non-contemporaneity of different peoples, whom Western culture wished to assimilate, while also looking down on them from the vantage point of the superiority it had acquired over the years.

This, therefore, is the cultural context the fetish developed in. Invented by the Europeans in order to designate African religious cults, this term does not, in actual fact, refer to anything particularly definite and clearcut. This is due to the fact that, within this context, it was the very arbitrariness apparent in the choice of the fetish objects that gave rise to an assumption of uncouthness and primitiveness inherent in the cult itself.

There is, however, an exception to this arbitrariness. It regards general fetishes and in particular the mountain fetish mentioned both by Bosman and des Marchais. Mountains, affirm Bosman and des Marchais, are worshipped as fetishes because the Africans believe them to be the place where thunder and lightning originate. Hence, at least in this case, the fetishization of a natural object depends on the relationship with a natural phenomenon deified by Guineans.

Within the field of philosophical discourse on religion, this kind of fetishization confirmed the idea that the genesis of religion was to be ascribed to the savages' and primitives' fear of *irregular natural phenomena*. This topic, borrowed by de Brosses from Hume, would become one of the bedrocks in his theory of fetishism and, in addition, attain wide credence throughout the eighteenth century. Once the comparative method had been systematized in a conjectural historical framework and once it had become essential in order to individuate the source and trace the *origins* of this very same framework, the fear of irregular natural phenomena provided an adequate explanation. It could not have been otherwise: irregular natural phenomena pertain to scientific analysis, to an explanation of the real causes of what is produced by nature. By deifying natural events which provoke fear and awe, primitive religion does nothing more than attribute erroneous causes to phenomena which do not present themselves as regular and, hence, are beyond the control a "savage" can exercise on the basis of his limited knowledge and limited experience.

Leaving aside any active intervention on the part of the devil, attention was then focused on the issue regarding a capacity for knowledge and the ability to control nature. Here again, of course, the idea of progress marks the transition and determines the manner of comparison among different peoples.

The description of fetishes; the comparative method; a historical discourse teleologically founded upon progress; a scientific approach to nature: all these elements constituted the basis for de Brosses's theory. Therefore, it is necessary to have a closer look at the theorizations that merged with the notion of the fetish and contributed to formulating the concept of fetishism, thus leading to a generalization which, as we shall see, Marcel Mauss would call "an immense misunderstanding."

The Comparative Method of Joseph-François Lafitau

The analogies de Brosses draws in his book on fetishism between contemporary "savage" societies and ancient peoples are usually seen as a model for the comparative method. From the early 1900s, de Brosses is usually mentioned immediately after the Jesuit Lafitau, who, on account of the remarkable breadth and systematicity of his analysis, is considered to be the real precursor of modern comparative theories.[44] Indeed, there is no doubt that to some degree de Brosses draws on Lafitau's thought and theorizations.[45] Nevertheless, it is necessary to clarify the extent of this influence. While it is true that Lafitau constitutes a fundamental basis for Brossian analysis, it is likewise true that the generalization of the concept of fetishism was made possible by virtue of the combination of Lafitau's contribution with a theory of history and progress as well as a series of hypotheses and conjectures, which are largely extraneous to the reflections, ideology, and beliefs of the Jesuit Father. The introduction of the idea of progress and a type of history that develops unilinearly implies, in some ways, a change in the form of the connections through which the comparison is made. Drawing comparisons across a temporal scale meant considering the results arrived at by Lafitau in a different theoretical context, a context in which it was possible to assimilate his method and his observations without, however, accepting his beliefs and *conjectures*.

Thus it appears necessary to clarify Lafitau's stance and contribution in order to not only highlight the aspects de Brosses would include in his analysis, but also grasp the nature of what would be excluded by him and by the formal connections of his theory. Each theory, each instance of the organization of formal connections, while including, on the one hand, the elements it is based on, inevitably *excludes* others. It is precisely by means of the exclusions that it is possible to compare historically the theories and methods that follow on each other. Should one proceed by analyzing only the elements that one theory incorporates and inherits from another, the outcome would be a mere history of influences, a history that excludes—pardon the wordplay—the exclusions. But if the need to comprehend differences pertains to historiographical analysis, then there is all the more need to include the exclusions, because this kind of inquiry is not supposed to imitate and mirror what has occurred in the history of ideas and theories. This is beyond its scope, and were it to give any idea to the contrary, it would not be doing its duty. Historical research is not concerned with the same subject matter ascribed to a theory that examines and tries to explain human systems or relationships. A theory cannot avoid excluding some elements, whereas historical research must necessarily take into account what has been excluded by other theories, since meta-theories can be taken as the object of historical research.

It is therefore necessary to consider Lafitau's theory in its entirety, that is, in the unreduced completeness—which he calls system—constituted by his method, conjectures, and beliefs.

An authority on the Hurons and the Iroquois, Lafitau, who had traveled extensively across Canada, exercised considerable influence throughout the eighteenth century by reason of his account of the customs and practices of American Indians compared to the customs and practices of "primitive times." Although heavily criticized by Voltaire[46] and by de Pauw,[47] the contribution of the Jesuit Father nevertheless soon became a point of reference for any philosophers who addressed the issue of "savages" in relation to forms of government, social systems, as well as the historical-evolutionary process of civilization. Goguet, Herder, Ferguson, Lord Kames, Adam Smith himself, Millar, and Robertson[48] refer to him as their source of information on the North American "savages." This is also true, needless to say, for President de Brosses. In the nineteenth century, despite advancing a thesis on matriarchy which was very close to that of Lafitau, Morgan makes no mention of him.[49] Taylor and Frazer refer to Lafitau as their source of information on particular topics.[50] It was in the twentieth century that the general aspects of Lafitau's contribution were reappraised; that is to say, his work was appreciated not only as a source of information on North American Indians, but especially for its comparative method. van Gennep sees him as one of the precursors of this research method in anthropology and affirms, with what may be considered slight exaggeration, that Lafitau had anticipated the method of Montesquieu.[51] Chinard underlines the importance of the Jesuit's thought precisely because of the analogies drawn between American Indians and ancient Greeks.[52] Meinecke goes so far as to say that, with regard to French thought, Lafitau took the place of Vico, who was not much read.[53] More recently, it was the scholars of classical antiquity who rediscovered Lafitau's work. Within the framework of the debate over the comparative method in the study of ancient history, scholars such as Vernant, Arnaldo Momigliano, Vidal-Naquet, and Detienne all mention Lafitau's work in their writings.[54]

As Pierre Vidal-Naquet has observed, Lafitau sees no contradiction between "the action of Time and the comparison, as we would say today, between 'diachrony' and 'synchrony'. It is legitimate to compare Indian and Greek customs because Indians and Greeks are both descended from Adam and Eve."[55] Lafitau's comparison derives, theoretically, from the religious assumption that all the peoples of the world stemmed from a common origin and that there are no human societies without religion. This assumption—polemically in contrast to Bayle's thesis[56]—formed the basis of his systematic analysis of the American Indians. The polemic against the atheists is very important not only from an ideological viewpoint, but also from a theoretical perspective, because, as we shall see, the comparative method proposed by Fontenelle was based on quite different assumptions, which have to be taken into account when discussing de Brosses's theory. Lafitau proceeded by using a method of *filiation*, so that his conjectures on the origins of the Indians would correspond to the Biblical texts. The idea that the American Indians and the Greeks had a common point of origin formed the basis and the diachronic premise for the application of his comparative method. Of course, this does not alter the fact that comparison remains the theoretical center of his analysis. Regarding this aspect, he is theoretically conscious that he is not restricting himself to a description or to a travel account. The originality and importance of his contributions consist precisely in the fact that they combine fieldwork experience with a method capable of organizing and systematizing this experience in broader and more general terms. Michèle Duchet affirms that "the structure of the discourse is neither that of the account nor of the description: *comparison* is the sole raison d'être for the text."[57]

Lafitau's book is significantly entitled *Moeurs des sauvages comparées aux moeurs des premiers temps* and its systematic approach is consciously expressed in the "Design and Plan of the Work," where it is stated:

> I have not limited myself to learning the characteristics of the Indian and informing myself about their customs and practices, I have sought in these practices and customs, vestiges of the most remote antiquity. I have read carefully [the works] of the earliest writers who treated the customs, laws and usages of the peoples of whom they had some knowledge. I have made a comparison of these customs with each other. I confess that, if the ancient authors have given me information on which to base happy conjectures about the Indians, the customs of the Indians have given me information on the basis of which I can understand more easily and explain more readily many things in the ancient authors.[58]

As we can see, the comparative intent literally opens up the field of inquiry. Not only does Lafitau refer to ancient texts in order to understand the Indians, but he also utilizes his direct knowledge of the North American Indians to understand ancient texts and what they narrate about the practices, customs, and habits of antiquity. Arnaldo Momigliano notes: "Following Herodotus, the French Jesuit Lafitau discovered a matriarchal society in America. His *Moeurs des savages amériquains* revealed to the world the fact that the Greeks had once been savages too."[59] However, even though the idea that the Greeks had once been savages can be traced back at least to Thucydides,[60] and despite the fact that Fontenelle's thesis on the savage origin of the Greeks was published in the same year as Lafitau's work, no one before Lafitau had outlined this in a systematic manner, with such an accurate focus on specific aspects and particular facts.

Lafitau is perfectly and programmatically aware of the fact that his inquiry and comparison are enclosed within a *system*, whose validity he intends to affirm and salvage, despite the prospect of possible mistakes or gaps in his research. Addressing his potential successors, he states:

> Perhaps by bringing my thoughts to light I shall open up, to those interested in the reading of these authors, some paths of investigation that they will be able to follow further. Perhaps I shall be fortunate enough to uncover the veins of a mine that will become rich in their hands. I hope that, in surpassing me, they may go still further and be willing to give an exact form, a fair dimension, to many things whose surface I shall only skim in passing. Some of my conjectures may appear light in themselves, but, perhaps, taken all together, they will make a whole, the parts of which will be held together by the connections obtaining between them.[61]

We are dealing here with a crucial statement of methodological intent, which highlights the essential gap between Lafitau and other travelers and writers: the whole, created by the relationship between the parts, becomes an entity that is superior to the parts. The comparison becomes a system because the ensemble of the relationships, the sum total of the relationships between the parts, becomes a system. In the chapter entitled "Americans. The Origin of the Peoples of America," he argues: "A comparison of the customs and folk traditions of the nations could lead us to a type of knowledge unique in itself."[62] But in Lafitau's work, what provides the foundation for this comparative system? To what extent is the systematic intent lacking in value judgment? How is it possible to recognize the difference between ethnology and ideology? Take, for instance, his description of the savages' character. He starts by disproving the idea that savages were nothing more than hirsute naked men, living like animals in the forests and lacking in any kind of social organization. He then distinguishes between the way they appear and the way they are. This point is extremely important, because appearance and being depend on the implicit comparison that the *observer* makes by using his conceptual framework:

> It is more difficult to grasp the character of their minds and spirits. There seem to be contradictions in it. The first glimpse is not favourable to them. Those who have judged them by it have painted for us a very unflattering picture of them. At the sight of these men lacking in everything, without letters, science, apparent laws, without temples for the most part, without regular worship and lacking the things most necessary for life, one might, it seems, judge that they are of such sort that the world had just been created for them or that they had just emerged from the mud of the earth or from the hollows of Dodona as the extravagant imagination of the pagans might have represented it. We should deem ourselves justified in depicting them as a people gross, stupid, ignorant, fierce, without sentiment of religion or humanity, given to all the vices which should naturally result from entire liberty, restrained neither by belief in a divinity, nor human law, nor principles of reason or education.[63]

Their appearance implies, therefore, that savages may be seen as standing at zero degrees of all specifically human qualities. In particular, zero degrees extends to letters, science, religion, and, above all, social ties, all the elements that create social relationships. The sentiment of religion, law, reason, and education: these elements determine the structure of social relationships. Significantly, the absence of such ties makes the savage look like the Hobbesian natural man. The scenario repeats itself in some measure: what would become of a man if he had no social ties? The answer is: pure and limitless individualism. One part, which contributes to determining the whole of society, itself becomes the whole. It is admitted as possible that the individual might exist without society. But whereas in Hobbes's theory the scenario is both hypothetical and operative at the same time,[64] here it arises precisely from the perception and description of a historical and social reality determined by a cultural model. Furthermore, it makes sense to speak of vices only if one assumes that virtues exist. But there is a decisive factor. As Lafitau notes, the basic mistake in this view lies in the fact that the observers fail to see social ties even when these ties are right in front of their eyes. They fail to do so because the *diversity* of the form of those ties, of the religious practices, the laws, the education, and the mode of reasoning has not been assimilated into the codes of the observers' cultural models. This diversity, then, becomes *absence*. Lafitau's operation consists precisely in the attempt to let others see and comprehend this diversity. This becomes possible only through a temporary *homogenization* between the observed object and the observer's model. *It is in this sense that comparison implies a determinate construction of formal connections.* The parallel drawn by Lafitau between "savages" and "men of primitive times" has exactly this aim[65] and the filiation he conjectures on the basis of his religious intent constitutes its guarantee and foundation.

In the meantime, let us quote again from Lafitau, who proceeds from appearance to being:

> This picture, however, would be inaccurate. They have good minds, quick perceptions and admirable memories. They all have at least traces of an ancient and hereditary religion and form of government. They think justly about their affairs, better than the mass of the people do among us. They reach their goals by sure paths. They act with cold common sense and a self-control that would wear out our patience. As a matter of honour and through greatness of soul they never [106] lose their tempers, seem to be always masters of themselves and are never angry. They have lofty and proud hearts, courage when put to the test, intrepid valour, heroic constancy under torture and an evenness of disposition which hindrances and ill success do not alter. Among themselves, they have a sort of code of manners of their own of which they carefully observe all the niceties, a respect for the aged, a somewhat surprising deference for their equals which is difficult to reconcile with the independence and love of liberty of which they are very jealous. They are not affectionate or demonstrative. But notwithstanding, they are very kindly, affable and exercise toward strangers and the unfortunate a charitable hospitality which would confound all the nations of Europe.[66]

So, in actual fact, savages do have religious and political obligations and, furthermore, notwithstanding the differences between them and the Western observer, they also have many qualities. It is interesting to note here an element that Lafitau sees as rationally inconsistent: respect toward equals—an element of social ties—is placed next to a sense of independence and freedom. There is, in short, something distinct from the picture offered by the system based on competition, where freedom and independence dynamically collide, instead of being interrelated with a sense of respect toward equals. He adds, moreover: "good minds, quick perceptions, admirable memories." Lafitau introduces another *comparison*: the way savages look after their affairs is superior to that of the Western lower classes. Coldness and self-control: qualities that contrast with a limited sense of the immediate and a reduction of the aim of life to the mere satisfaction of one's most immediate needs. He shows that the qualities of the savages are actually similar to those admired by Western people, but—and this is the point to emphasise—these qualities are developed in a completely different (nowadays we would say symbolic) context.

> We should doubtless be happier, if we had, like them, that indifference which makes them treat scornfully and remain unaware of many things

which we should not be able to do without. Perhaps also their poverty is the result of that natural laziness which renders them so indolent that they would rather do without the very advantages which they envy in us than take the necessary trouble to procure them. However that may be, since their first contact with Europeans, the use which they have been able to make of such improvements has not inspired them to alter their ancient folkways and they have gained fewer of the skills which would put them at their ease and make them more comfortable than they have lost in imitating our vices.[67]

In this process of comparison differentiation, on the one hand Lafitau describes the nature of savages compared to that of civilized men and highlights their, shall we say, "positive" faculties and qualities. On the other hand, however, he is unable to explain the structural context within which these qualities and faculties acquire a sense. The disregard savages show for many of the objects brought by the Europeans is then explained naively by their natural laziness, which makes them impervious to the possessions aspired to by those who are a part of commercial societies. This is the reason provided by Lafitau in his attempt to explain why savages prefer to deprive themselves of the advantages conferred by Europeans, despite recognizing their importance. The concept of "natural laziness" constitutes here a connection through which Europeans can understand the savages' way of life, but it is a connection predicated on the assimilation of a model of perception typical of the Western observer. Indeed, "natural laziness" provides a way to explain the different attitude savages have toward work and life in general, but this diversity is seen as being at zero degrees of the Europeans' attitude toward work and life. The comparison is subsumed here into the perceptive model to the same extent to which the observers criticized in their turn by Lafitau subsumed savages, depicting them as naked and hirsute, and lacking in both the law and religion. The inadequate receptiveness to the advantages conferred by Europeans is not explained through the diversity of social types—that is to say, through the different types of relationship which develop in a given social context, possessed of their own dynamic means of self-preservation and identity—but rather through a specific characteristic "inherent" in the savages. Different categories—such as different qualities and faculties—acquire a sense within a social type in terms of the form assumed by the relations. This is the reason, for instance, why work is something to which different societies and cultures attribute different meanings, as Malinowski was the first to show,[68] and the reason why categories such as exchange, commerce, and currency develop and formally interrelate in a different way, as Karl Polanyi has shown.[69] *The ability to formally understand the systemic aspect of the relational role played by categories in a given sociocultural context makes it possible, in some measure, to avoid developing the comparison in an analytical way, to avoid assuming the homogeneity of the context, while articulating the differences in an evolutionary key of category enrichment, which are always formally arranged in the same way.* If one says that the savages are "naturally lazy," it means that the homogeneity on which the comparison and the difference are to be built is in this case assumed. It precedes and is removed from the formal connections that preside over comparison. This implies that the homogenization is based here on implicit value judgments and ideological grounds. The savage is "naturally lazy" because he does *not* work as Europeans do: this negation is already part of the context of homogenization. At the level of logic, the judgment "naturally lazy" is only apparently positive: the quality (or failing) of laziness is explained only in relation to the quality of industriousness as it is perceived in the Western world. Anthropology will show that this is not so, that what we see as "natural laziness" is, in fact, a different attitude toward work, which can be explained only if the opportunity to study the different formal arrangement of the categories at stake in the various social systems is included in the observational model.

It is only by taking this problematic point into account that the role of *time* in comparative analysis can be discussed: time has, in fact, an epistemological function, since it produces a homogenization on the diachronic plane. Consequently, the basic assumption of the comparison consists in the structural *fixity* of the interrelated categories and in the fact that differentiation shifts, in the given context, from zero degrees to the higher level of these very same categories.

It is in this theoretical frame that Lafitau's great contribution should be evaluated. He built a system in which men from primitive times could be compared to savages from distant places. When compared with the primitive, the savage will become primitive.[70] If, on the one hand, this practice favored the expansion and enrichment of comparative analysis—which was now able to draw comparisons between people distant in space and time—on the other, it was grounded in a religious assumption that in turn required confirmation from research. Starting with the assumption that there are no human societies without religion and that all human races descend from a common type—thus implying a diffusionist hypothesis for the distribution of human cultures across the world[71]—Lafitau establishes a connection between the Iroquois and the Pelasgians, peoples who are distant in chronological, yet close in evolutionary, time. From this derives the opportunity for Europeans—as the cultural descendants of the ancient Greeks—to understand savages. As a matter of fact, the Greeks had originated from the very same primitive Pelasgians from which the Hurons and the Iroquois descended. Descendancy becomes filiation and filiation becomes a criterion for homogenizing humanity, a criterion for building comparisons and individuating differences. This fact constitutes the basis on which comparative analysis has developed: the use of a systemic and structural dimension while simultaneously acknowledging the limit that this systemic and structural dimension has been unable to overcome: up until the moment, that is, when *time* becomes an internal and relational category within the forms structurally acquired by social types, and thus ceases to be an external category that shapes the homogenization of the forms into an extra-structural assumption and an a priori foundation that conditions.

Lafitau, the Conjectures, and the System

Lafitau elaborates a system in opposition to Huet's *Demonstratio Evangelica*, where all religions are shown to have originated in Mosaic history.[72] In the "Design and Plan of the Work," he states:

> The study which I have made of pagan mythology has opened up to me another system of belief and made me go back far beyond the time of Moses to apply to our first ancestors, Adam and Eve, all that the author of whom I have just spoken applied to Moses and Zipporah. This religious system, which will appear new although it should not, seems to me based on substantial enough evidence. Although I have not developed my conjectures as far as I might be able to, I am convinced that they will be found solid enough and that people more capable than I will be able to add to them proofs that will strengthen mine.[73]

Lafitau's system is based on the following conjectures:

(a) Thef irstf athersw ereg ivena p urer eligion.
(b) Public worship has existed from the time of man's creation.
(c) The religion of the first fathers has passed down from generation to generation. It was not spread by the Egyptians after the deluge. Religion was present at the origin.
(d) The religion of the first fathers was corrupted by ignorance and passions. Ignorance has invented uncouth myths in order to explain the meaning of the hieroglyphs (of the Indies) to people who no longer knew their meaning.
(e) In spite of the alteration of religion, there is nevertheless a certain uniformity in the myths of all peoples.[74]

Lafitau argues, furthermore, that his conjectural system has one last advantage: he aligns pagan mythology and symbolic theology, the hieroglyphs and the symbols, to the Divinity, to the principles of the Christian religion and not, as pagan philosophers did in the final stages of paganism, to an explanation of the physical world that provided an ideological weapon for atheism:

> The atheists can oppose my conjectures with their novelty and say that, in the explanations I give of pagan mythology, I establish a whole system of thought on a matter that, in itself, is very obscure. I should be able to protest against this so-called "novelty," which I find to be based on the theories of other writers whom I cite and very likely on conjectures. Nevertheless, despite being simple assumptions, they do not fail to make a very strong argument and amount to a sort of proof, should one wish to bring them all together as proof of this same point of view.[75]

Therefore, the power of the conjectures also depends on the fact that they are *systematically* brought under a single point of view. The truth of the conjectures is reinforced, according to Lafitau, by the relations existing among them. These relations are substantiated in the main theoretical element of the work: the "comparaison"—a "comparaison" that does not limit itself to drawing analogies between the peoples of North America and those of "primitive times," but conjecturally refers to the whole globe. Nor could it have been otherwise, given the initial assumption based on a sole, pure, and originary religion and on a public cult existing from the time of man's creation. Starting from this assumption, he undertakes an investigation of various contemporary savage peoples and various ancient peoples, looking for traces of this originary mark in their beliefs and their customs.

This global "comparaison" does not concern only religion, but, starting from religion, takes in the whole way of life of "savages" and "primitive" people:

> It is not only in the chapter on religion that I show that the peoples of America regarded as barbarians have a religion. We shall see several similar and curious features of it in the other chapters, those on their government, marriages, warfare, medicine, death, mourning and burial, so that it seems as if formerly and at the beginning of time, religion played a part in everything.[76]

Religion plays a part in everything. In this regard, much recent anthropological research is relevant, as it is based specifically on the idea that the division of activities typical of the Western system cannot be applied to so-called savage or primitive societies, where social facts must be seen as a whole. The disavowal of the originary *homo oeconomicus*, an image first disproved by Malinowski[77] and then further refuted in Marcel Mauss's

The Gift,[78] finds its roots, in substance, in Emile Durkheim's reflections and polemics against utilitarian economic assumptions.[79] But it is based, in particular, on the rejection of a feature of economic anthropology's formal connections, and regards the development of the comparative method subsequent to Lafitau, and in particular a specific reaction to his work. As a matter of fact, Lafitau's system is built on the assumption that traces of a common origin are observable in all peoples; this, in turn, is based on the belief in an originally pure religion given by God to the first fathers and altered over the course of time by ignorance and passion, which led to its dispersion and degeneration. Despite the dispersion, this religion managed to leave a mark, albeit hidden and diluted with crude explanations of symbols and mysteries. Lafitau states:

> Of all the religions of which we have knowledge in the East and the West Indies there is not one which is not hieroglyphic and whose theology is not full of symbols, [a fact] which serves as the basis for my conjecture and which I shall develop at greater length, namely, that it was our first ancestors themselves who believed that they should exalt matters pertaining to God with a mysterious language to which men's vanity added much of their own. Thus religion found itself mixed up with an infinite number of absurd folktales.[80]

This, therefore, is the conjecture used by Lafitau to make the comparison—an all-embracing comparison between savages and the peoples of antiquity, an ability to systematically connect customs, practices, and usages of people widely separated by centuries and continents. Of course, today it is quite easy to focus on the naivety of his main thesis, but from a historical point of view the issue at stake is that by refuting this thesis, subsequent theories attempting to explain the origins without falling back on revelation have actually contributed to modifying the comparative system. Warburton argued that the origins of language could be studied by drawing on the theories of Diodorus Siculus and Vitruvius, that is to say, without any need to refer to the Bible.[81] Warburton's theory of hieroglyphs[82] was soon translated into French and adopted by Condillac in his *Essay on the Origin of Human Knowledge*.[83] From this arises the need to explain human and social origins through facts and observation. Shortly afterwards Condillac himself published his *Treatise on Systems*, where he criticizes philosophical systems based on conjecture instead of observable facts.[84] This crucial work[85] contains a number of highly influential reflections:

> Systems are older than philosophers. Nature creates them, and there were no inadequate systems when nature was man's only teacher. For then a system

was and could only be the result of observation. It had not yet been suggested that everything could be explained. Man had needs, and he sought only the means for satisfying them.[86]

Human beings noticed the facts related to their needs because the needs were few and primary: "Man was rarely mistaken or at least his errors could only be short-lived: he was soon alerted to these errors since the needs went unsatisfied."[87] But even when they outgrew the stage of primary needs, men still proceeded in a similar manner by groping their way forward. Supposedly, initial observations aroused suspicions, which were later confirmed or disproved by other observations. But if we remain at the level of suppositions, we make the mistake of confusing the means we have for discovering the system with the principle of the system itself. Hence, the mistake lies in confusing means with principles. The suppositions, therefore, alter the system only insofar as they present themselves as substitutes for observable facts, but maintain their role as a means for reaching those facts:

> On the other hand, hypotheses or suppositions (for we use these words interchangeably) are not only means or hints in the search for truth, they can also be principles, that is, first truths that explain others. They are means or hints because observations, as we have remarked, always begin by groping around in the dark... But hypotheses are principles of first truths once they have been confirmed by new observations that cannot be doubted.[88]

This does not entail prohibiting the use of hypotheses—provided they are used with due caution—"[to] intellects keen enough to get ahead occasionally of experience":[89]

> If Descartes had offered his ideas merely as conjectures, he would still have provided an opportunity for making observations. But by presenting them as the true system of the world, he committed everyone who adopted his principles to error, and was instead responsible for placing obstacles along the path to truth.[90]

If we compare Condillac's theories with Lafitau's statements—who certainly does not build systems of the world but, rather, applies his system (which is based on conjecture)—we can see that, on the one hand, Lafitau shows caution since, as we have seen, he does not confuse his conjectures with the description of observable facts; while, on the other, he affirms the validity of his conjectures insofar as they can be grouped under the same viewpoint, that is to say, to the extent that the systematic connections between them are taken into account. But the fundamental difference between Lafitau's method and Condillac's analysis consists in the fact that the *Treatise on Systems* is based on a *conjecture*, a conjecture advancing the idea that knowledge derives from needs. What is more, Condillac delineates the development of the systems and their tendencies on the basis of a pattern—which has continued to exercise its influence up to the present time—according to which culture only develops once humanity's basic needs have been met. *Utility* thus becomes the underlying concept of this pattern, the axis around which—independently from revealed truth—the reconstruction of history and its origins rotates. This idea may already be found in the ancient authors and if Warburton argued that the origins of language could be studied by drawing on Diodorus Siculus and Vitruvius, in Lucretius we find an account of the development of human social life and a critique of superstition.[91] "Utilitas expressit nomina rerum,"[92] affirms Lucretius.

This is the same Lucretius who explains the origin of the idea of divinity and superstition: "Praetera cui non animus formidine divom / contrahitur, cui non correpunt membra pavore, / fulminis horribili cum plaga torrida tellus / contremit, et magnum percurrunt murmura caelum?"[93] And if the origin of language derives from "utilitas," superstition derives from *fear*. And fear derives from *ignorance*, from the incapacity to explain natural phenomena. The link between fear and religion, caused by ignorance, would subsequently be discussed by Hobbes in his *Leviathan*:

> This perpetual fear, accruing from an ignorance of causes and which has always accompanied mankind, keeping him in a sort of darkness, must needs have something for an object. And therefore when nothing can be seen, nothing remains to be indicated as the source of man's good or evil fortune but some *power* or *invisible* agent: it is perhaps in this sense that some of the old poets said that the gods were first created out of human fear: which, said of the gods (that is to say, of the many gods of the Gentiles), is veryt rue.[94]

Vico, at least on this point, echoes his view.[95] And, before the publication of Hume's *Natural History of Religion*, which returns to issues raised by Hobbes (issues I shall examine later in more detail), Condillac also dedicates a fundamental chapter of his *Treatise on Systems* to "The Origin and Development of Divination," where he speaks of fear as a source of prejudices and a fount of ignorance:

> If people only realised that everything in the universe is connected, and that what we take for the action of a single part is the result of the combined actions of all its parts—from the largest bodies down to the tiniest atoms—they would never think of regarding a planet or constellation as a basic cause of what happened to them. They would realize how unreasonable it is in explaining an event to take account only of the smallest part of

its contributing causes. But fear, the first principle of this prejudice, does not allow for reflection; it shows the danger, magnifies it, and we are only too happy to be able to ascribe that danger to any cause whatsoever. It gives us a kind of relief from the evils we suffer.[96]

While Fontenelle's comparison, in analyzing the history of oracles and the origin of the "fables," was based upon the assumption that it is possible to trace common traits in people over space and time,[97] and while Lafitau (despite still believing in demons)[98] also demonstrates the uniformity of human nature—even though, unlike in Fontenelle, this uniformity is still tied up with the way in which God had given and then spread the truth—Condillac expands on the greater scope for autonomy (thus following Fontenelle) affecting the understanding of origins, and shifts these away from divine intervention,[99] arguing that similarities between people derive from needs and utilitarian behavior. There is a link between the needs, which become the keystone of the analysis, and fear, which motivates first beliefs. This link is parallel to the one concerning conjectures and observations. Let us see in what sense.

Condillac does not deny the importance of conjectures and hypotheses, but rather criticizes the tendency to see them instead as substitutes for the truth. As D'Alembert would argue,[100] Condillac sees conjectures and hypotheses as a means for inquiry, needed when more accurate observations are lacking. The error of the systems consists in confusing these means with the principles, without being supported by observations. Indeed, in the first case, conjectures and hypotheses encourage research, while in the second they hinder it. The problem of confusing the means with principles presents itself when men have already outgrown the stage of primal needs, because there are few observations to be made at this stage, and they are thus easily verifiable. If the need is not met, the observation is erroneous. But divination is a system that provokes this confusion: this means that divination develops subsequent to the primal needs stage and is generated by fear, which hinders knowledge and inquiry. On the one hand, fear is produced by ignorance, while, on the other, ignorance is strengthened by it.

But why fear? And why does fear make men stop at conjectures, hindering them from going further in the observation of phenomena? Bayle, Fontenelle, Mandeville, Condillac, and Hume all agree in relating beliefs and superstitions to the *irregular phenomena of nature*.[101] The same is true for Giambattista Vico.[102]

In the *Treatise on Systems* Condillac states:

> Among the evils we are heir to, for some the causes are evident, while for others, we do not know what to attribute them to. The latter evils were a

source of conjectures for people who thought they were examining nature when they were merely consulting their own imaginations. This way of satisfying one's curiosity, still so common today, was the only one for people unenlightened by experience. This, then, was the first intellectual undertaking. As long as the evils affected only a few individuals, none of these conjectures gained enough ground to become generally held beliefs. But are they more widespread? What if, for example, the plague were to devastate the earth? Then this phenomenon would hold everyone's attention and men with imagination would succeed in getting their systems adopted. Now, to what cause can still-primitive minds attribute the evils assaulting us if not to beings who find pleasure in inflicting misery on mankind?[103]

Lightning, plague, monstrous births. The irregular phenomena of nature generate fear; fear hinders knowledge and makes men confuse conjectures with observations. But in this case fear depends on the incapacity to control these phenomena, while beliefs create the illusion of being able to do so. From this follows the fact that the beliefs, similarly to the systems of divination, are a naïve means to the basic end of human existence: attaining mastery over nature so as to satisfy one's needs. How is this mastery achieved if not through observation and experience? If a system is based on conjectures (which take the place of observation and experience), it actually hinders the progress of knowledge, whose aim is satisfying and refining human needs through a constantly growing mastery over nature. So what do Lafitau's conjectures, and even more so his system, have to do with history and ethnology? What counts in his writings are the descriptions and the observations, and these, after all, are well grounded. And even though Voltaire and de Pauw ridicule the Jesuit's conjectures, Montesquieu, Ferguson, and Adam Smith make use of his accounts.

But is it enough, in Lafitau's work, to separate the conjectures based on his religious belief from the descriptions he gives of the Iroquois and the Hurons? The "comparaison" is, in fact, to be found between the conjectures and the descriptions; it is even possible to argue that it becomes meaningful in the French Jesuit's reflections in relation to his beliefs. Indeed, the idea that it is possible to globally compare contemporary and noncontemporary savages is based on his hypothesis that originally true religion was given by God to the first fathers, that this religion was then lost, and that the fables and the ensuing explanations are uniform across all peoples. Without the idea of uniformity, it would not have been possible to conceive of the "comparaison," and, consequently, to envisage the complexity of the descriptive system of the customs and practices of "savages" compared with the peoples of "primitive times." The fact that the inquiry has to do, and indeed can do, without the conjectures about the corruption of religion and the degeneration of men, does not exclude the alleged uniformity of men. Fontenelle, the other precursor of comparativism, states: "Since all men resemble one another so greatly, there can exist no people whose foolishness should not make us tremble."[104] The starting point for Fontenelle, who draws a comparison between American savages and early Greeks, is opposed to Lafitau's, but is nevertheless based on the idea that the fables of all peoples resemble one another because men are similar to each other. But isn't this also a conjecture? A conjecture that can do without god, but a conjecture nevertheless. From an epistemological point of view both Lafitau's and Fontenelle's conjectures foster inquiry and observation; yet, the former was set aside, whereas the latter gained ground. The assumption of the uniformity of men and peoples can do without god and the unfortunate circumstances of his revelation, but, from an epistemological point of view, this is not without consequences. On what is this uniformity and resemblance to be based, once divine intervention has been dismissed? By means of the account of revealed truth—lost and then reestablished thanks to Christianity—human history had already reached a goal by means of which it was possible to examine events as part of a supernatural plan. Aside from this, the uniformity of men asserts itself when facing nature. The confrontation with nature opens up an opportunity for knowledge, safety, and exploitation aimed at satisfying one's needs. Without this, there is fear, a fear that transfers to the gods the incapacity to explain and control the irregular phenomena of nature.[105]

In Lafitau, the "comparaison" derives from his religious assumptions, thus shifting his epistemological field. "Primitive" religion appears as a prescientific explanation of the things of nature, in an ideal course of history where men expand their knowledge and make progress. The question shifts: if it is possible to find analogies between American savages and the early Greeks, how can the situation arise that some peoples have outgrown this stage and others have not? In "Sketch of the Second Discourse," Turgot observes:

> The people that first acquired a little more knowledge quickly became superior to their neighbours; and each step in their progress made the next one easier. Thus the development of one nation accelerated from day to day, while others stayed in their state of mediocrity, immobilised by particular circumstances, and others remained in a state of barbarism. A glance over the earth confronts us, even today, with the history of the human race, showing traces of all the steps and monuments of all the stages through which it has passed from the barbarism, still in existence, of the American peoples to the civilization of the most enlightened nations of Europe. Alas! Our ancestors and the Pelasgians who preceded the Greeks were alike the savages of America![106]

Although Lafitau's influence and thesis is evident here, the conceptual scheme of the "comparaison" is closer to Fontenelle than the Jesuit's line of thought. Starting from the assumption of the uniformity of men, Turgot proceeds to consider the issue of the differentiated stages of progress experienced by a people and bases his explanation on the various capacities for acquiring knowledge, along with the development of scientific and technological understanding. We find ourselves in a different epistemological field here, since the formal connections unfold from a stadial perspective.[107] But what must be underlined here is that, even though the theoretical starting point may be found in Fontenelle, it is Lafitau who, despite his conjectures, provides the real material for the comparison. Indeed, were it not for his idea of "comparaison," it would not have been possible to distinguish the difference between the Jesuit and the other travelers. The ethnographic material he provides acquires an additional value because it does not contain only plain description, but field observations, even though they are arranged according to his system of observation, which is based on conjectures. And although one might reject the conjectures, this still would not entail the reduction of his work to description. Therefore, the problem of the relationship between the conjectures, a theoretical system of observation, and comparative observations descriptions remains open.

Should analysis be restricted to a mere distinction between theory and its concrete application, then we might argue that Fontenelle's highly successful theory played an influential role—in particular in France and Scotland—in the development of eighteenth-century thought, whereas Lafitau's work was appreciated mainly for its ethnographic material. In this case, such an approach would lead to a rigid separation between theory and observed facts, as if the facts were completely independent of theoretical assumptions. This may indeed be so, but only to a limited extent. Let us see in what sense.

The Conjectures, the System, and the Problem of Observation

In Lafitau's work one must distinguish between the conjectures on which the theoretical comparative system is based (the system itself within which the facts are arranged and gathered) and the facts that have been observed in a comparative manner.

The conjectures can, in fact, be taken into consideration separately: even though they ensure the construction of the system and the observation of the facts, they are just inquiry hypotheses on which the ideological elements and the beliefs are focused. Lafitau's conjectures are based upon ideas that, ultimately, are guaranteed by the veracity of God and the Christian religion. They are a means of shedding light on facts, starting from their plausible conformity to the Scriptures as revealed truth. But the possibility of separating the conjectures does not immediately concern the observed and described facts. Rather, it regards the system of observation, which, for that matter, is also based on conjectures. Lafitau's system of observation is built upon a "comparaison" capable of structuring the formal connections within which the facts are made visible. Now, when Condillac associates the systems with the conjectures and juxtaposes them with the observations taken from experience, however much this gives rise to a methodological moment of critical importance, since it delimits the value of the conjectures in relation to the inquiry, he does not take the fact into account that conjectures can be substituted by observations only within a system of formal connections which makes these connections visible. From a historical-genetic point of view, Lafitau's system is not arbitrary since it originates from his conjectures and his beliefs; from an epistemological point of view, it is possible to separate the conjectures from the system, provided we admit that the juxtaposition between conjectures and observations must always be theoretically mediated by the system within which the observations are organized and connected. This is not without consequences from the historiographical point of view, because the real historical problem with the reception of Lafitau's work in the eighteenth century not only concerns the rejection of his conjectures and beliefs, but also bears on the issue of his system of formal connections, and thus on the way the "comparaison" is structured. We have already seen this in Turgot. The "comparaison" between American savages and Pelasgians—the ancestors of the Greeks—is already structured into a different system of formal connections, which in turn is founded upon other conjectures. The growth of human mastery over nature determines the different level of progress and explains why the American savages did not move beyond what, for the peoples from whom the enlightened civilization of Europe would spread, was merely a primitive stage. The "comparaison" is no longer rooted in religious assumptions, but rather in anthropological ones, whose purpose is to make conjectures about the uniform behavior of men in certain circumstances and the inequalities in the progress made by different nations. So it is the idea of the relationship between the theoretical and practical knowledge of nature that structures other formal connections within which the theoretical acquisition of the "comparaison" is integrated, and thus altered.

But there is another epistemological aspect that confirms the necessity of the relationship between the system of formal connections and the observed facts. If it is true that the observer cannot be separated from the observation,[108] that is, if it is true he is part of it, then this depends on the fact that the observer has a system of observation whose properties cannot be reduced to his beliefs or to his ideology, even though beliefs and ideology may provide the original impulse for the constitution of the system. Therefore, the evaluability of a system of observation is not bound to the ideology that supports this system while not exhausting it as such—but rather to its formal structure, that is to say, to the *way* in which the observer has built the vantage point from which he can see specific things. Nowadays epistemological reflection bases itself on the problem of the observing system's limits and on its possibilities of self-observation.[109] This aspect can be applied to the historical field even when the problem is not posed epistemologically, but presents itself as such in theoretical practice. The power and the limits of a system's observability represent a crucial point for a historical-philosophical type of reflection that does not wish to limit itself to mere critical-ideological judgments. This is also true for the problem of the comparison between the different formal connections within which the observations are organized. The story of the reception of Lafitau's work during the eighteenth century is, to a considerable extent, the story of the transformation of the "comparaison" system within which the observed facts may be inserted. It is true that Lafitau laid the foundations for transfiguring the savage into a primitive person. Nevertheless, these foundations were actualized in another story, where another system of formal connections was built. To a great extent this story parallels that of the famous *homo oeconomicus*, whose end would be proclaimed only in our century. This is a story in which the importance of Lafitau's system of observation would be in part undermined in favor of the reinforcement of other observations, and it would be undermined not only by criticizing the naivety of his conjectures, but also by downscaling the scope of the comparison. In Lafitau the comparison is comprehensive: it involves economic life, forms of government, and religions. The system of comparison changes in Turgot and the Scottish scholars. The theory of time and the theory of history become part of the issue of the social relationship between man and nature and are included in the hypothesis concerning the behavioral uniformity of men in conditions of parity. The search for an axis of observation through which to move the arrow of time would entail attributing more importance to one of the aspects of the ways of life as a cardinal moment of the comparison.

It is admittedly true, for instance, that on account of his theory of the shared similarities of peoples and his analysis of the American Indians' economic life—which would play an important role in the "subsistence theory"[110]—Lafitau can be considered as one of the predecessors of the "Four Stages" theory. Nevertheless, if we limit the analysis only to the possible influences, we would come up against historicism's old continuistic vice, which tends to delineate a field of inquiry by arbitrarily limiting the analysis to the influences and by disregarding the changes, breaks, and losses. Consequently, by underestimating the reasons behind the historiographic recovery of lost authors, only those elements upon which they exerted an influence are emphasized when, in its turn, the theoretical field was undergoing a transformation. Furthermore, this would fail to throw light on the specificity of whatever thought succeeds in altering the preceding one at the precise moment it begins to gain ground. The fact is that Lafitau's system was altered: the comparison made by the Scottish thinkers differs to the one developed by him, even though it originates from and is undoubtedly influenced by Lafitau's work. After Lafitau, the scope of the comparison is narrowed down precisely because it is necessary to take into consideration the *time* in which the comparable processes have historically differentiated themselves and thus ensure an explanation that—irrespective of individual factors—does not refer to conjectures that happen to fall outside the field of what is specifically human. Ultimately, this is the only truly, and, above all, independently observable field.

Two Hypotheses for the Comparison: Lafitau and Fontenelle

The year 1724 is an important date for the rise of the comparative method. It is not only the year of publication of Joseph-François Lafitau's *Moeurs des sauvages*, but also that of Bernard de Fontenelle's already-famous brief essay *De l'Origine des Fables*. As precursors of the comparative method, what links them is the comparison they drew between the so-called American savages and the early Greeks (we have already seen this in Lafitau) and, independently of each other, the theoretical generalization they made. And indeed, the originality of their respective contributions lies in the theoretical systematicity with which the comparison was conceived, in the awareness that the method they were proposing to adopt could generally be used in the inquiry which juxtaposed and drew parallels between worlds and forms of life so distant in time and space.

Lafitau, as has already been said, made a fundamental methodological and theoretical contribution to the bilaterality of the relationships between contemporary "savages" and the peoples of antiquity. As, on this issue, did Fontenelle.

Hes tates:

> This shows that the Greeks were, for a while, savages, just as much as were the Americans; that they were lifted from barbarism by the same means; and that the imagination of these two peoples, so far apart, agree in believing that those who have extraordinary talents are children of the sun. Since the Greeks, for all their intelligence [*esprit*], when they were still a young people thought not all that much more rationally than the barbarians of America, who were, to all appearances, quite a young people when they were discovered by the Spaniards, there is reason to believe that the

Americans would have come eventually to think as rationally as the Greeks, if they had had the time.[111]

But if, in general terms, what links Lafitau and Fontenelle is the factor of systematic comparison—in particular the strong belief about the similarities in practices, customs, and thinking of the Americans and the early Greeks—perhaps the most important fact is that the systematicity they respectively put forward through their comparative theories is expressed on the basis of quite different conceptions, beliefs, hypotheses, and points of view. This can be seen in the passages quoted above: whereas Lafitau expresses in a methodological manner the possibility of throwing light upon the ancient Greeks by analyzing the ways of life of the American Indians, Fontenelle goes further. He goes as far as to say that if the Spaniards had not arrested the evolutionary time of the Americans, they would perhaps have taken the same road as the Greeks. Fontenelle hypothesizes thus that the internal stages of a society's evolution are the same for all peoples, except for outside interferences, which can arrest or deviate the course. He refers to the period when the Greeks "were still a young people" and speaks about the Americans as "quite a young people when they were discovered by the Spaniards."[112] Subsequently, he would refer to the Phoenicians and Egyptians as peoples "older than the Greeks.[113] So, it is possible to trace the antiquity of a people by taking into account the degree of the "sottises," of the stupidities reiterated in the "Fables." The comparison is thus grounded in the idea that the times of a people correspond to the degrees of their mind's evolution. The "Fables" allow us to find these correspondences. Hence, he hypothesizes a sequence of stages of evolution and improvement that in some way rigidly succeed each other, unless external events interfere and change their development. In this regard, the communication between peoples belonging to different evolutionary times has the effect of transforming stories into "Fables." Accordingly, since the Phoenicians and the Egyptians were older peoples than the Greeks, their stories passed to the Greeks—still a young people—and were transformed into "Fables."[114] When writing was invented, Fontenelle goes on to say, the increase in opportunities for communication helped to disseminate the "Fables" and "to enrich one people with all the stupidities of another; but one gained from it in that the shifting traditions became more or less fixed, and the bulk of the fables, remaining pretty much in the state in which the invention of writing found them, degenerated no further."[115]

On the contrary, Lafitau's argument is based on the assumption that the first Fathers had received a pure religion, which was then corrupted. Therefore, from the viewpoint of the notion of time, the fables or the myths are alterations of an originary knowledge. But the former still bear traces of the latter. Unlike Fontenelle, who attributed the similarities discernible in fables to the level reached by a people in their evolution, and who saw in them traces of historical truth which, however much it may have been altered, was passed on from an ancient to a younger people, Lafitau explains the same similarities through the idea of the dispersion of an originary knowledge of which there are still traces.

From this point of view—that is, from the viewpoint of the idea of time capable of justifying comparative inquiry—the distance between Fontenelle and Lafitau is immense. The explanation for and justification of the comparative method they came up with, which were so very dissimilar, would have remarkably diversified historical consequences. This is attributable, as has already been mentioned, to the different assumptions they start from in order to arrive at similar results.

Lafitau is a traveler, a fieldwork researcher whose work results from his firsthand experience with the Iroquois and the Hurons. He systematically describes all the aspects pertaining to the American Indians' way of life: occupations, religion, customs, kinship system,[116] warfare, and education. But the crucial point is that he was not content simply with description.[117] Lafitau organizes the facts and the knowledge according to a comparative method that is rooted in his religious belief. As a Jesuit, Lafitau starts from the assumption that there are no human societies without religion and that it is possible to draw parallels between the Iroquois and the early Greeks on the basis of the biblical dispersal of humankind and the ensuing diffusionist idea.

In this framework of convictions and assumptions, Lafitau structures the comparison in accordance with the *genetic* model that explains the similarities of crude fables across the most diverse peoples, starting from the idea of a faulty reception—ascribable to passion and ignorance—of an originary source of communication common to everybody—not so faulty, of course, as to hinder the retrieval of traces in the altered stories. In any case, even though peoples may be differentiated in accordance with the way the stories are altered, the persistence of similarities depends on the fact that the transmission of stories and the communication between peoples have moved along a temporal ladder whose highest rung is occupied by the originary religion of the first fathers.

This is the context that enables Lafitau to maintain that traces of the originary religion or, in any case, the persistence of the belief in god are discernible in the beliefs and the religions of all peoples, even the most primitive ones. It becomes clear that, from the point of view of time, the comparison drawn by Lafitau is still based on the intervention of god and on the intervention of the devil as elements capable of accelerating or hindering the progress toward truth and perfectibility. In this respect, notwithstanding the original unity of peoples, their routes become differentiated over the course of time, thus leading to either degeneration or perfectibility.

Fontenelle is a free thinker, a defender of reason, an enemy of opinions based on tradition, and the author of the 1686 *Histoire des Oracles* and of a fragment entitled by the editors *Sur l'Histoire* to which *De l'Origine des Fables* is closely connected.[118] Unlike Lafitau, Fontenelle does not place religion at the origin,[119] because religion is produced by ignorance and by a sense of the marvelous.[120] When faced with the prodigies of nature, error originates from the search for a cause without ascertaining the facts.[121] Disregarding god, Fontenelle draws the comparison on the basis of an assumption about human nature.

As we have seen, Lafitau assumes the existence of demons, whereas in his *Histoire of Oracles* Fontenelle shows that demons may in no way be considered as the authors of oracles.

The differences in the convictions and the assumptions held by these authors who systematically use the comparative method have to be emphasized not only so as to draw attention to the different ideological assumptions that have given rise to this method, but also so as to foreground the fact that these differences produced diverse ways of organizing the formal connections upon which the comparative theories would subsequently rely.

Times, Formal Connections, and Conjectures

For Lafitau, as for Fontenelle, fables, or myths, are coarse representations people have made of themselves, their history, and their origin. But the difference between them consists precisely in the structuring of time. Whereas Lafitau considers the fables, or myths, to be remnants of an originary knowledge possessed by the first fathers and given to them by god (and hence as traces of a previous time), Fontenelle considers the fables or myths as the first or originary attempt at explanation, as the temporal starting point for the perfectibility of peoples.

In the absence of a hypothetical history bearing the marks of god's intervention, as instead is the case with Lafitau, Fontenelle has to focus on a different assumption: the universality of human nature and, thus, the similarities between peoples, who, if placed in conditions of parity, act in the same way and tend to progress over time.

By placing human nature at the center of the issue, and by underlining the similarities of all peoples under the same conditions, Fontenelle must consequently find a single explanation at the origin that may be valid for the various peoples who lived independently of each other at the primitive stage.

From this starting point Fontenelle refers to the prodigies of nature and the sense of the marvelous as moments that gave rise to the first crude systems of explanation. Religion is born when natural phenomena are attributed to divine power, and the very crudeness of the explanation depends precisely on the fact that the causes are attributed to these phenomena without properly ascertaining the facts. But what needs to be underlined is that Fontenelle attributes the origin of religious beliefs and, as he terms them,[122] the first philosophical systems to the impact the *irregular phenomena of nature* had on savage and primitive men. It is worth quoting directly from Fontenelle, who challenges a statement made by Canguilhem in an important essay on de Brosses's and Comte's concept of fetishism. In this text Canguilhem attributes a conception of the origin of religious belief to Fontenelle that is based on the uniformity and regularity of nature.[123] It is certainly true, as Canguilhem argues, that in *De l'Origine des Fables* Fontenelle states that the prodigies of nature are usually explained through ideas taken from very familiar objects.[124] But this only means that the savages and the primitive peoples attempted to give a reason for the irregular phenomena of nature by relating them to the order and the regularity that belonged to their experience and their conceptual world,[125] and not that the fables mirror the course of nature's regular phenomena. In fact, Fontenelle states: "The first idea that men had of some superior being was based on extraordinary effects, and not on the regulated order of the universe, which they were incapable of recognizing or admiring."[126] It is clear that everything that was outside their experience was considered by the first men to be prodigious, but this was the effect of their ignorance,[127] which enlarged on those initial explanations in the fables.[128] The savages and primitive peoples used a system of explanation analogous to that of modern man: that is to say, they attempted to relate the explanation of phenomena to their experience and their conceptual world. But the difference lies in the limited experience, which hindered the ascertainment of the facts and, therefore, led them to attribute an erroneous cause to the variousp henomena.[129]

Furthermore, it is by taking into consideration the idea of the irregular and extraordinary phenomena of nature that Fontenelle is led to assert that for the savages and primitive peoples the image of a superior being was closely connected to *power*[130]—the first form of social relationship they had. By imagining the divinities as beings more powerful than themselves, capable of throwing thunderbolts, stirring winds, raising the waves of the sea,[131] the savages and primitive peoples attributed to them the only social form they were familiar with—the idea of power—and barely considered any other attributes such as wisdom or justice:[132] "Nothing could more effectively prove," says Fontenelle, "that these divinities are very old, and nothing could better mark the road taken by the imagination in forming them. The first men were utterly unaware of any quality better than bodily strength. Wisdom and justice did not even have names in ancient languages, nor have they today among the barbarians of America."[133]

Hence, the antiquity of the belief in divinities imagined as more powerful human beings is proved by assuming the growth and development of the process of thinking itself, which, in turn, derives from the growth and development of practical experience. Once these phases of growth and development have been established—according to a scale at the top of which, in terms of time, stands the notion of power, seen as physical power[134]—it is possible to make conjectures about the antiquity of the beliefs, the way they succeeded one another, the way they developed and, thus, draw a comparison between savages and ancient peoples.[135] According to Fontenelle there are, therefore, parallel times within which a people can develop, following a fixed pattern, unless an external factor such as discovery or invasion by other peoples interferes and changes this course.

According to Fontenelle, the initial idea of divinity had its origin in the irregular phenomena of nature, and the error arose on account of the attribution of causes without having first ascertained the facts. This is what definitely sets him apart from Lafitau, who considered the act of attributing divine powers to thunder to be a specific case.[136] In fact, Lafitau argues that the Iroquois make a clear-cut distinction between a superior being and minor gods, depicted as the authors of natural phenomena.[137] Under this aspect, the assumptions on which Lafitau's comparative method rests are quite different from those of Fontenelle. This issue plays a decisive role in the further development of the comparative method and depends on the *conjectures* that were to be accepted and taken up again. Indeed, what is considered by Lafitau to be just one particular case is seen by the authors of the so-called conjectural history as the originary case of the birth of religion.

The Irregularity of Natural Phenomena, Fear, and "Conjectural History": David Hume's Theory of Religion

The idea that religion arises from primitive man's fear of the irregular phenomena of nature is, as we have seen, rooted in antiquity. In the modern era, starting from Hobbes, it was progressively related to a critique of the superstitious forms of religion. In actual fact, although projected back to the origins, this criticism concerned the struggle going on at that time to give greater autonomy to the quest for scientific knowledge. Furthermore, Condillac's *Treatise on Systems* delimits the field of the conjecture: it is useful only when there are not enough facts to be observed. And certainly the issue of the origin of religion, if explored autonomously, that is to say outside of revealed truth and sacred texts, could not avoid lending itself to conjectures, since the facts concerning primitive men were few and far between and could be obtained either by reading ancient texts or by studying contemporary "savages" and, thus, by drawing comparisons through time between primeval mankind and American Indians, African Negroes, or Laplanders. These facts could be used for formulating a conjecture about the possible course of history.

Furthermore, doing without gods and demons as actors who intervene in time and history implied finding explanations that were not only capable, as in Fontenelle, of shedding light on the similarity between the fables of the ancients and those of the savages, but that could also give a reason for the progress of some peoples. Undoubtedly, the assumption of a universal standard of human nature, which—under the same conditions—always follows its due course, provided an ideal framework for imagining the human being as increasingly capable of assimilating natural phenomena within his conceptual order—phenomena that, since they were irregular, he could not initially account for. The growth of practical experience expanded his horizons of knowledge and, thus, his familiarity with the world, and these were factors that contributed to an increasing capacity to assimilate phenomena and ascertain the facts, so as to attribute them to the right cause. But what governed this growth of experience? How were the leaps forward made? Here, as well, the factor of *time* was to play a role of pivotal importance.

In the *Natural History of Religion* David Hume returns to the topic of fear in order to explain the origin of polytheism and relates it to the issue of the irregular phenomena of nature:

> But a barbarous, necessitous animal (such as man is on the first origin of society), pressed by such numerous wants and passions, has no leisure to admire the regular face of nature, or make enquiries concerning the cause of objects to which, from his infancy, he has been gradually accustomed. On the contrary, the more regular and uniform, that is, the more perfect nature appears, the more is he familiarised to it, and the less inclined to scrutinise and examine it. A monstrous birth excites his curiosity, and is deemed a prodigy. It alarms him from its novelty; and immediately sets him a-trembling, and sacrificing, and praying.[138]

The image of a barbarian pressed by numerous needs and passions provides an explanation for the polytheistic origin of religion, since—as Hume believed[139]—if human nature is uniform, then man's behavior depends upon the circumstances he finds himself in. Therefore, according to Hume, fear and the attention toward the irregular phenomena of nature depended on an environmental situation in which primitive people were pressed by needs and passions. The factor of *time* is implicit in the discourse: indeed, the circumstance of pressing needs and passions means that primitive people did not have time for thinking, save in a superficial way, because they were unable to pause and search for the real causes of those phenomena. Hume will argue[140]—and so will Adam Smith[141]—that under these circumstances, the relationship with nature is not based on contemplation but arises, rather, from a concern for the events of life, fears, and hope. For so long as human beings remain entirely preoccupied with controlling the problem of satisfying their immediate wants, their experience will remain limited to precisely that. This is the reason why their idea of deities cannot but depend on this limited experience. And since "there is a universal tendency amongst mankind to conceive all beings like themselves, and to transfer to every object those qualities with which they are familiarly acquainted, and of which they are intimately conscious,"[142] it is natural that they should attribute to deities features and qualities deriving from the extent of (and indeed limit to) their capacity for knowledge. In particular, they attribute a typically human will and intentions to nature, except they are more powerful. The absurdity, Hume argues, of ascribing human qualities to gods, appears when:

> we cast our eyes upwards; and transferring, as is too usual, human passions and infirmities to the deity, represent him as jealous and revengeful, capricious and partial, and, in short, a wicked and foolish man in every respect, but his superior in power and authority. No wonder, then, that mankind, being placed in such an absolute ignorance of causes, and being at the same time so anxious concerning their future fortunes, should immediately acknowledge a dependence on invisible powers possessed of sentiment and intelligence. The unknown causes, which continually employ their thought, appearing always in the same aspect, are all apprehended to be of the same kind or species. Nor is it long before we ascribe to them thought, and reason, and passion, and sometimes even the limbs and figures of men, in order to bring them nearer to a resemblance with ourselves.[143]

The pressure of needs and passions, a limited experience, the inability to explain the causes of natural phenomena and of life events: all these elements contribute to creating the scenario given by Hume on the origin and progress of religion. For Hume, as for Fontenelle before him,[144] the power of primitive imagination depends on the limits of men's experience of the surrounding world. This is the point where imagination takes the place of precise knowledge of natural phenomena, which, consequently, are divinized according to specific schemas.

On these grounds Hume argues that the first religion of mankind must have been polytheism. *And it is precisely with this assertion that he combines facts with conjecture.* In the first place, Hume delimits the universality of religious belief: as Bayle before him, he admits that—"if travelers and historians may be credited"[145]—there have been atheistic peoples. If this is so, and if another fact to be considered is that no two nations have ever had the same opinion on religion,[146] then it is possible to deduce that religion does not arise from a natural instinct, such as self-love, affection between the sexes, love of progeny, gratitude, or resentment, that is to say from instincts that are, effectively, universal.[147] Religion is not universal and its first principles must therefore be secondary.[148] And if the first principles have been historically acquired, then it is in the historical records that one must find the possible origin of religion. And according to the records and the facts the first religion was polytheism:

> It is a matter of fact incontestable, that about 1,700 years ago all mankind were polytheists. The doubtful and sceptical principles of a few philosophers, or the theism, and that too not entirely pure, of one or two nations, form no objection worth regarding. Behold then the clear testimony of history. The farther we mount up into antiquity, the more do we find mankind plunged into polytheism. No marks, no symptoms of any more perfect religion. The most ancient records of the human race still present us with that system as the popular and established creed. The north, the south, the east, the west, give their unanimous testimony to the same fact. What can be opposed to so full an evidence?[149]

Hume then argues that "mankind, in ancient times, appears universally to have been polytheistic."[150] But how can the assertion of the universality of polytheism be reconciled with the delimitation of the universality of religious belief? The reason is obvious: in the first case the universality is delimited—by asserting that there have been and there are atheistic peoples—in order to include religion in the history of society and civilization. Religion is, in fact, an element acquired by mankind, an element acquired during the course of mankind's historical development. In the second case, the universality of polytheism indicates the first historical stage of this acquisition—a stage all the peoples go through on their journey toward civilization. Indeed, the assumption of the universality of polytheism is opposed to the idea that this belief was preceded by monotheism: the belief, which was then abandoned, in only one being. We have seen, for instance, that Lafitau bases his conjectures—by coordinating the facts and the comparison—precisely on the idea of an originary monotheistic religion.

On the contrary, as far as mankind is concerned, Hume argues:

> As far as writing or history reaches, mankind, in ancient times, appear universally to have been polytheists. Shall we assert, that in more ancient times,

before the knowledge of letters, or the discovery of any art or science, men entertained the principles of pure theism? That is, while they were ignorant and barbarous, they discovered truth; but fell into error, as soon as they acquired learning and politeness.

But in this assertion you not only contradict all appearance of probability, but also our present experience concerning the principles and opinions of barbarous nations. The savage tribes of America, Africa, and Asia, are all idolaters. Not a single exception to this rule.[151]

After all, these facts and testimonies are in tune with the idea of natural progress. Is it possible to imagine, Hume argues, that men inhabited palaces before huts or studied geometry before agriculture?[152] "The mind rises gradually, from inferior to superior."[153]

Therefore, both the facts and the idea of mankind's natural progress strengthen the conjecture of the polytheistic origin of religion.

But this combination of facts and conjectures implies a decisive element: religion is a fact of civilization and an acquisition of society. Its progresses and developments are to be studied historically. Hume's "conjectural history," as it was termed by Dugald Stewart,[154] shifted the scope of the analysis of a phenomenon such as religion away from hypothetical and merely speculative explanations toward religion's social implications. It is the social circumstances and the stage of progress reached by civilization that are able to explain the status of religion, that is to say the scope of the experience gained by a people in the arts and the sciences, or rather in the ability to control and master natural and, consequently, social events. This field of experience has, nevertheless, different levels even within the same nation. This explains why polytheism resurfaces even among developed nations, where people are still living in ignorance.[155] Although there is a progressive tendency toward the refinement of the idea of religion, this nonetheless does not exclude relapses and different levels of growth within the same nation. Once again, to the comparison over a course of time marked by progress is added the comparison between different classes of the same nation. The poorer classes bear a certain resemblance to the "savage" and "primitive" peoples. This is a constant feature of the enlightenment theories of progress.

Before taking into consideration the relationship between the contribution of Hume and the theory of de Brosses, it is worth underlining the importance of Hume's writing for the Scottish stages theory, based on the "modes of subsistence." The act of connecting religion and its progress to the social circumstances within which nature's irregular phenomena were explained paved the way for an approach toward the notion of civilization which explored the succession of these social circumstances—that is to say, an approach which examined ways of mastering nature and organizing needs, both from a technical and a scientific point of view. This issue developed contemporaneously in France—in particular with Turgot and Goguet[156]—and Scotland, where Hume's writing provided an informing methodological impulse. During the same years, in fact, Adam Smith would write a series of essays, which would be published posthumously, in which he established a relationship between the primitive explanation of nature's irregular phenomena and the first people's or "savages'" conditions of subsistence[157]—the very same Adam Smith who would divide civilization into four stages on the basis of the modes of subsistence.[158] Lord Kames and John Millar would take the same approach.[159] The comparative method was definitively and systematically subordinated to the unilinear time of progress and the way the contemporary "savages" organized their material life provided a basis for relegating them to primitivism. But the rigid subdivision of history into stages—the Age of Hunters, the Age of Shepherds, the Age of Agriculture, and the Age of Commerce—that is to say, the simplification used for supporting the universality of progress—was proved wrong precisely by the facts.[160] But in any case this is an extremely significant aspect of the relationship between the comparative method and the notion of time based on progress: that is, of the contemporary "savages'" systematic reduction to primitive man. This relationship, as far as religion is concerned, is central to Charles de Brosses's theory of fetishism.

Chapter Two
Charles de Brosses's Theory of Fetishism

Definition of Fetishism

In the previous chapter I introduced some of the premises of de Brosses's theory. Before the president of the Assembly of Dijon set out to write on fetishism, discussions of Guinean fetishes had already appeared, alongside descriptions in travelers' accounts, and had been compared to similar phenomena common among other "savage" peoples. As the comparative method was gaining ground, it became clear that its connection to theories on the progress of humankind impinged on the question of religion and its possible origin.

Some of the authors cited earlier, such as Bosman and des Marchais for the Guinean fetishes, the Jesuit Lafitau for the comparative method, as well as David Hume with his *Natural History of Religion*, were among the main sources of de Brosses's analysis (Hume in particular, as we shall see below).

Nevertheless, the reduction of primitive religion to the notion of fetishism implies a peculiar combination of these sources, especially with regard to Lafitau. de Brosses is typically mentioned alongside Lafitau as one of the forerunners of the comparative method.[1] Yet such an approach would not be historically complete, if one does not take account of the profound theoretical differences, which relate to a particular way of developing the comparative method, through conjectures and ways of proceeding quite different from those used by Lafitau, and which were gaining ground at the same time as the analyses of the Jesuit Father. Besides, if the publication of the work by Lafitau and the short essay by Fontenelle in 1724 make this a landmark year, it must be remembered that the attempt to apply the comparative method through conjectures and hypotheses unconnected to the Revealed truth—that is to say through a notion of human nature and its behaviors devoid of any divine or demonic intervention—had already been developed a long time before. Bekker, v an Dale, Fontenelle himself, and others had fought the battle for independent historical knowledge, and Fontenelle had supported, as we know, the theory of progress.

de Brosses, like Turgot and Hume, belongs to the tradition of Fontenelle: the primitive expressions of humanity, such as religion, were to be analyzed according to the notion of a gradual progress from barbarism to civilization, parallel to the gradual development of the human mind from the concrete to the abstract. With reference to Turgot, Manuel says:

> By the theological stage, Turgot—writing in the tradition of Fontenelle and paralleling the works of his friends Hume and de Brosses on the natural history of primitive religion—meant the propensity of men to project intelligent divine power into all manner of objects and forces in nature.[2]

This propensity, which was typical of the first stage in the progress of humankind, is precisely what de Brosses will identify with the term fetishism.

In 1756 President de Brosses, known for his *Voyage en Italie*[3] and for his *Traité sur la formation mécanique des langues*,[4] which Turgot would shorten for the *Etymologie* entry of the *Encyclopédie*, published a *Histoire des navigations aux Terres Australes*, a work in two volumes, in which he had collected and summarized the travel diaries of the various captains, who had visited and described these lands between the sixteenth and the first half of the eighteenth century. On several occasions in this work de Brosses expresses the view that if some of the ancient peoples had been able to progress, then the same could happen to all the others. The colonial intent of this hypothesis emerges clearly in the second volume, where de Brosses tries to explain that there is no such thing as indomitable peoples and therefore none unsusceptible to education and progress.[5] More than in the philosophical treatises, it is here that de Brosses makes clear the colonial implications of the term *progress*. And it is just a few pages after these observations that the word *fetishism* can be found with reference to the cult practiced by the inhabitants of the island of Manila. They belong to the oldest people among those found in all the other foreign colonies of the area, the colonies being the reason that pushed them toward isolation in the inaccessible rocks and woods of the island. Among these black people it is customary to venerate certain round stones, tree trunks, and "various other types of *fetishes*, like the African Negroes."[6] They also seem to share this custom with some of the most ancient peoples, who had a similar cult of "Baetyles,"[7] "which is a type of *fetishism*, resembling that of modern savages."[8]

We encounter here a foretaste of what would become a general theory in the work published four years later, which had also been the subject of a *Dissertation* in 1757.[9] Not only are the fetishes among the Negroes in Manila similar to those among the African Negroes, they also resemble the cult of the most ancient peoples. In conclusion, what we find here are all the elements of a comparison, in space and time, between the "savage" peoples of his time and ancient peoples. Lafitau's lesson has been adapted and transformed in a work where the notion of progress is imbued with mercantile and colonial overtones.

When we approach the work itself, which was published anonymously in 1760, we may be led to believe that the comparison is confined to the African Negroes and the ancient Egyptians, as the full title reads: *Du Culte des Dieux fétiches ou Parallèle de l'ancienne Religion de l'Egypte avec la Religion actuelle de Nigritie*. In reality, although the bulk of the analysis revolves around this parallel, de Brosses's argument extends to include both other "savage" peoples and other ancient peoples.

Let us now turn to the definition of fetishism, a concept that de Brosses uses more generally to refer to a form of primordial religion, common among ancient peoples and "savages."

Primitive peoples' dogmatic opinions and ritual practices all focused "either on the cult of the stars, known under the name of Sabeism, or on the cult, perhaps not less ancient, of certain terrestrial and material objects called *fetishes* by the African negroes among whom this cult exists, and which for this reason I shall call *fetishism*.".[10] Immediately after this, de Brosses adds that even though the term fetishism, in its proper sense, refers to the Africans' belief, he will use it "in speaking of any other nation whatsoever, where the cult objects are animals or inanimate beings that have been deified, even in speaking sometimes of certain peoples for whom objects of this sort are less gods, properly speaking, than things endowed with a divine virtue; oracles, amulets, and preservational talismans."[11]

de Brosses intends to set this type of religiosity apart, especially because both Sabeism and fetishism are more ancient than idolatry proper.[12] Besides, these types of lore deserve a different analysis and classification from that employed for deified men. In addition, when exploring the Egyptian cult of animals, one finds that this type of cult is common among many ancient peoples.[13] It is therefore possible to classify this cult of inanimate objects or animals as the first stage of religion, that is to say, the stage before idolatry and deification of human beings, representing but a primordial aspect of it.

It is obvious, of course, that fetishism, being a form of original cult, is engendered by fear compounded with ignorance.[14] Classifying fetishism as the first stage of the evolutionary spectrum of religious thought and practices does not explain why contemporary "savage" peoples—the living proof of this ancient cult—persist with the lore; alternatively—the flipside of the coin—why had some peoples gone beyond this stage. On this point de Brosses's explanation is very ambiguous. On the one hand, he excludes the "chosen race" from this stage: "With the exception of the chosen race, there is no nation that has not been in that state, if one considers them only from the moment when one sees the memory of Divine Revelation entirely extinguished among them."[15] On the other hand, he dwells upon an argument which appears to give credit to the theory of degeneration, a theory which postulated an original monotheism, which later degenerated and became contaminated. This thesis was found in Lafitau, as discussed earlier. de Brosses says:

> The human race had first received from God Himself immediate instructions conforming to the intelligence with which His goodness had endowed mankind. It is so astonishing to see them later fallen into a state of brute stupidity that one can scarcely avoid considering it a just and supernatural punishment for the forgetfulness which they had made themselves guilty of toward the kind hand that had created them.[16]

This statement appears, however, like a cautious rhetorical device. In actual fact, de Brosses says, God had given no truth, but rather instructions in compliance with human intelligence. Human beings have not been able to take advantage of it, and that is why one cannot help thinking that the state of brute stupidity into which they have fallen must be some divine punishment. This thesis is not accepted as the conventional historical narrative based on the sacred texts. It is instead a hypothesis that is plausible in its own right. After all, how was it possible that some nations had remained at that stage, whereas others, after having passed through it, managed to go beyond it? de Brosses takes great care not to allow God to intervene in these matters. He says that

> a part of mankind has remained until this day in that unformed state: their customs, their ideas, their reasoning, their practices are those of children. The rest, after having passed through this state, have sooner or later come out of it by means of example, education, and exercise of their faculties.[17]

The fact that some nations have remained at the stage of fetishism may lead us to believe in divine punishment, but in fact the explanation can be found, firstly, in their state of isolation, which prevents them from following the example of others—in the *Histoire des Navigations*, as mentioned, the fetishist Negroes from the island of Manila were isolated—secondly, and consequently, in the impossibility of being educated and thus exercising their faculties—again in the *Histoire des Navigations*, he stated that any people can be educated and disciplined in exercising their faculties. The colonial principle made de Brosses as optimistic on the communication of progress as he was rendered assertive in accusing of brute stupidity all the peoples devoted to fetishism.

Yet the general principle de Brosses adheres to, and on which he bases the comparison between the modern savages and the ancient peoples, is that similar actions demand similar principles:

> After having shown the present-day fetishism of modern nations, I shall compare this with that of the ancient peoples, and since that parallel will lead us naturally to judge that the same actions have the same principles, we shall demonstrate quite clearly that all these peoples had the same way of thinking about the matter, for they had the same manner of behaving, which is a logical consequence of that premise.[18]

A Theory of the Primitive Mind

de Brosses's argument on the opportunity of development that education and example would offer primitive peoples, and its corollary, the permanence of fetishism caused by isolation, does not imply a diffusionist theory like in Lafitau. Taking the Bible as evidence, the Jesuit had supposed that, among the many migratory movements that followed the Deluge,[19] America had been populated through Asia, since he believed in the single origin of humankind. Historically there exists a genetic thread linking all the peoples who have gradually populated the different places on earth. In Lafitau's view, this is the hypothesis that underpins the assumption that, even though these scattered peoples have strayed from the truth of the original religion, they have preserved traces of it in their myths. These are weak traces, he concedes, but this is because of humans' decline into ignorance and corruption. The concept of trace allowed Lafitau to compare the various myths and lore, and to regard them as memories of the same narrative. In conclusion, Lafitau's diffusionism implied, on the one hand, the notion of a single origin of peoples' history; on the other hand, it allowed an interpretation of their lore as going back to the initial truth. His method is genetic.

According to de Brosses things are different. He bases his comparison on a theory of the primitive mind, as Fontenelle had done before him. In the first section of his book, de Brosses describes the current fetishism among Negros and other savage nations, from those in America to the Laplanders. When comparing these different nations, and after mentioning the Ethiopians, de Brosses notes, with regard to the cult in Yucatan:

> Another country, far removed from this one, provides us with an example of the manner in which the savages come to choose their deities; at the same

time it gives us proof of how much this ridiculous cult, spread so far away and yet shared by peoples who had not been in communication with each other, can easily come to mind to coarse persons.[20]

While discussing the topic of fetishism among ancient peoples, de Brosses adds a further point to this notion of the primitive mind leading the most diverse peoples to the same cults, despite the lack of contact between them. In explaining the reason why he has repeatedly mentioned the Egyptians, the most ancient people with fetishistic cults, de Brosses states: "It is natural, in effect that an opinion which is widespread among all barbarian climates, be equally so in all the centuries of barbarism."[21] For a theoretical justification, the projection of fetishism in time depends therefore on its universality as a phenomenon in the contemporary savage world. The theory of the primitive mind implies the assumption that humans, who have the same way of thinking, are clearly at the same level of development and therefore carry out the same actions. Having established the universality of the fetishistic practices in space, that is, among contemporary savage peoples, and having noticed that this practice occurs in "all climates," there is nothing more logical than to think that it has occurred over time. And so the theory of the primitive mind uses "savage" contemporaries as evidence for ancient peoples. The generalization of the concept of fetishism as a universal practice in contemporary space and in the time past depends therefore on this theory.

> All the evidence derived from the argument appear to indicate, as I shall say later, what we are here presenting as factual evidence; that is to say that Egypt had been as savage as many other countries. The factual evidence that show us an Egypt worshipping animals and vegetation, what I call, in short, *Fetishism*, is no less abundant than precise. And since the customs, cult and actions of the Egyptians were almost the same as those of the Negroes and the Americans, is it not natural to conclude that they have all acted by virtue of an almost uniform way of thinking, and therefore conclude that there lies precisely the mystery of an enigma for which we have long sought a word?[22]

This argument of the primitive mind implied the hypothesis of its development and its progress. Indeed, the idea of finding the origin of religion, of searching for primordial cults that correspond to the primordial mind of men, is informed precisely by a classification, along the ladder of progress, which aligned the human mind with that of human society. The resulting diachronic primacy of this classification meant that the differentiation of cults and religious rites was informed by the notions of "before" and "after." Along this ladder, fetishism predates the worship of heroes and the building of statues, which is, in practice, an idea of the development of the human mind from the initial stage of its faculties—a boundary stage [23]—to their high stage—such as that of civilized peoples. With regard again to the Egyptians, de Brosses insists on the precedence taken by fetishism and Sabeism:

> Fetishism and Sabeism were then the only two religions accepted in Egypt... the erection of statues of human figures had rarely been in use, or had not yet taken place, nor had the idolatry of deified persons; and as for the latter... Egypt has hardly ever been prone to it, likewise it has similarly no presence in Negritude.[24]

Fetishism and Sabeism predate idolatry and the cult of heroes, as well as the erection of statues. There are stages of development in the human faculty of symbolic representation, and fetishism is the lowest stage, one where the choice of objects of worship does not involve the reproduction of figures or images. It becomes clear then how the arbitrary nature of fetishes, often mentioned by voyagers, is here placed within an evolutionary theory of the human mind, which defines it in relation to a primitive use of its faculties.

Fetishism in Remote Antiquity

The anxiety generated by this overarching classification, designed as an evolutionary ladder, leads de Brosses in search of the oldest evidence of fetishistic cult, so as to show how this has taken precedence over time. While Lafitau and Fontenelle had declared that the Greeks had been savages, de Brosses adds that the Egyptians had been savages, too.

The antiquity and authenticity of the fragments by the Phoenician Sanchuniaton, reported in the *Praeparatio Evangelica* by Eusebius of Caesarea, who had drawn them from Philo of Byblos,[25] was the subject of debate and speculation at the time.[26] In particular, Sanchuniaton talks about "Baetyles," "animated stones" crafted by the god Uranus.[27] According to Huet[28] and Bochart[29] these "Baetyles" come from the stone used by Jacob: to make the sacred pillow he poured in oil and called the place "Bethel."[30] On this basis Bochart suggested that the "Baetyles" were not "animated stones," but rather "anointed stones."[31] Etienne Fourmont in his *Réflexions sur l'origine, l'histoire et la succession des anciens peuples* denied that the "Baetyles" had originated from the Stone of Jacob and claimed that they predated that time.[32]

As I have already mentioned, de Brosses in the *Histoire des Navigations* had referred to "Baetyles" as fetish objects of worship.[33] And in *Du Culte des Dieux fétiches* it is the "anointed stones" he dwells upon again to support his thesis of the primordial nature of fetishism. On the one hand, de Brosses accepts Bochart's suggestion and uses "anointed stones" rather than "animated stones."[34] Indeed, "animated stones" implied the idea that the "Baetyles" were idols, representatives of a god, whereas "anointed stones" indicated the peculiarity of fetishism, that is, their direct deification. On the other hand, however, de Brosses, unlike Bochart, maintains that the "Baetyles" predate the Stone of Jacob.[35] In fact, the Jews had inherited primordial cults from other peoples, more ancient cults that continued to exist alongside those new. That is why one can often come across a mixture, for example, between fetishism and polytheism, but in it one can single out those older elements that have survived and that coexist with the new ones.[36] The classification of the cults in the evolutionary timeline becomes a method of investigation and interpretation.

de Brosses therefore goes in search of these "anointed stones" throughout ancient mythology. In fact, together with their respective cults, they are part of the myths of all ancient peoples, and the myths narrate the origin of religion. Even the Jews have inherited this narrative,[37] and so have the Egyptians, Syrians, and Chaldeans.[38] And even though their myths differ in the details, it does not follow that these peoples disagree on the general facts concerning fetishism.

> One can see that they have all written down the traditions they have received, and almost against the same backdrop of ideas; if this is nothing but the truth, which one can find in its pure form among the Jews, it is often omitted or disfigured among the neighbouring nations. As for the details surrounding the circumstances, they no longer agree, which is very natural. Does the same thing not happen also in the tales of recent events which converge on the essentials of those occurrences? Nothing would be more in vain than the efforts and suppositions which we would want to make so as to give a total conformity to the opinions of antiquity. Every country has its myths, which are not those of another country, and should be left to them.[39]

After analyzing these ideas among the oriental peoples, including the civilized ones, where the arts and philosophy flourish, and where in the early centuries of barbarism the same theory proves true,

> would we not be surprised to find it in Greece, which we know as far as its infancy? We should not hold a different view on the savage Pelasgians, who inhabited it up to the time when it was discovered and populated by the Oriental seafarers, from the one we have on the Brasilians or the Algonquins.[40]

And it is thanks to the history of Greece that de Brosses's arguments on the primordial nature of fetishism become more precise.

The lesson of Lafitau and Fontenelle, according to which even the Greeks were savages, is taken up again here. Above all, in his theory of the "primum movens" of the lore and religious practices, de Brosses uses the comparison that Lafitau made between Algonquins and ancient Greeks, and between American Indians and Pelasgians. His analyses' shifts in time unfold in an attempt to differentiate fetishism from idolatry through the hypothesis of the gradual progress of the primitive mind in its ability to represent and symbolize. In this sense, relying on Herodotus, he insists on thef act

> that Greece would later give the old anointed stones the names of the foreign gods, that the stones and the other animal fetishes do not represent anything, and that they were divine by their own divinity.[41]

This last point is very important: against the idea that Baetyles were representative of human figures, de Brosses argues that they did not have this quality: they were "anointed stones," not "animated stones." As such, they did not represent any gods; they were deified as themselves. This is for de Brosses the main feature of fetishism as a form of primordial religion.

Fetishism before Polytheism

Fetishism precedes polytheism in time, because it precedes it in the development of the human mind. Even when fetishism and polytheism are mixed, it is possible to distinguish one from the other. In fact, while in fetishism the objects themselves are the deities, in polytheism they have turned into representatives of the deities. This is probably the turning point of de Brosses's theory:

> The representation of once important things cannot today be found but as a symbol that is routinely added to the image of the gods, which are, in terms of date, secondary.[42]

The theoretical classification arranged diachronically defines fetishism for its peculiar and primordial character of deifying objects. Of all the things travelers had said about fetishes, that they were general and particular, that they were arbitrary and concerning the exteriority of religion, de Brosses offers a theoretical generalization by subsuming the comparative method under the idea of progress of the human mind and society. Arbitrariness in the choice of fetish objects and exteriority of primitive religion: these descriptive attributes, given by travelers, recur in de Brosses's theory. In addition, they are a confirmation of, and even reinforce, the notion of fetishism built on the idea that a primitive mind has poor and limited ability to symbolize and represent. What is more, the comparison between "savages" and "savages" and between "savages" and the ancients in turn confirmed the conformity of customs and practices and supported the primacy of the diachronic classification, the subordination of space to time. If all contemporary "savages" had practiced a religion similar to that of the African fetishes, then this was a first theoretical step that ensured consistency in space. If in addition, having proved such a consistency, and having made such a generalization, the same consistency in practices was to be found in primitive times, then the second theoretical step would be possible, the step that would link the spatial generalization to the temporal one. From this point of view, it is not just the diffusionist theory, such as Lafitau's, which ensures *genetically* the consistency of the comparisons of the spatial kind with those of the temporal one. A theory of the primitive mind that accepts the assumption of progressive stages of development of human faculties can come to the same conclusions, too—*with one major difference, though.* Lafitau thought that pagan religion was the result of corruption and ignorance, and that the falsehoods it was full of derived from the inability to understand those symbols that the early Fathers knew well. This only meant one thing that primitive pagan religion *substituted* the creatures with the creator. Natural phenomena were thus deified, starting with the sun.[43]

But Lafitau interpreted this decay process in line with his hypothesis of a monotheistic origin of religion, and in virtue of the fact that despite the fall, *traces* of the original religion had remained among polytheist peoples. Moreover, he says that many "savage" peoples do not have any idols,[44] nor any of the ancient peoples' excesses of idolatry. There is therefore an important distinction: no matter how broadly he speaks of idolatry,[45] the fact remains that the forms of divine representation are differentiated by the presence of idols, or lack thereof. Yet Lafitau's theoretical position on this point should be clarified, and for a substantial reason: the absence of idols does not imply the lack of representativeness of invisible beings in visible objects. On the contrary, Lafitau goes in search of traces of the forgotten God in all the deified objects. In effect, his monogenetic hypothesis implies that the forgotten or disfigured truths are not such as to prevent a search for the divine wisdom originally passed down to humans. In the end, even when talking about inferior deities or subordinate tutelary gods[46] Lafitau implies that these live alongside the "savages" belief in a higher being, and therefore they cannot possibly form the basis for a generalization of the idea of a primitive religion that deifies things without them representing invisible beings. The Manitous, which Lafitau compared to the fetishes, remain in any case, from the outset, subordinate entities.

To de Brosses, in contrast, fetishism is the origin of religious belief, and it is characterized by lack of representativeness. When objects are deified as representing invisible beings, then they are to be classified as a more advanced phase. de Brosses takes to the extremes the ascending trend of the diachronic interpretation. Fetishism is the first, crude form of religion precisely because objects are deified in themselves. The theory of the primitive mind and the hypothesis of the progressive course of human societies take to the extreme consequences the subordination of the comparative method to unilinear time. The sequence of steps in his argument is flawless, and it is thanks to such assumption that it is possible to investigate methodically and to discover, for example, in polytheism, mixed forms of fetishism and therefore the traces of a previous form of religion.

But this search for the "primum" in fetishism (defined as the deification of things) meant, from the point of view of the theory of time and the course of history, that this form of religion, found in lands where the unsophisticated mind of humans has no faculty of representation, was not a substitution of God with things. Such a substitution would have meant that things had previously represented the invisible gods. This form of religion was instead an attribution of divine powers to things. The primacy of the diachronic framework inevitably led to this conclusion.

Before questioning this point and drawing all the theoretical consequences, it is still necessary to dwell on the plurality of fetishism, and of its temporal precedence with respect to polytheism.

More on Fetishism and Polytheism: de Brosses and Hume

In 1757 Diderot wrote to de Brosses to say that he had read the manuscript on fetishism and that he was pleased with it. "You are right," Diderot writes, "fetishism was certainly the first religion, general and universal. The facts must necessarily agree with the philosophy."[47] Diderot had grasped the theoretical element in de Brosses and accepted it. de Brosses had connected the facts in a theory that allowed the generalization of the concept of fetishism. Immediately after this, Diderot compares de Brosses's manuscript with the *Natural History of Religion*: "You have completed the proof of the natural history of religion by David Hume."[48] As Madelaine David points out, in the third section of his *Du Culte des Dieux fétiches* de Brosses related entire passages of Humes's *Natural History of Religion*, which appear superimposed when compared to the rest of the work.[49] Diderot's letter confirms the fact that de Brosses had read Hume after writing at least part of the first two sections of the work, which were to form part, in all likelihood, of the *Dissertation* on fetishism presented in 1757.[50] Diderot brings Hume's work to de Brosses's attention, and de Brosses draws from it to strengthen the general philosophical theory, central to his analysis of the concept of fetishism. In effect, as Diderot had observed, the theory of fetishism appeared to complete Hume's theory of the origin of religion. Fetishism, as the first form of lore and religious practice, appeared as a specification and a further clarification of the Humean theory, according to which the origin of religion was polytheistic. Yet this specification and clarification that fetishism was said to represent in relation to polytheism has some problematic implications.

But let us examine for the moment the third section of *Du Culte des Dieux fétiches* entitled "Examination of the causes to which Fetishism is attributable." Here de Brosses summarizes the principles on which his analysis was based and the general conclusions he had reached:

> So many similar facts, or facts of the same type, establish with the utmost clarity that what is today the religion of the African Negroes and other barbarians, was formerly that of ancient peoples, and that in all centuries, as well as all over the earth, one can perceive the dominance of this worship directly rendered, without images, to animal and vegetable productions.[51]

Having asserted the universality in space and time of this primordial cult, de Brosses claims that it is fear and folly that lead the human spirit to take on those superstitions. But how was it possible that such cults were so common among all peoples? Without denying the possibility of dissemination and communication from one people to another, for example, between ancient Egyptians and African Negroes, de Brosses propounds the theory of the primitive mind and claims that it is possible that fetishism established itself at the dawn of humanity wherever people's state of mind was psychologically coarse.

> When one sees, in centuries and in climates so far apart, men who have nothing in common with each other, but their ignorance and barbarity, having similar practices, it is all the more natural to conclude that man is so made that left in his natural brutal and savage state, not yet formed by any reflection or imitation, he is the same as regards primitive manners and customs in Egypt as in the Antilles, in Persia as among the Gauls: everywhere there is the same mechanism of ideas from which comes that of actions.[52]

The savage human is uniform everywhere;[53] this assertion is the basis of the generalization of the concept of fetishism. *It is also the basis of the observation*: diversity of customs and traditions is homogenized by the theory of the primitive mind. The savage human is uniform everywhere: the entire observation, in space and time, of different worlds can be connected, thanks to this principle. The reduction of the network of comparisons in space to a form of classification based on diachrony does not need a genetic, diffusionist theory. The savage is uniform everywhere because of his coarse mind, which produces the same actions. From this point of view, de Brosses embarks on a critique of the theories that argued that the worship of animals or stars was never direct; it symbolized instead divine beings. According to de Brosses, "this way of thinking reverses the natural order of things."[54] In fact, thinking that all peoples have started with an "intellectual religion" which was later contaminated

> does not conform at all with the natural progress of human ideas, which is to go from physical objects to abstract knowledge, and from what is near to what is far, tracing back from the creature the creator, not tracking down from the creator he does not see, the nature which is under his eyes.[55]

The distance from Lafitau's hypothesis is obvious and is based on the Humean principle, according to which, in the natural order of things, we move from the concrete to the abstract. After the Deluge, humanity started again from scratch, from its childhood. It makes no sense, therefore, to look for a link between the first religion and the contaminated religions, to try to find clues to retrace an original monotheism. It started all over from the beginning, and it is from this real beginning that the investigation of the peoples must start.

Next, de Brosses relates Hume's passages on fear and on the unusual natural phenomena that produce early forms of religion.

Theory of the primitive mind, transition from concrete to abstract as the natural course of progress, and fear of unusual natural phenomena: these themes are gradually linked together in the comparative observation in time and space of the ancients and the "savages." On these points the commonality of ideas between Hume and de Brosses is very clear. Nevertheless, the analysis cannot stop at this finding. It would appear in fact, given the same principles, that the theory of fetishism completed Hume's theory of polytheism, as Diderot said. But when one takes a closer look, some complications arise when linking these principles within the interpretive grid of progress as a function of time. In fact, fetishism is a specification or a completion of the Humean analysis of the polytheistic origin of religion, precisely in the sense that it *predates* polytheism as such. But this precedence in time, within the transition from the concrete to the abstract, within, as Diderot would say, the connection of events in philosophy, implies the substantial fact that while Hume talks about the deification of visible objects or phenomena, which represent invisible beings to which people attribute intentions, de Brosses talks about objects that are deified in themselves and do not represent invisible beings. de Brosses's procedure undoubtedly takes Hume's analysis to the extreme consequences: it is perfectly logical within the idea of the natural transition from the concrete to the abstract gradually accomplished by humans. Alternatively, going backwards, fetishism turns out to be, effectively, the end point of the concrete, or, in other words, the starting point of the progress in the course of things. It is the first level of the symbolic and representative faculty of humans facing those events of nature they cannot find a "rational" explanation for. The savages are uniform everywhere in this regard.

The turning point given by Hume to the subject of the origin of religion had another consequence: that the analysis based on degeneration was wrong. According to said analysis idolatry and polytheism were based on the *substitution* of the Creator with the creatures, of the represented with the representatives, of the Supreme Being with the objects that symbolized him on Earth. But such a substitution process presupposed a notion of history on a downward trend, so to speak, that is, as a transition from the original truth to its decline and contamination. And this simply meant building a historical timeline that could be reconciled with such theoretical assumption. In fact, when one refers to *substitution*, it is assumed, of course, that something is replaced with something else, and when this something else is considered an unsuitable substitute, an abnormal fact, then it follows that the "normal fact"—that which has been replaced—was there *before*, in its function and role of what it stands for. Similarly, idolatry is just a substitute for the monotheistic truth, which logically precedes idolatry and polytheism. From such an assumption then, a notion of history as confirmation of this truth is unraveled. The theoretical assumption materializes in the hypothetical historical process, which goes from the original monotheism to polytheism and idolatry, by degeneration. Divine truth determines history.

Hume's hypothesis, on the contrary, showed that the practice of attributing divine intentions to natural phenomena and life events derives from the low level of knowledge and experience of men who "generally tend to conceive of other beings as similar to themselves." Hume's hypotheses ruled out any possibility of active intervention of either God or demons. Even the latter's evil intentions, which Lafitau would still seriously consider, fitted perfectly with this typically barbaric tendency to transfer typically human attributes to other beings.

But it is at this point that the *origin* question becomes thorny: by making historical research on religion autonomous, by removing from it the revelation of the divine word, the problem of the *before* in history emerges, that is to say, the problem of when history begins, and when it may actually be defined as history. The framework offered by Hume, based as it is on the idea of progress, of human knowledge as a sequence of successive and progressive steps, changes completely the theoretical problem of substitution. It is no longer a matter of considering polytheism as a replacement of divine truth, but rather as a replacement of a scientific truth. That change is crucial. Hume argues that the attribution of divine features to inexplicable events, to the unusual natural phenomena, derived from the limits of knowledge and experience that allowed only an imperfect assimilation of those events and phenomena in the system of normality built by primitive men. Fear stems from the limits of their cognitive and conceptual system. It is for this reason that Hume, in his analysis, contrasts the usual order of things and family—order that does not affect the poor savage—with the unusual phenomena that he cannot rationally master. Progress is then marked by the growth of this mastery, which means a greater ability to assimilate the unusual phenomena into the cultural and conceptual category of the usual devised by humans as they enhance their knowledge. The procedure described by Hume presents the following sequence:

(a) Human beings are affected by an unfamiliar phenomenon and are afraid of it.
(b) Human beings transfer onto this phenomenon a power that is familiar to them.
(c) Human beings give this power a superior strength, although of the same quality that they possess.
(d) Human beings come to deify this phenomenon, *assimilating it into their conceptual world, precisely because it is recognized as foreign. Hume determines here the contextual limits of the universe of the "primitive mind."*

The deification, therefore, of unusual natural phenomena reflects this dual, conflicting feeling among "savages": they assimilate these phenomena into their poor conceptual universe, but they do so having recognized their extraneousness and superior might.

The transfer onto things of those features peculiar to humans has, by that very fact, the function of *substitution*, but the objects of substitution have changed. It is features of humans being reflected in natural phenomena and taking the place of the real causes that produced them. And the process of their deification creates and at the same time hides this substitution.

In Hume, too, there is a logical *primum* that materializes in history and structures its *observation*: the deification of natural phenomena replaces their scientific understanding. Their extraneousness is treated as such. This logical "primum" becomes the historical "primum," since what belongs to observation—that is, the idea of a substitution of scientific truth with deification—becomes description of the historical process. Now, the *origin* of religion can be structured in this way, of course, if, and only if the ancients and the "savages" were observed through an idea of progress that is defined by the growth of knowledge and the mastery of nature. Here too, therefore, the idea of substitution pertains to the observer and to his formal connections, and not to the person being observed, for whom this is not to do with substitution, but with truth. The way one looks behind their truth and conscience always depends on how the observation from the outside is structured and how it is made to fit inside their world. And Hume structures it according to the principle of assimilation to his own cultural world, which recognized the "others" and their diversity within the framework of the timeline of progress.

Charles de Brosses's fetishism would narrow down Hume's procedure, by articulating an additional step: the first stage of religion, which predates polytheism proper, consists in attributing features of men to things, which become deified and therefore recognized as extraneous but at the same time assimilated in the conceptual universe of the ancients and the "savages." de Brosses, proceeding on his own account, had found in Hume a similar theoretical observation, which would further strengthen his argument.

In 1763, Hume wrote to de Brosses:

> You may easily believe, that it gives me great Pleasure to see the few Principles, which you had deignd to borrow from my Writings, and in a Light so much stronger than I was able to throw upon them; and I was equally surprized to observe the great Accumulation of Facts, which your superior Learning had enabled you to collect. I dare not flatter myself, that I have not been mistaken in the Conclusions which I drew from the natural Progress of the human Mind; and tho not by my own Force, yet by that of my Ally, I dare boast of my Cause as invincible.[56]

Observer, Observation, and Observed Facts

The deification of those things, to which typical human characteristics are attributed, is therefore twofold, as it is defined on the basis of both alienation and assimilation. Something, an object, a phenomenon are deified precisely because it is at the *limit* of the conceptual universe of the savages. But this definition is made possible by an idea of knowledge as the process of assimilation of the world, a world where objects and extraneous natural phenomena are dominated and mastered. By placing them in the realm of natural causes and effects, they are deprived of their nature as gods.

From this point of view, fetishism is a bad symbolization; as a theory it produces a twofold conflicting effect: on the one hand, there is, in the attribution of typical human characteristics to things, a process of symbolic human reversal; on the other, this reversal process is reduced to the effects of the poverty of the conceptual and symbolic universe of the "savages." In the former, the objects become, unconsciously, a mirror of the processes of the human brain; in the latter this mirror reflects those distorted and magnified characters symbolizing natural phenomena.

It is necessary at this point to discuss de Brosses's theory of fetishism from the point of view of the observer-observation relationship.

If we consider the scenario offered by Brossean theory with regard to a primitive world devoted to the worship of fetishes, we can see in what way the boundaries of this world are established. The deification of objects and unusual natural phenomena determines the limits of both "savages" and primitives' power of observation. It is worth repeating here that the deification of things defines their assimilation as entities that remain *extraneous*. But who defines these limits within which primitive human beings act the way they do? Clearly, this is done by an outsider, an external observer, whose knowledge informs the creation of that scenario and whose observation includes parts of his personal identity and his culture and excludes other aspects of observable reality. And his knowledge is based on the idea that the progress of the human mind moves forward through scientific knowledge and the mastery of nature. This idea is in turn projected onto the observed world, thus determining the scenario. The observer here, unlike that in the theories of fetishism by Marx and Freud, is outside the observed world; yet, he must necessarily internalize it and assimilate it to make it meaningful to the symbolic world he is part of. And the internalizing of this external world, this object of observation, is achieved here through the theory of unilinear time. If the "savages" stand as evidence of a past world, this means that both "savages" and ancients are homogenized in a time that belongs to the interpretive framework of the observer. Observing the "savages" means looking back at one's own past, and this looking back gives a universalizing meaning to the process of observation. The external observer introjects the observed world, and by doing so he applies the kind of observation that is culturally shaped by his conceptual universe. Given that this conceptual universe is based on the assimilation of external nature to his practical power and knowledge, its projection into a different world will reveal only *a certain diversity*, one measured on the stages of development of that practical power and knowledge. This explains why the definition of fetishism takes as a starting point the relationship between human beings and, above all, nature, and why the observed world appears, in origin, beset with fear of unusual natural phenomena. In Western culture, scientific knowledge begins to take the place of religion and its traditional role as a safe harbor for humans: by contrast, the savage and primitive world is originally defined as beset by fear. This definition, that dates back to ancient culture, now includes the "savages," who thus come to bear the brunt of the battle taking place in the Western world between scientific knowledge and religion, between rationality and superstition. This happens precisely because such a battle is projected into the universe, in worlds that are other, because the Western culture of the eighteenth century tends to reduce all the surrounding space to a mirror image of its own past, thus imposing *its* history as universal history. The "savages," projected into the past, represent evidence of people one can come across in this journey backward to assert one's own future. The way in which the external observer *enters* "savage" worlds is determined by an idea of history and time which, by including those worlds, at the same time excludes. Arbitrary objects, outward rites, personal fetishes, and general fetishes: all these items are included simply like this, that is, by excluding any other possible explanation. What would be the point, when we are clearly confronted by primitive minds that tremble in the face of natural phenomena?

Nevertheless, the inclusion-exclusion process, described as degrees or stages of evolutionary time and progress, presents itself as a strong theory of the observer, especially when we compare it, historically, to those theories that combine the observation, through biblical lenses, of "other" worlds with the hypothesis of a single original religion, later contaminated, for all peoples. In this respect, the gap between de Brosses and Lafitau is quite significant. The Jesuit, basing his analyses on a genetic notion of human history derived from the Bible, had turned his conjecture of the existence, originally, of an early religion of the fathers into a method of investigation, which he used to find in all "savage" and primitive religions *traces* of that early religious form. In addition, by applying his conjecture to the comparative method, he had discovered Platonic and Cartesian ideas among the Iroquois.[57] de Brosses, on the assumption that the natural order proceeds from the concrete to the abstract, not only denies that conjecture, but exposes the fallacy of those theories that apply to the "savages" the ideas of the cultural universe of the observer, as they twist the interpretation of the indigenous words in order to discover meanings that make sense only within the culture of the observer. "When reasoning about their way of thinking, one must [...] beware of attributing to them our ideas, as they are now attached to the same words as those used by them, and one must not lend them our principles and our reasoning."[58] Savages' and primitives' ideas of the divine have a distinctive meaning that depends on their universe, experience, and needs. The external observer must therefore explain savages' and primitives' ideas by setting them in the context of their environment and at the stage of their development. The fundamental problem of the historical and social situatedness of cultures and beliefs is, to a certain extent, introduced here. A few years later Scottish philosophers and historians, friends of Hume, would theorize the need to refer the customs, habits, and culture of peoples to their respective means of subsistence.

However, the subordination of the idea of situatedness to the notion of a unilinear time of progress, that marked, after all, the dissolution of the constraints imposed by the power of God on scientific knowledge, and offered another cultural universe and an alternative ideology, involved taking on a new self-awareness whose universality was to be imposed, through diachronic assimilation, to the world. It was a notion of progress conceived, more and more, as mastery of nature, and one that would produce, in a future already visible, individual and social happiness. The awareness of freeing oneself from natural bonds meant the acceptance, on an individualistic basis, of the primacy of the man-nature relationship, which would consequently lead to the man-society relationship.[59]

Marcel Mauss's suggestion to banish the concept of fetishism from ethnographic discourse would be made in the name of another model of observation, a method of investigation that would seek to describe fetishistic practices as symbolic systems of regularity in social relations. In other words, it would shift the field of investigation from the primacy of the man-nature relationship to the primacy of the man-society relationship. And in this realm there would be no place for a concept such as fetishism, by now historically linked to a scholarship that tended to include observation in a scenario where the man-nature relationship still prevailed. In this sense, in opposition to Wundt, he argued that fetishes could not be arbitrary, but rather ruled by the code of religion and magic, an eminently social code.

The "immense misunderstanding," which Mauss would talk about, had therefore a very specific history, a history that, through the worlds of the other, would slowly shape the so-called self-consciousness of bourgeois culture. It is not surprising then that a concept created within the emergence of said self-consciousness would be so successful throughout the nineteenth century, a time when the social sciences were based on the ideology of progress.

After de Brosses

When Kant uses the concept of fetishism in 1793, he talks about it as a well-known concept.[60] Heyne mentions Manitous and fetishes in 1764,[61] but these two words had already been used by Rousseau in *Émile*.[62] When Dupuis discusses fetishism, he sets against it the worship of the stars as the possible origin of religion[63] and Destutt de Tracy supports him.[64] Leroy, on the other hand, echoes de Brosses's line of argument.[65] From Comte to Spencer fetishism is placed at the beginning of the ladder of progress.[66] Meiners takes up de Brosses's core argument and Marx's sources include de Brosses, Meiners, Böttiger, and Constant.[67] Hegel confines fetishism to Africa, "the childhood of history."[68] McLennan draws a distinction between fetishism and totemism.[69] Lubbock suggests that fetishism occurs after atheism in the trajectory of progress.[70] Alfred Binet's essay on fetishism in love will be one of Freud's sources.[71] The popularity of fetishism, in the late eighteenth and throughout the nineteenth century, is huge, yet always problematic. Nevertheless, the name of de Brosses, who invented it, disappears from the stage, or rather his fame enjoyed a lesser renown than the concept. Briefly acknowledged in a footnote or blatantly ignored, as in the case of Comte—in many ways one of the closest to de Brosses's theory—who cites instead Hume and Adam Smith among his sources,[72] de Brosses, as author of *Du Culte des Dieux fétiches*, has hardly existed and still does not exist. But the spread and popularity of fetishism testify to what extent this concept fitted into an ideology and a way of thinking that was already in de Brosses, in his theory of progress and in his use of the comparative method. It was in this context that fetishism arose and later became widespread.

Two authors have, to some extent, changed the context: Marx and Freud. They analyzed phenomena from within, as *internal observers*, phenomena of a society they culturally belonged to. For this reason they faced the opposite problem compared to de Brosses and the others: they had to turn the insider's observation into that of an outsider so as to provide an implicit comparative framework that could shed light, by analogy, on the observed phenomena. Commodity fetishism and sexual fetishism refer back to religious and ethnological fetishism, that is, to the context that was an "immense misunderstanding." Yet, despite the altered context, the changed framework of observation, as well as the standpoint of the observer and the nature of the observed phenomena, that "immense misunderstanding" had nonetheless provided a crucial landmark and source of knowledge. This proves that any misunderstanding, having established itself in history, becomes irreversibly part of a culture and a language, even when its inherent deception is revealed.

Chapter Three
The Concept of Fetishism as a Theoretical and Historical Problem

The Concept of Fetishism in Ethnography: An "Immense Misunderstanding"

In 1907, Marcel Mauss put an end to the role that the concept of fetishism played in the field of ethnology and in the history of religions. In reviewing a book by Dennett for "Année Sociologique," Mauss observed:

> When the history of the science of religions and ethnography comes to be written, one will be astonished by the unmerited and fortuitous role that the notion like that of the 'fetish' has played in theoretical and descriptive works. It corresponds to nothing but an immense misunderstanding between two civilizations, the African and the European; it has no other foundation than a blind obedience to colonial usage, to the *lingua francas* spoken by Europeans on the West coast. One has no more right to speak about fetishism concerning the western Bantu than one may be accustomed to speaking about it with regard to other central or eastern Bantu. Equally one does not have the right to speak of Negro fetishism: Guinean or Congolese idolatry (this is very rare), Congolese witchcraft, the ownership taboo, and others, are not found to be, in the Congo or Guinea, of a different nature than that of other religions or other societies. On the contrary, it is really remarkable that the fact of what appears to be the very truth concerning the notion of the fetish had been known since the seventeenth century.... The success of the book by de Brosses had to be due to some sort of simplicity, of mistake, perhaps necessary, in which the science and the study of religions, African religions in particular, have existed up ton ow.[1]

When Mauss wrote these words, the concept of fetishism was still used to describe one of the forms of primitive religion. Wundt, still in 1904, in his *Völkerpsychologie*, spoke of fetishism as a specific form, more precisely as an involutional form of totemism.[2] In this respect, Wundt deviated from the classical theory that considered fetishism as a primitive form of religion. However, Mauss himself, when reviewing Wundt's work in 1908, observed that the German thinker, while conceiving fetishism as a next step in the development of primitive religions, in fact remained in thrall to the classical theory that considered this religious form as absolutely primitive.[3]

But still in the 1930s, the historian of religions and ethnographer Wilhelm Schmidt had to insist on the inadmissibility of fetishism as an autonomous religious phenomenon, noting that where fetishism is found, it is never a primitive phenomenon, but a phenomenon that belongs to already-advancedc ultures.[4]

More recently, Valerio Valeri's discussion of some of the most important theories of fetishism has narrowed down the theoretical field of anthropological investigation for the word fetish, and has defined it as an individual object, whose validity rests in its nonsubstitutability in the context of symbolic values, and whose occurrence, in these terms, can be found in all socialc ontexts.[5] Meanwhile Joseph Goetz, for his part, insists that

> it is false to think that there are people whose religion is animism, fetishism, or magic: these are cultural phenomena present in varying degrees in every religion, especially when considered unilaterally in a superficial and popular sense, as is too often the case when studying the religions of others. But in no case can it be said that one of the above-mentioned phenomena, or even all of them together, constitute the entire religion of a particular people; in no case can these phenomena help us understand the meaning that the practical wisdom and morality of these people gives them.[6]

As one can see, the trend in anthropological studies is to remove the specificity of the concept of fetishism as a religious phenomenon, independent and identifiable in some particular society. The sharp criticism moved by Marcel Mauss undoubtedly effected a turn in the theoretical reflection also on this point. But up until Mauss the concept of fetishism enjoyed great popularity that lasted precisely from 1760 until the early 1900s. This is because, from the beginning, fetishism was conceived as a form of primitive religion. On the characteristics of this form, there were very different theories, in relation to both classification and type. However, there is no doubt that fetishism maintained a general character that enabled it to embody one of the stages of human cultures from the state of barbarism to the state of civilization. Indeed it can be said that fetishism is considered one of those key concepts that have characterized the kind of anthropological investigation that was built on the general idea that the comparison and classification of social systems ought to be informed by the notion of the stages of transition that humanity went through in its path toward civilization, which of course meant Western civilization.

The very fact that the concept of the fetish was, as Mauss said, an "immense misunderstanding" constitutes in itself an important historiographic and philosophical problem. How was it possible that such a notion, built on a "misunderstanding," could become so important in the field of theoretical history of ethnography and history of religions? Could it simply be explained, as Mauss stated, with the oversimplification and error that characterized Science and its description of religious and social phenomena?

Mauss's response appears, in effect, hasty and insufficient. Let us begin first from Mauss's observation cited above, according to which the concept of the fetish in ethnography corresponds to an immense misunderstanding between two civilizations, the European and the African, and derives from the colonial use of European languages spoken in the West coast. But perhaps precisely because of this origin, this concept, more than any other, allows a reflection on an aspect of the *inner* history of Western thought, of its consolidation in certain *structures of observation* of the "other"—an aspect, which undoubtedly includes the colonial and ideological dimension of the word's origin, but from the point of view of the historical-theoretical investigation, it is not limited to this.

In fact, if we were to confine the analysis of the concept of the fetish to its ideological origin, we would certainly make some accurate comments, but perhaps we would miss something out, that is, the fact that this concept has been included in a large conceptual context, in a system of formal connections[7] that underlie certain theoretical processes of a comparative nature. From this perspective, the discussion becomes complicated, since the issue is not only the origin of the term, but also the relationship between the term (with its origin) and the conceptual context in which it has historically been included.

If we do not set out from this consideration, we run the risk of undermining the issue. If the history of the concept of the "fetish" is the result of an "immense misunderstanding,", one must explain how, historically, such a "misunderstanding" has come to existence. The spread and popularity of the concept of fetishism can be explained because this concept summarizes the inclusion of the notion of the fetish within a given complex theoretical and conceptual structure that attached the comparative method to the Western view of world history as progress. If the concept of "*civilization*" that was gaining ground in the second half of the eighteenth century subsumed Western universalism under the dynamics of historical-evolutionary processes (i.e., it subordinated other societies' time to bourgeois time).

the concept of "fetishism" established the Western view of the "other," of the savage reduced to a primitive. The subordination was achieved, by showing that those practices of objects worship belonged to the first step of the ladder of progress. The generalization of the concept of fetishism for all ancient and savage peoples could thus become essential evidence in support of the dynamic Western universalism: it allowed a classification of the most diverse peoples at the primitive stage of progress. The concept of fetishism realized, therefore, the possibility to use the effects of the comparative method, which had already broken what could be called the isolationism of Western history (which Bossuet, for example, still stood for),[8] to broaden the scope of the universality of the Western world, of its history and of its time.

Matters of Methodology: The Issue Concerning Historiography

The word "misunderstanding," used by Mauss to brand the notion of the fetish in ethnography, is therefore reductive. On this subject, it is worthwhile to look at another work by Mauss. In his long, sustained analysis of Wundt's *Völkerpsychologie*, Mauss criticizes Wundt's explanation of the concept of fetishism. Against the instability of Wundt's analysis that, among other things, linked the choice of the fetish object to the strangeness of its shape,[9] Mauss says: "The object that serves as fetish is never, no matter what has been said, any random object, chosen arbitrarily, but it is always defined by the code of magic and religion."[10] To paraphrase this statement by Mauss, one can say that the choice of the concept of fetishism in the ethnological theories between the second half of the eighteenth century and the end of the nineteenth century was not arbitrary, but dictated by a code that was becoming established in conceptual frameworks of observation and theories' formal connections.

The above paraphrasing of Mauss's observation actually intends to determine a field of inquiry that is, within certain limits, different from the one in which he writes. Mauss's accurate comment that it is Wundt's mistake—typical of ethnological theories—to consider the choice of the fetish object as arbitrary is a comment that *concerns the observer-observation relationship vis-à-vis the object observed*. In fact, when Mauss says that the choice of the fetish object is not arbitrary, since it always depends on the code of magic and religion, he criticizes a *mode of observation* of the observed object. But in this case, the observed object is an object of ethnographic observation. Wundt's analysis and Mauss's criticism represent in effect two different modes of ethnographic observation, competing for the same observed object. But when one turns to the problem of the "immense misunderstanding," the object in question is no longer ethnographic, but historiographic. *The object in question is actually a concept*, that of fetishism, that is, a phenomenon that is intrinsic to the modes of observation themselves; it is neither an object (an external phenomenon), nor a social-symbolic practice.

One must of course concur in the fact that such a distinction cannot be but theoretical and formal. It is obvious that there can never be an ethnographic issue devoid in itself of a confrontation between theories, as one is never presented with a historiographic problem devoid in itself of associations with external reality. And yet this distinction appears necessary. When Mauss criticizes Wundt's mode of explaining the fetish object and comes to the conclusion that the object cannot be described by the term "fetish," because the specificity that it aims to define does not exist, and when he disputes the idea of arbitrariness in the choice of the fetish object, he effectively sets his own mode of observation, his own theory against Wundt's. The relationship with the external object, with the object called fetish, depends on the theoretical parameters within which it is observed. Although the conflict is between theories, the link with the external phenomenon to be described still remains—even in the case when it is doubtful if the same term actually designates the same object.

But when Mauss, criticizing Wundt's theory, wonders how the term fetish and its counterpart and consequent concept of fetishism have managed to become established in the history of ethnography, he effectively moves the investigation to the specific field of historiography. What he calls the "immense misunderstanding" marks the location of the transition to another field, and what he defines as an "oversimplification" and a "mistake" of ethnography is in fact an epiphenomenal statement about something, whose explanation falls within another form of investigation. He already implicitly refers to another object of study, which requires the specific tools of the historiographic method.

Having thus determined the kernel of the distinction, it is important to emphasize that this can be found within a unified whole that can be defined as the field of *meta-theory*, that is, the theoretical observation of theory as an object of investigation. Ultimately, we could reverse the order of the two aspects—the object and the mode of observation—which define, on an ethnographic level, the meaning of Mauss's critique of Wundt. We said earlier that even though this critique targets the mode of observation, that is, the theory, it deals nonetheless with an external phenomenon, one for which the term "fetish" is either appropriate or not. We also added that this dealing could provide, albeit in a theoretical and formal way, the distinction between the ethnographic and the historiographic fields. But if we now hypothetically focus on the modes of observation, rather than on the external phenomenon, then the distinction between ethnographic field and historiographic field undergoes a qualitative change. Both ethnography and history deal with meta-theory: the mode of observation is the subject and object of analysis, but as an object, it is defined on the one hand, by the critique of another mode of observation (e.g., in our case Wundt's) and, on the other hand, by the *history* of how that mode determined by observation came into existence—a history that is both a search for "precursors" of the proposed mode of observation, and a search for a network of errors of a rejected mode of observation; either way this history appears as an integral aspect of self-reflection of the theory adopted. The possibility itself of knowing and describing the object depends on the kind of relationships established by the chosen mode of observation. Even when one analyzes an external phenomenon, a social practice, a "social fact," that is, an object that pertains specifically to ethnological and ethnographical theory, when one goes beyond the mere acceptance of the external referent, what is brought into the equation is the system of associations that the mode of observation establishes with itself and with other modes of observation. The historiographic moment, in turn, intervenes when the referent is no longer the external phenomenon, nor the "social fact" (with its objective aspects and its other aspects defined by the mode of observation), but it is rather the relationship that is created between the mode of observation and its internal and external history. The historiographic moment deals therefore with the problems connected to the associations that the mode of observation creates on the meta-theoretical level, but it does not deal, in the first instance, with the external referent, that is, with the problem in itself of knowing and describing this referent. The historiographic moment's referent and object is a concept or a network of concepts in the making, which also includes aspects of discontinuity and rupture. But while the ethnographic moment must presuppose rupture and discontinuity as *exclusion* from its field in order to define itself and to relate to the external referent, the historiographic moment *comprises* within its field exclusion itself. Ultimately, this is what appears to be the outcome of Michel Foucault's historiographic thinking. Every object is excluded and at the same time constituted because it belongs to the self-defining field of discourse; yet, the exclusion is part of the historical observation; otherwise the analysis would be reduced to the presupposition of external discursive entities, in themselves full and ontologically alternative; which is what Foucault himself has fought against. It is precisely the incorporation of exclusion within historical analysis that distinguishes Foucaultian reconstruction of general grammar, natural history, and analysis of wealth, from general grammar, natural history, and the analysis of wealth.[11]

Undoubtedly, the historiographic moment whose object is a concept or a network of concepts must, to some extent, reiterate the assumption whereby a concept cannot be stated arbitrarily, that is, outside of complex theoretical contexts. And, more specifically, it poses again, but from a different angle, the issue of the relationship between observer and observation. Lévi-Strauss has discussed this issue in his *Introduction* to the collection of Mauss's most significant writings,[12] including what is perhaps the Maussian masterpiece, the essay *The Gift*, with its concept of "total social fact." Among other things, he observes:

> An appropriate understanding of a social fact requires that it be grasped *totally*, that is, from outside, like a thing; but like a thing which comprises within itself the subjective understanding (conscious or unconscious) that we would have of it, if, being inexorably human, we are living the fact as indigenous people instead of observing it as ethnographers. The problematic thing is to know how it is possible to fulfil that ambition, which does not consist only of grasping an object from outside and inside simultaneously, but also requires much more; for the insider's grasp (that of the indigenous person, or at least that of the observer reliving the indigenous person's experience) needs to be transposed into the language of the outsider's grasp, providing certain elements of a whole which, to be valid, has to be presented in a systematic and coordinated way.[13]

But this method discussed by Lévi-Strauss assumes that the "external" observer's analyses refer first and foremost to the *morphological* structure of the "social fact," in which it is possible to discern the evolutionary factors and transformations. *The gift* is a model of the primacy of morphological structure. The "total social fact" logically precedes the evolutionary elements that are placed in it according to the dynamics of the assumption which define the whole as greater than the sum of its individual elements. The "total social fact" implies what Gregory Bateson has termed the "pattern which connects."[14] The adjectives that qualify the "fact," that is, "social" and "total," depend on the mode of observation that connects the elements, which become observable through that connection. Without this, the "fact" would be nothing but the mere statement that there is something outside the observer. It is in this sense, the same that will lead him to develop his analysis of the gift, that Mauss can deny the arbitrariness of the choice of the fetish object and can make that choice hinge on the code of magic and religion. The identification of a fetish object depends, for Mauss, on the connections determining a code. The problem for the observer is then a matter of being able to connect the mode of observation with those connections that determine a code. This seems to be the way Lévi-Strauss interpreted it. But in any case, all this still has to do with objects and external social practices, and therefore with observable entities.

It is true that vis-á-vis objects and social practices to observe, the observer carries out the analyses from the inside and from the outside, through the transposition, as Lévi-Strauss says, of internal subjective learning into external subjective learning, "providing certain elements of a whole which, to be valid, has to be presented in a systematic and coordinated way."[15] And this means precisely that transposition is the process that allows the mode of observation to show the whole, *and therefore it can and must become itself the object of investigation and critique.*

The theoretical problem in historiography arises at the point of analysis of the modes implemented in such transposition, which is carried out in certain systematic and coordinated ways, whereas the theoretical problem in sociology or ethnology concerns more directly such transposition in relation to the object observed. In a word, the theoretical problem in historiography concerns essentially the *events* in the field of history of ideas, not as a mere description of them, but as a meta-theoretical problem, as a matter that concerns the modes of connection and observation. In the end, a book such as Thomas Kuhn's *Structure of Scientific Revolutions* concerns events exactly in this field. The discussion of paradigms and the question concerning the psychology of scientific communities are nothing more than ways of explaining how an event in the realm of natural science has been or can be produced. It is clear that the problem is meta-theoretical and should concern the analysis of how a scientific community works and thinks, but from the historical point of view such concern is invariably informed by the need to explain such events through connection and observation.[16] From this point of view, the historiographic moment is essential in epistemology, but not in the sense of pure commentary of what "actually happened" or what happens, but rather in terms of that decisive aspect in epistemology that concerns the meta-theoretical problem of every mode of connection and observation.

Notes for a History of the Concept of Fetishism

This differentiation between the ethnographic moment and the historiographic moment plays an essential role for a history of the concept of fetishism. In fact, fetishism disappears from the field of ethnology, just when ethnological theories cease to link their comparative method to classifications of a diachronic kind, and start to separate the structural analysis of societies from the constraints of a historical-ideal reconstruction of social, economic, and religious forms as a single evolutionary process of humankind, that is, from the more or less open aspiration to a universal human history. It is at this very moment that the concept of fetishism can become the object of historical investigation, that is, when it ceases to be an ethnographical question.

The rise of fetishism is closely connected to a comparative method that avails itself of conjectural histories. It links, for example, the mode of observation to a hypothetical history of humanity based essentially on the teleological idea of progress. This idea was undoubtedly suitable to connect the different social systems and to homogenize them diachronically so as to allow a comparison between them, but it was also prone to be manipulated ad hoc, so to speak, and to be turned into a history whose beginning was already teleologically determined by its point of arrival.[17] What has been called the "obsession with origins,"[18] or the search for origins as primary historical-structural problem, fits perfectly with the assumption that it is possible and necessary to develop a universal history, within whose framework the course of evolution and the transformations of the object being investigated and analyzed supposedly correspond to its theoretical-structural determination. The search for the origins reveals only the claim of finding a firm anchor, a foundational starting point on which to pin the origin of the processes of change. It claims to give substance to a process of historical investigation, which is in fact invalidated by teleologism, and it is this very claim that reveals the uncertainty of such a process, one that is completely geared toward the discovery of a "primum movens" of a history already determined by its arrival point, which is ultimately the true starting point of the investigation.

Wittgenstein regarded the process informed by the genetic-evolutionary framework as *one* form of argumentation, as *one* way to build formal connections, and pointed out the importance of meta-theoretical analysis in this regard. In discussing the concept of "perspicuous representation,"[19] which mediates our understanding (built around the act of seeing the connections), Wittgenstein stresses the importance of the "connecting links" that in a genetic-evolutionary process, for instance, are important to reveal the connections and similarities between the various phenomena being observed. He states:

> But an hypothetical connecting link should in this case do nothing but direct the attention to the similarity, the elatedness of the *facts*. As one might illustrate an internal relation of a circle to an ellipse by gradually converting an ellipse into a circle; *but not in order to assert that a certain ellipse actually, historically, had originated from a circle* (evolutionary hypothesis), but only in order to sharpen our eye for a formal connection.[20]

Here Wittgenstein highlights in particular the fact that the genetic-evolutionary process is a mode of the observation and connection of facts. The importance of Wittgenstein's meta-theoretical assertion rests first of all in the distinction drawn between the process and the presentation of the "acts," the observed reality—a distinction mildly tainted by the genetic-evolutionary hypothesis—and secondly in the need to consider the very mode of observation and connection as the object of reflection.

Much of the history of the concept of fetishism, from its inception in the eighteenth century up until the nineteenth century, is closely linked not only to the genetic-evolutionary hypothesis, but also to the consequence of such hypothesis, that by hiding its meta-theoretical moment, represented as actually evolving "acts" what were only formal connections. The possibility to observe the observer and to take into account the fact that the observer is also part of the observation was effectively prevented.[21] Fetishism at its inception was the "lowest" possible form of religion to be found among peoples: it was the first stage of an evolutionary plan that, by confusing the "facts" with the mode of observation, granted the observer the possibility to disguise the formal connections. It is precisely in this disguise that ideology can be found, colonialist ideology in this case. That is to say, not in the conscious and instrumental application of a mode of observation, but in the exclusion of the meta-theoretical moment that informs the mode of observation. This meant the exclusion of the possibility to question the observer's conditions of observation and representation. If this were not the case, then some things would remain unexplained. For example, there is no doubt that the evolutionary hypothesis was founded on the ideology of progress: the facts were connected and compared on the basis of a diachronic classification of the social phenomena observed. Yet such an explanation, which refers the mode of observation back to the ideology of progress, seems insufficient. What must be explained instead is the fact that the evolutionary hypothesis built on the ideology of progress was based on the assumption of uniformity and equality of human nature. Humans are equal by nature; it is the circumstances that determine their different behaviors. Once human nature became the founding principle, then it could also become the epistemological criterion of homogenization with which to show the differences, which could be explained by the sociohistorical circumstances. These could be compared to one another according to criteria of similarity and difference within the evolutionary time ladder, which therefore formally connected the facts on the basis of an egalitarian principle. This groundbreaking principle, equality of human nature, allowed the acknowledgment of the "other." But while ensuring, on the one hand, the inclusion of the "Other"—that is, the savages—within the Western conceptual framework, on the other, the act of connecting the facts according to the evolutionary ladder also ensured that the Other be included with the stigma of inferiority—an inferiority derived not from nature, but from history.

In the attempt of keeping the comparison separate from the formal connections built on the evolutionary and teleological hypothesis of progress, Radcliffe-Brown has emphasized the distinction between the historical method and the comparative method:

> History, in the proper sense of the term, as an authentic account of the succession of events in a particular region over a particular period of time, cannot give us generalizations. The comparative method as a generalizing study of the features of human societies cannot give us particular histories. The two studies can only be combined and adjusted when their difference is properly recognized.[22]

The point to emphasize here is not so much the schematic excesses of the English anthropologist's methodological statement, because we could observe, with Wittgenstein, that the use of the comparative method as a generalizing mode is nothing more than *one* way to connect formally the facts. The striking fact here is that Radcliffe-Brown makes a clear distinction between two methods which, for much of the history of philosophy and ethnology, were one. Denying the generalizing power of the historical method marks the end of a conceptual system in which history and comparison were bound together by the teleological hypothesis of progress. As a result, thanks to the distinction between the two methods, the historical from the comparative, the distinction between evolution and progress starts to take shape. With regard to Morgan's theory, Radcliffe-Brown had this to say:

> These theories of successive stages in human development are frequently referred to as "evolutionary anthropology". They are really based on the conception of progress. Morgan, for example, thought of the history of mankind as a process of steady material and moral improvement. Such theories are in direct conflict with the idea of social evolution, for an essential feature of evolution is that it is a process of divergent development, just as insects, birds and mammals represent the end results of the divergent developments of organic evolution. Progress, on the other hand, as a process of improvement, is conceived as unilinear, as being the step by step improvement of the conditions of social life.[23]

Leaving aside the flavor of positivistic dogmatism in Radcliffe-Brown's observations, there is no doubt that the distinction between progress and evolution is central. Among other things, with the idea of progress as improvement, the evolutionary hypothesis can be summed up as the gaze of the observer who sees, and makes others see, the whole (including the differences) through a convergent process, which is a way of organizing formal connections.

That "immense misunderstanding," embodied by the concept of fetishism, derived from philosophical theories based on an idea of history as phases or stages, built in turn on the "progress" and "improvement" of human civilization. There is a clear link between this and colonialism, in spite of appeasing and apologetic interpretations, geared toward the glorification of the ideology of progress, on the one hand, and, on the other, toward the use of a historical method in itself teleological and unilinear.

It was in 1929 that Mauss himself, with his lecture on the "civilizations," definitively broke away from the idea of a unilinear development of humankind as a prerequisite for ethnological investigation.[24] He also implicitly separated the comparative method from the idea of homogenizing all peoples within a single evolutionary and progressive history. He argued that a "civilization" was to be understood in its difference and individuality, which subverted the epistemological relationship between homogenization and difference in the comparative method. In the progressive-evolutionary hypothesis, the gaze provided by the idea of progress and improvement served also as homogenizing factor for all the peoples compared. The differences were placed on the time ladder on the basis of that homogenization. For Mauss instead a "civilization" is to be compared to another precisely because it is first and foremost assumed as different. It is this difference that is inherent in the very idea of "civilization," which is defined by its unique and peculiar characters.

Nonetheless, having grasped the original link between anthropological investigation, progress, and colonialism, no doubt present in the first author who generalized the concept of fetishism, the President de Brosses, I must reiterate that it is not enough, for a historiographic study, to limit the scope to ideological criticism—firstly, because ideological criticism cannot explain the particular combination between fetishism, progress, and colonialism that occurred and established itself at some point and secondly because colonialism existed before the systematic takeover of the ideology of progress.[25] With this premise an attempt was made earlier to discuss that particular combination that grew into a theoretical and conceptual system.

The Concept of Fetishism in Marx and Freud

It seems useful here to expand on what has been stated before, namely, that the fetish becomes a historiographic issue when it ceases to be an ethnographic problem. It is not a matter of considering the history of a phenomenon at the end, once it is over. As far as the object under consideration here is concerned, there is another reason for our interest in the question of fetishism. At least on two occasions fetishism left its place of origin to become an adequate concept for the study of phenomena in and on Western society, phenomena in which the observer is part not only of the observation, but also of the very phenomenon observed. I am referring to the one theorized by Marx as commodity fetishism and the other theorized by Freud as sexual perversion.[26] Beyond the fame that the two theories still have, the fact remains that Marx and Freud have inadvertently confirmed that the concept of fetishism is an invention of Western thought, and they have done so simply by looking at the transformations the concept has undergone in its transition from the analysis of religious practices of the so-called savage world to the analysis of the practices of the so-called civilized world.

It has been observed[27] that there are similarities between Marx's theory and Freud's theory, but a historiographically and theoretically important fact is the relationship that has been created between the original meaning of the concept of fetishism and the meaning it has taken on in Marx and Freud, thanks to the transposition in the analysis of social and psychological phenomena endogenous to the observer. The original meaning of the concept of fetishism (the worship among some so-called primitive peoples) plays a *theoretically* decisive role in Marx's and Freud's analyses, precisely for its *analogical* and *metaphorical* function. What is interesting to notice is that the phenomena described by Marx and Freud are identified through the transposition of a term and a concept from a field of inquiry, the ethnological, to another field, the sociological and psychological, respectively. But this transposition takes on an epistemological value that is autonomous from the actual descriptive value of its original meaning. In essence, even when the concept of fetishism has dissolved in the ethnographic field, its residual value continues to retain relevance, in its analogical and metaphorical function, in the social field with Marx, and in the psychoanalytic field with Freud.

With Marx and Freud, ethnology's "immense misunderstanding" becomes a tool for sociological and psychological analysis, and it does so, on a theoretical level that, in some ways, is parallel to Mauss's own theoretical assumptions, that is, those very assumptions that determine, in the ethnological field, the need for the disappearance of the concept of fetishism. In fact, in Marx and Freud fetishism takes on a symbolic meaning precisely because the phenomenon it describes—albeit with substantial differences between Marx and Freud—concerns *structural synchronic moments* (for social relations in a given system in Marx, for the individual in his relationship with the social object in Freud) and not or not only a phase of a given diachronic sequence. It is in this sense that the historiographic problem arises when the ethnographic one is dissolved: this is not because, as I said, historical conclusions are drawn at the end, but because the concept of fetishism has been radically transformed. If, as mentioned, historiographic investigation must include rupture and discontinuity, here we are confronted with rupture and discontinuity in the history of a concept. The theoretical reasons adduced to refute fetishism in ethnology are similar to the theoretical reasons that have introduced it in its true place of origin: the Western world.

Marx's and Freud's processes, by contrast, could not take on a synchronic structural value or a descriptive power, without the link between the original meaning and the new meaning that the concept of fetishism had taken on. Indeed, if it is true what Jakobson has said, that is, that every sign is a reference ("tout signe est un *renvoi*")[28], then we must conclude that the new meaning relies on the reference to the original meaning. When we call "fetishism" an inversion between things and people, or an exchange between a part and the whole of the sexual object, that is, when we connote with this term the phenomena analyzed, we effectively characterize our description by the *analogy* and *metaphor* existing between these and the phenomenon identified in ethnology. And this is made possible precisely by the fact that fetishism has a history, a history that can be referred to in order to determine the *context*[29] within which the facts observed by Marx and by Freud can be described. So what has been recognized as ethnography's "mistake" translates into descriptive theories that have a different object and different analytical processes. The analogy here is structured in diversity and difference. In describing as fetishism a phenomenon of inversion between things commodities and people, or a phenomenon of displacement of a sexual object, the *context* of interpretation of these objects of analyses, in themselves specific and unique, is effectively structured through the analogy with the religious phenomenon of so-called primitive peoples.

Let us clarify this point, through a schematic recapitulation of the three definitions of the concept of fetishism:

(a) Fetishism is the name given to the cult of so-called savage and/or primitive peoples who worshipped inanimate beings and/or animals (de Brosses).
(b) fetishism is the name given to the attribution to things commodities of what are in fact social relations (Marx).
(c) Fetishism is the name given to that perversion that replaces the normal sexual object with one of its parts or something that belongs toi t(Freud).

It is evident that Marx and Freud use the same term used by ethnologists, but to describe different objects. But it is equally evident that the use of the same term implies at least the fact that these different objects represent phenomena that, at least approximately, are considered similar. Marx and Freud in fact borrow the term from the ethnographic field. Yet a situation where different objects can express similar phenomena immediately presents itself as problematic. Starting from the assumption that analogy is a relationship of similarity between different things, it can be claimed that de Brosses, Marx, and Freud were analyzing different objects that expressed phenomena resembling each other in something, and de Brosses's, Marx's, and Freud's is effectively fetishism. Those by Marx and Freud are theories of fetishism, not of something that looks like it. Marx and Freud build their theories from an analogy, but their descriptive process does not resemble de Brosses's or the other ethnologists'. What is similar is only a certain arrangement of the elements in the various objects studied, or, to be more precise, it is a process of *substitution* in the fetish thing, which from being a representative of something else (a strange and unusual natural phenomenon, people's relations, the normal sexual object) becomes the very object and point of arrival of symbolic human activity. The fetish things—the commodities in Marx or the feet, hair, shoes in Freud—precisely because of their relationship of contiguity and belonging with the object that they originally represent, precisely because they stand as *traces* of it, they can replace it. But for Marx and Freud fetishism is not mankind's primordial religious cult (de Brosses), nor a form of "survival" (Taylor), but rather the *fixing* of an image, one that has been inverted in the symbolic process. Connections, to take up Wittgenstein's argument again, are not structured in a historical-evolutionary form as in de Brosses or in nineteenth century's ethnologists, but rather in a synchronic form.

We thus find ourselves confronted with theories that use different formal connections to describe similar phenomena in different objects. And all of them are theories of fetishism. The analogy function, which allows us to subsume different objects of study under the term fetishism, plays a decisive epistemological and semiotic role: if on the one hand we find that the formal connections, used by Marx and Freud to describe their objects, are organized differently from de Brosses, on the other hand the use of the same term "fetishism," in revealing the analogy of the phenomena in question, ensures that certain meta-descriptive connection make the description itself meaningful to those who are meant to receive the information. Now, if analogy is a relationship of similarity between different things, it clearly establishes a *reference* from one thing to another, and in our example, from the phenomenon described by de Brosses and the ethnologists, to the phenomena described respectively by Marx and by Freud. A relationship of similarity between different things is actually *a comparison*; hence, within the formal connections established by Marx's and Freud's theories of fetishism there is a comparison between the phenomenon described by de Brosses and the phenomena described by Marx and by Freud. It is a comparison that has a *meta-communicative* role, one very similar to that described by Gregory Bateson with the phrase "this is play,"[30] that is, to the moment between speakers when the *context* is defined and their communication starts to make sense. In order to include some items of information in the context it is essential that some other items are excluded and placed outside the context. And in fact the relationship between the formal connections and the acceptance of the analogy between the phenomena—relationship that defines Marx's and Freud's as theories *of* fetishism as not as theories that refer to fetishism—is what allows Marx and Freud to study their respective object of analysis both from the outside and from the inside, as Lévi-Strauss would say with regard to Mauss. Thanks to the comparison between the phenomenon described by de Brosses and the ethnologists, and the phenomena described by Marx and by Freud, the latter can be observed by internal observers as if they were outside. Analogy, as a comparative reference, takes on, with regard to formal connections, a *meta-theoretical* or *meta-contextual* role, that is, it indicates the context in which the theory operates, which therefore has a communicable descriptive function.

In conclusion, in Marx's and Freud's theories, fetishism describes phenomena similar to the one described by ethnologists, but they are *internal* objects of analysis for the observer. The observer is part not only of the observation—as in the case of the anthropologist who must describe phenomena external to his historical, symbolic, and social context—but also of the object he describes. He is to bring to light those processes that, originating from the unconscious activity of individuals, must be part of the communication code that is common to him and the subjects observed. Marx attributes to relationships between things what are in fact relationships between people, and Freud's attribution of sexual satisfaction through a part or a trace of the "normal sexual object," are forms of fixing that have to deal with this problem. To put them under the lenses of observation, a meta-contextual moment is required, a moment that turns the observation as if from the outside. The concept of fetishism that arises from the analogy with the ethnological phenomenon and is structured in formal connections that differ from those in which it arose originally has precisely this meta-theoretical and meta-contextual function. Thanks to the fact that the concept of fetishism retains traces of its origin in an external observation (in a world or context that is different from that of the observer), it is possible to consider phenomena internal to the observer as if they were from the outside. In a sense, when compared to the process analyzed by Lévi-Strauss with reference to Mauss, this is an *inverted* process.

Here, too, one is dealing with processes that originate in unconscious activity, but while the object must be observed as if it were from the inside, in Marx and in Freud the object should be observed as if it were from the outside. Therefore, the comparative effect between ethnologists' fetishism and Marx's and Freud's fetishism has a decisive role for the observer relying on formal connections of a structural-synchronic type. The history of the transition from formal connections of a diachronic type, as in the ethnologists, to formal connections of a structural-synchronic type, is here phylogenetically assimilated by the latter. The formal structural-synchronic connections, through the implicit comparison with the original concept of fetishism, incorporate that history that the observer reuses, so to speak, to determine the context through which he makes his observation a communicable one.

If we consider this argument from the point of view of the historical method, that familiar statement, at least from Marx onwards, that the historical analyses of the past can be carried out through a self-criticism of the present, can be taken to mean that history is only possible when the observer has externalized through his observation, the present of which he is part. Or, as once was said: he has determined the historicity of the present, in the sense of making a reference to the dimension of *time* when determining the meta-contextual moment. If this reference is not made explicit, then what happens is that the way in which formal connections are organized—for example, diachronically through the idea of progress and improvement that structures the scenario of the unfolding of things—comes to be confused with the organized facts. Everything appears as if things actually happened that way. What is lost in the process is the "frame"[31] that defines the context and that allows people to distinguish, for example, a fantasy or myth that simulates a denotative narrative from a denotative narrative as such.[32] On the other hand, if it is true that myth and fantasy have a logic, it is not surprising that, for example, the ideology of progress and improvement may belong to a myth of our era, that is, ideology shapes associations between different levels of discourse, once it has hidden the meta-contextual moment that allows people to distinguish between information and messages, and hence to master communication.[33]

Mauss's "immense misunderstanding" is here transformed and takes on a significant epistemological role. If we confined ourselves to describing the steps of the various notions of fetishism in the history of thought, following the diachronic framework, the assimilation of a concept, when it switches from the original context to a new one, would escape our notice, and it would escape our notice even more the fact that the switch has a decisive epistemological function, that is, to communicate the new context to the observer, precisely because the original concept, as a trace of the new one, *does not manifest itself as a residue or surviving entity, but rather it establishes, through the comparative process implied in the switch, the new semiotic level.*

More on Marx and Freud

It is worth looking at this problem by comparing Marx's theory with Freud's somewhat more directly.

The Marxian theory of commodity fetishism, as is well known, assumes that an *inversion* occurs in the capitalist mode of production: social relationships among people appear as economic relationships among things (commodities). The Freudian theory of fetishism, instead, relies on a *displacement*: the object of love is not the person, but one of his/her parts, or rather, something that belongs to him/her.[34] In both cases, however, the commodities or the fetishized object of love appear as *traces, signs*, where the relationship between signifier and signified is contradictory. The sign must retain its relationship with the thing it represents, but at the same time it is hiding that very thing, transfiguring it into something else. This transfiguration in turn ensures not a distortion, but the functionality of a symbolic process that becomes a system. If this were not the case, then we should categorize the phenomenon of fetishism in the field of "oversights," of "bad symbolism." We would be looking at an epistemological incongruity, since "oversights" or "distortions" presuppose a *straightforward* view of things, a "correct" interpretation. In this case we would have no reason to speak of symbolic and symbolic process: inversion and displacement would only be pathological effects of the mind, not phenomena of its processes.

At a closer inspection, in effect, Marx's and Freud's theories themselves exist within this ambiguity. But we will return to this point later, when discussing the role of the *observer* in the analysis of symbolic phenomena of displacement and inversion. For the time being it is perhaps useful to clarify what has been argued so far, and to take Freud and Marx as our starting points.

In the first of the *Three Contributions to the Theory of Sexuality*, Freud defines the phenomenon of fetishism. Freud speaks of the "normal" sexual object being substituted by another "which is related to it but which is totally unfit for the normal sexual aim." So the fetishistic object is in relation with the "normal" sexual object, but it is not appropriate for the same purpose. Shortly afterwards he adds:

> The substitute for the sexual object is generally a part of the body but little adapted for sexual purposes, such as the foot, or hair, or an inanimate object in demonstrable relation with the sexual person, and preferably with the

sexuality of the same (fragments of clothing, white underwear). This substitution is not unjustly compared with the fetich in which the savage sees the embodiment of his god.[35]

In these observations by Freud we should highlight the following:

(a) the "normal" sexual object is replaced by an equivalent *substitute*;
(b) the substitute is a *part* of the "normal" sexual object, or is in contact with␣it;
(c) that part of the body is, according to Freud, rather unsuitable to represent the sexual object; and
(d) these substitutes can be compared to the fetishes of the savages.

We have here the notion of equivalent or substitute, but this equivalent or substitute is represented by a part of the object or by a contiguous object. It is a part which, while being equivalent, appears little suited to the representation of what it replaces.

The Marxian theory of commodity fetishism (which must be kept separate from the concept of fetishism that Marx uses before the *Capital*) describes the situation in which relationships appear as social relations between things.

In Marx, too, we find the notion of equivalent or substitute, that of part, and that of not appropriate representation. In fact:

(a) "normal"␣s ocialr elationsa rer eplacedb yr elationsb etweent hings;
(b) thingsc ommoditiesa re *part* of the social labor in two ways: firstly, because they are crystallized labor, that is, dead labor as opposed to living labor; secondly, as they become dead labor, they are labor taken away from the laborer;
(c) their representation of social relations is not appropriate, precisely because it is the dead labor that replaces the functions of the living relationsb etweenp eople;also:
(d) the inversion process that affects people in the capitalist system is similar to the phenomenon of religious fetishism.

As one can see, the analogy between the theory of Marx and Freud's theory is, under this respect, self-evident. It is specified at the semiotic level, and also in the common assumption that the two phenomena of fetishism described are expressions of a particular symbolic process.

This semiotic level, however, should be clarified further, since it will be within its realm that the limit of Freud's and Marx's theories can be found, a limit depends on the use of the concept of fetishism in its analogy function.

In fact, the notions of equivalent or substitute, of part, of not appropriate representation, can fit perfectly in what constitutes a semiotic process. The substituted sexual object or the substituted social relations, as a *part* of the normal sexual object or normal social relations, represent a sign, a trace of the latter. Their being a *part* and, at the same time, their becoming substitutes, implies a contradictory situation that provides their semiotic value. They, at the same time, refer to things of which they are a part and which they represent, and *yet they hide this reference.* The phenomena analyzed by Freud and Marx are part of the unconscious. The seemingly paradoxical dimension of a sign that refers to something, and at the same time hides it, is the semiotic assumption that makes the observation communicable. If, as Jakobson says, the sign is always a reference to another sign, everything relies not on the relationship sign thing, but on the context or on the system within which the relationship sign thing is structured. Both systems, Marx's and Freud's, take as a reference point the substitution of the part with the whole, that is what we might call an all-encompassing claim of the part. This substitution has practical consequences in the kind of sexual enjoyment for the fetishist, or in the maintenance of a certain form of social and labor relations. In both cases, the replacement of things with the sign—the sign becoming the thing—must be explained by the particular meaning that it takes on in the two contexts. But how?

Let us take another instance where, in the semiotic process, the part does not replace the whole, and let us use Charles S. Peirce's framework. Pierce distinguishes between "Icon," which resembles the object's characteristics, "Index," which is factually connected with the object, and "Symbol," which denotes the object through interpretive habit. At some point Peirce says:

> The footprint that Robinson Crusoe found in the sand, and which has been stamped in the granite of fame, was an Index to him that some creature was on his island, and at the same time, as a Symbol, called up the idea of man.[36]

The footprint as a sign is an Index because it is factually connected with the man who left it, but it is also a Symbol because it calls to Robinson's mind the idea of man. It should be added, however, that Robinson's idea of man depends on his mindset and intellectual habit. Here we find ourselves in a situation where the footprint has actually been left by a specific individual; however, this link between the sign and the object to which the sign refers is mediated by the idea of man that Robinson is allowed to have by his own mindset. And yet there can be no substitution here of the whole with the part: the footprint does not replace the individual who left it, nor the idea of man held by Robinson.

If we now turn to Freud and Marx, in their case it is as if the footprint had replaced the individual: it does call to mind the idea of man, but only as if it were a fetish. On the other hand, the footprint example as the sign is not so farfetched in relation to the problem we are trying to analyze here. As a matter of fact, Lotman, the Russian semiotician, takes up the same footprint example when discussing magical practices of so-called primitive societies. He observes:

> Magic performed by sorcerers on human footprints is a practice which ethnographers have remarked on in many different cultures, and it has usually been explained by reference to the archaic consciousness which allegedly cannot distinguish part from whole and which regards the footprint as something that is in principle the same as the person who imprinted it. We suggest another explanation as follows: because the footprint while being the person at the same time obviously is not the person, and because it is cut off from the whole mass of its everyday and practical associations, it can be included in a semiotic situation.[37]

The question of distinguishing and not distinguishing part from whole encompasses the instances described by Freud and by Marx. However, these instances not only include the normal practical associations, but these associations actually constitute a decisive factor. Does this mean then that it is the first assumption described by Lotman that applies to their instances? Is it true that the fetishism described by Freud and the one described by Marx, relying on the confusion between the part and the whole, are referring to the idea of an archaic consciousness that cannot distinguish between the part and the whole? In a sense it is, but only up to a point. If we were to adhere to the distinction described by Lotman, we would be forced to make a drastic choice vis-á-vis the concept of fetishism used by Freud and Marx. We would either reduce their theories to an analogy of the phenomena in question with a given idea of archaic consciousness, or, in the second case hypothesized by Lotman, conclude that the simultaneous identification/nonidentification of the part with the whole implies a sort of neuter semiotic situation. We would be confronted with a theoretically untenable situation: either the loss of credibility of Marx's and Freud's theoretical analyses or the loss of specificity of the phenomena in question, a sort of indifferent status: Freud's fetishism and Marx's fetishism would become indistinct semiotic situations like many others. Instead, we must endeavor to escape such context, without losing sight of the ambiguities, limits, and internal contradictions in Freud and in Marx.

The problem can be approached in another way, by focusing our attention on the semiotic processes, that is to say, by shifting our focus from Freud's and Marx's respective objects of analysis to the processes, their mode of observing and describing those objects. At a closer inspection, it becomes evident that the concept of fetishism is like an analogy. It is actually the transposition from one context of meaning to another in which it acquires meaning. Fetishism is a phenomenon originally descriptive of particular religious practices in Western Africa and used as a generalization for all those defined as "primitive" religions. When fetishism is applied to the sexual realm or the realm of commodities, it assumes the heuristic function that is implied in its being, in itself, a reference and an implicit comparison. In order to designate as fetishism a certain sexual deviation or a certain way of seeing and imagining social relations, I give meaning to the phenomenon to the extent that I can refer, within this sign called fetishism, to its original meaning, and therefore compare it with this original meaning. Here, too, the trace of its origin must remain, as it is the persistence of such a trace that allows us to include it in a context of observation that differs from its origin, and, at the same time, to observe this context as if from outside. These two aspects—inclusion in a new context and observation from outside of the context itself—guaranteed by the implicit persistence of the trace of its origin from a comparatively different context, is what establishes the link, in my opinion, between observer and observation. Without it one could not explain phenomena that do not emerge in the consciousness of those who experience them, but only of those who observe them, or even in the consciousness of the same person who experiences them.

But if we hypothetically assume that this is so, the persistence of the trace of the original meaning of the concept of fetishism may cause an influence of meaning also in the new context in which it is included. That is, the original meaning can affect the description of the new context, weakening the purpose for which the concept was used analogically. The trace does not completely guarantee the observer to be outside the observation, and this therefore implies further analysis of both, the observation and the observer. To this regard Pierce claims that the mindset,[38] through which one observes, determines the observation, and Lévi-Strauss argues that the relationship between observer and observation depends on the split between subject and object even within the subject itself.

The Context and the Observer

Gregory Bateson has discussed the notion of context by taking "stories" as a starting point. The context is the "pattern through time."[39] H es ays:

> What happens when, for example, I go to a Freudian psychoanalyst? I walk into and create something which we will call *context* that is at least symbolically (as a piece of the world of ideas) limited and isolated by closing the

door. The geography of the room and the door is used as a representation of some strange, nongeographic message.

But I come with stories—not just a supply of stories to deliver to the analyst but stories built into my very being. The patterns and sequences of childhood experience are built into me. Father did so and so; my aunt did such and such; and what they did was outside my skin. But whatever it was that I learned, my learning happened within my experiential sequence of what those important others—my aunt, my father—did.

Now I come to the analyst, this newly important other who must be viewed as a father (or perhaps an antifather) because nothing has meaning except it be seen as in some context. This viewing is called the *transference* and is a general phenomenon in human relations. It is a universal characteristic of all interaction between persons because, after all, the shape of what happened between you and me yesterday carries over to shape how we respond to each other today. And that shaping is, in principle, a *transference* from past learning.[40]

Bateson says here that the stories of the interaction in human relations shape a new *context*—that between the individual and the analyst—through the *transference* of those same stories in the new relationship's interaction. It is evident then that the transference takes the implicit and hidden form of the comparison between the original relationship's interaction of the individual with his father and the new relationship's interaction of the individual with the analyst. At the same time, the assimilation of the original story in the new context between the individual and the analyst hinges on this comparison. Similarity and difference between the two contexts thus interact in the new one, where one can observe, as if from the outside, the internal stories of the individual. The latter, thanks to the new context determined by the interaction with the analyst, can be both object and subject of his own stories, observed object and observing subject. But in order for this split to take place (a split that has always put in doubt the objectivity of the humanities and social sciences),[41] it is essential that the observer be included in a new context that determines the scope of the observation according to the dialectic outside/inside. To see the object as if it were from the outside involves a complex process capable of giving meaning to the description.

Batesons ays:

> By referring to psychoanalysis, I have narrowed the idea of "story." I have suggested that it has something to do with *context*, a crucial concept, partly undefined and therefore to be examined.
>
> And "context" is linked to another undefined notion called "meaning." Without context, words and actions have no meaning at all. This is true not only of human communication in words but also of all communication

whatsoever, of all mental process, of all mind, including that which tells the sea anemone how to grow and the amoeba what he should do next.

I am drawing an analogy between context in the superficial and partly conscious business of personal relations and context in the much deeper, more archaic processes of embryology and homology. I am asserting that whatever the word *context* means, it is an appropriate word, the *necessary* word, in the description of all these distantly related processes.[42]

This generalization of the notion of context that Bateson asserts opens up an extremely important theoretical space for the analysis of the concept of fetishism, precisely because it is the *transference* of this concept from its original theoretical history, that helps to determine the new context where the new and different formal connections take on *meaning*, connections on which to build the description and the observation of phenomena that differ both for the methods of observation and for the position of the observer. The comparison that remains between the original fetishism and the new fetishism is, from an epistemological point of view, the trace of assimilation in the new context and, at the same time, the point at which the new context is perceived by the observer, who can thus give meaning to the phenomena described.

As far as the observer is concerned, the importance of the comparative effect is essential. Maturana and Varela, in developing their idea of "Autopoiesis," have established a number of theses on cognitive function and role of the observer. In particular, they claim that

> for the observer an entity is an entity when he can describe it. To describe is to enumerate the actual or potential interactions of the described entity. Accordingly, the observer can describe an entity only if there is at least one other entity from which he can distinguish it and with which he can observe it to interact and relate. This second entity that serves as a reference for the description can be any entity, but the ultimate reference for any description is the observer himself.[43]

Maturana and Varela here assume for the observer the need of comparative reference with another entity so as to describe the entity in question. But when they say that the ultimate reference is the observer himself, we must understand this to mean, for the purposes of our argument, the observer's formal connections, connections that, as I have tried to show, have a definite epistemological relationship with the moment of comparison. It should be added that in the case of "fetishism," the entity taken as comparative reference has in itself *a story* that comes from previous formal connections, those made by ethnologists within the framework of diachronic primacy. Similarly, in the observation of a physical or biological object, the observer always stands behind the comparison between his own formal connections and those belonging to the other observers who have preceded him.[44] It is not a matter of any random entity, here, but of an entity that has a historical link with the entity in question. It is this link, in my opinion, that determines the meta-theoretical and meta-contextual relationship between the formal connections and the comparative effect through which these connections indicate the descriptive processes of inclusion and exclusion.

Chapter Four
Marx's Theory of Fetishism

The Theoretical Problem of Commodity Fetishism

Marx's theory of commodity fetishism has generally been addressed and examined from two main points of view: that of its relation to the notion of alienation and that of its connection to the theory of value. In both cases, however, the central problem—or, if one wishes, an obstacle to be overcome—has been and continues to be that of the social process which leads to the phenomenon of commodity fetishism and, consequently, to the theoretical practice used by Marx for describing the phenomenon. In one of the sections of Marx's *Capital* entitled "The Fetishism of the Commodity and Its Secret" (Chapter I, section 4) the notion of fetishism assumes an *analogical* function and, as is known, once again puts forward the problem of *appearances*, that is to say, of the gap existing between a social being and the "nebulous and fantastic" images it assumes when seen and conceived of by men. This topic recurs throughout the evolution of Marx's thought and takes on a specific value dimension within the theory of commodity fetishism, since in this case Marx's analysis is not carried out in general terms, as in *The German Ideology*. It does not involve, in other words, a general discourse about the application of historical materialism within the framework of the relation between "real life" and "conscience," but rather entails an analysis within a specific context such as the one embodied by the capitalist mode of production.

In this case, precisely because Marx's analysis concerns a phenomenon circumscribed to a specific social system, it is possible to individuate two important phases in the theoretical practice that give rise to the description of the phenomenon of commodity fetishism. Although interconnected, these two phases should be analyzed separately. The first one can be defined as *comparative*, whereas the second as that of the *relation between the observer and the observation*.

In the chapter devoted to commodity fetishism the comparative stage is found on two levels: the first is the analogical function performed by the notion of fetishism in both the religious field and the field of commodity production, whereas the second consists of the comparison Marx draws between a system based on the capitalistic mode of production and four cases of production relations: two historical ones (production relations within the feudal system and production relations within patriarchal peasant industry) and two imaginary ones (Robinson's island and the association of free men). What these four cases have in common is the absence of the phenomenon that, on the contrary, characterizes the capitalistic mode of production.

The relation between the observer and the observation is a phase that raises the issue of how it is theoretically possible to grasp the phenomenon of fetishism; that is to say, the inversion according to which relations among men take the form of relations among things, beyond the conscience of the social actors who find themselves within the context and are subjected to that particular phenomenon, as well as to a specific system of interaction. In other words, how is it possible for the observer—who is able to grasp the reality that lies beyond and outside the subject's conscience—to stand simultaneously both outside and inside the observed phenomenon?

This second phase leads us to the well-known issue of the link between being and conscience, between material reality and ideology, a topic repeatedly addressed by Marx in *The German Ideology*, in the Preface to the 1859 edition of *Contribution to the Critique of Political Economy*.

It must be added, furthermore, that the two phases examined so far, that is to say, the comparative phase and that concerning the relationship between observer and observation, are connected with each other, since the observer's position largely depends on a theoretical, or at least partially imagined place, which lies outside of the observed system. Therefore, the observer's position depends on the implicit conjecture that he himself, at least partially, is part of an ideal system (if compared to the observed one), which is situated on the opposite side. The theoretical links between exchange value and use value, between a commodity society and an association of free men, between a nebulous and fantastic world and a transparent instance of reality, can be analyzed starting from the comparative effect produced by the simple models in which it is assumed that the observed phenomenon is not present within the system under consideration. What remains to be seen is whether these models have an ontological value in Marx's writings or a merely regulative one. This leads us to the issue of Marx's general philosophical assumptions.

But before going to the heart of the matter, it is necessary to consider Marx's sources and reflect on the way he used the concept of fetishism, before applying it to the commodity sphere.

Political Critique and the Shift of the Observer

In 1842[1] Marx read and made excerpts from some texts devoted to the issue of fetishism. These texts included a German translation of Charles de Brosses's book.[2] He also made excerpts from Meiners's treatise on comparative religion,[3] from Böttiger's *Ideen zur Kunstmythologie*[4] and from Benjamin Constant's *De la Religion*.[5] In this period, as mentioned in the Preface of the *Contribution to the Critique of Political Economy*, Marx was engaged in a political battle, which he fought on the pages of the journal *Rhenish Gazzette*.[6] In presenting his intellectual biography Marx states that his interest in economic issues arose precisely through the study of these political matters.[7] The corrosive critique of his articles was often due to the comparison he drew between figures and ways of being that were characteristic of the society of his time and figures and ways of being characteristic of the so-called savage world. This comparison played both a critical and an ironic role and was used in order to deride and show contempt for the German middle class, its politics, its morality, and, above all, the cultural presumption with which it justified all the rest. The context in which Marx places those authors dealing with fetishism is mainly a political one.

In light of this, an article published by Marx in the *Rhenish Gazzette* (Rheinishe Zeitung) with the title "Debates on the law on thefts of wood" is particularly significant. In this article Marx explicitly draws on his reading of de Brosses's book. In fact, one of the points relevant to our analysis concerns an excerpt made by Marx from *Du Culte des Dieux fétiches*. The article in question ends as follows:

> The *savages of Cuba* regarded gold as *a fetish of the Spaniards*. They celebrated a feast in its honour, sang in a circle around it and then threw it into the sea. If the Cuban savages had been present at the sitting of the Rhine Province Assembly, would they not have regarded *wood* as the *Rhinelanders' fetish*? But a subsequent sitting would have taught them that the worship of animals is connected with this fetishism, and they would have thrown the *hares* into the sea in order to save the *human beings*.[8]

If one looks beyond Marx's ironic tone, one perceives that the image of the Cuban savages, drawn from de Brosses's book,[9] is placed in a scenario which anticipates, even though only partially, the analogy drawn in *Capital*. Not so much in the more apparent sense of attributing the notion of fetish to the Spaniards' gold, *but rather in the sense that this attribution is structured in a comparative way, starting from the mental and cultural universe of the Cuban savages*. In fact, in Marx's scenario, Cuban savages integrate the Spaniards' relation to gold, according to their conception of fetishes. de Brosses refers to this phenomenon when discussing the fear that Spaniards provoked in Cubans. But the integration of the relationship Spaniards had with gold within the cultural universe of the Cubans is, in de Brosses, a sign of the misunderstanding. In Marx, on the contrary, this example is extrapolated with a hint of irony with the aim of ridiculing the Rhenish provincial orders and their culture. Here the irony depends on a hypothetical shift on the part of observer into the cultural universe of the Cuban savages. Marx's object is dissimilar to de Brosses's: Marx's object coincides with the cultural universe of the middle class, whereas that of de Brosses coincides with the cultural universe of the savages. The issue of a misunderstanding is not present in Marx; on the contrary, the shift of the observer enhances a critical understanding of his world. In fact, the shift of the observer enables him to walk out of the frame of the observed world—the world in which the Rhenish provincial orders sentence people for wood theft—and reenter it from another point: a point of observation whose different conceptual and cultural universe enables an implicit comparison and, thus, a display of the relativity (and of the absurdity) of the values held by the Rhenish orders.

It must be said that the way Marx uses the concept of fetishism here is very far from a comparative theory of a teleological nature. The notion does not originate in a framework where the concept of fetishism is placed on a lower rung of a hypothetical development in human society, as is the case, for instance, in Comte. In this case the comparative method is unquestionably synchronic. It implies the problem of the integration of a phenomenon that lies outside the observing system (that is to say, the importance of gold for the Spaniards) within the conceptual and cultural universe of this very same system (that is to say, the system of Cuban savages). But this observing system is purely hypothetical (it consists in imagining the way Cubans would react when faced with Rhenish wood). The observer, that is to say Marx, needs this so as to be able to define the context, that is, the manner in which he reads the world he is observing and is actually a part of. Ultimately, by means of this method, Marx observes a phenomenon that is internal to his cultural universe as though it were external. He does so by using a reference that connects and defines the structure of the observation, thus making the observation communicable to the reader in its critical and ironic sense.

It goes without saying that Marx's idea cannot be generalized; it cannot provide absolute proof of the fact that, despite using de Brosses as a major source, he applied a different meaning to the concept of fetishism, a meaning that also differed from the way the concept had been used throughout its development in nineteenth-century philosophy and ethnology. So, if it is true that rhetorical and literary devices are not mere embellishments but crucial elements of communication, then Marx's scenario cannot but have a crucial meaning of its own. Of course, the article on wood theft does not yet come under the vaster and much-debated field of inquiry concerning the comparative method in historical materialism and, successively, in the theory of the modes of production. Nevertheless, by linking the analysis to the concept of the "observer," this early political writing already engages with an issue that was to become of central importance in Marxist thought. It can be illustrated by this question: how is it possible to observe the conscience of a society *from within*, if, by means of ideologies, its forms are capable of exteriorizing what this society thinks of itself? How indeed is it possible if ideologies—the self-same products of a society—appear as crystallized projections, as deforming mirrors, as exteriorized and autonomized images of what men as social creatures think of themselves? In the field of Marxist discourse this question has been answered in several mostly deleterious ways. These range from the idea of "a class point of view" to the "proper" type of ideology—from the idea of science being in opposition to ideology, to the notion of economics and economic relations as "the truth" of ideologies. All these hypotheses are based on the assumption of having found the proper, neutral place of the internal observer. But there again, the answers Marx gives to this question also seem contradictory. And it could not be otherwise. Nevertheless, the central issue lies in the fact that Marx's parameters are our starting point for a discussion. The question remains open, while also constituting a framework for both a theoretical and a political problem.

By means of the shift on the part of the observer, the scenario described by Marx in the article on wood theft leaves only a faint trace of a problem that would subsequently undergo theoretical development.

The Observed Conscience: Money and Religion

In 1844 Marx copied extensive excerpts from James Mill[10] and wrote out his own critical reflections. Going beyond Mill's discussion of money as the medium of exchange, Marx argues:

> The essence of money is not primarily that it externalizes property, but that the *mediating activity* or process—the *human* and social act in which man's products reciprocally complement one another—becomes *alienated* and takes on the quality of a *material thing*, money, external to man. By externalizing this mediating activity, man is active only as he is lost and dehumanized. The very relationship of things and the human dealings with them become an operation beyond and above man.[11]

As has already been noted by Rosdolsky,[12] Marx's text anticipates the theory of commodity fetishism: the relationship of things becomes an operation above and beyond man. This process concerns men's conscience, since they transfer and project their relationship with things upon an alien entity.

This problem—the projection and transfer of man's relationships upon an alien entity—thus precedes the general theory of ideology that Marx was to formulate together with Engels within a materialist conception of history. But how is it possible to observe this phenomenon of projection and transfer if, on the one hand, it occurs beyond man's conscience and if, on the other, the observer is situated within the social context of this phenomenon? The question lacks a theoretical answer, but the way Marx proceeds shows that *this* is indeed the problem. Marx observes what men *see* in money by means of what they *do not see*; whereas the observed men follow an inverse course: they do not manage to see because of the nature of what they are looking at.

> Through his *alien mediation* man regards his will, his activity, and his relationships to others as a power independent of himself and of them—instead of man himself being the mediator of man. His slavery thus reaches ac limax.[13]

But this seeing is indeed a not seeing, because in projecting his will and his activity upon a material thing—money—man's slavery reaches its apex, and the mirror that reflects him acquires the capacity autonomously to counteract him. The image of his will and his activity—deposited in things—replaces the person that has produced it. At this point Marx returns to the topic of the processes of conscience and the way they occur in religion:

> It is clear that this *mediator* becomes an *actual god*, for the mediator is the *actual power* over that which he mediates to me. His worship becomes an end in itself. Apart from this mediation, objects lose their value. They have value only insofar as they *represent* it while originally it appeared that the mediation would have value only insofar as *it* represents *objects*. This inversion of the original relationship is necessary.[14]

While money originally represented objects, now the relationship is inverted: it is the objects that have value, only insofar as they represent money, that is to say only insofar as they are bearers of exchange value. The intermediary element—money—acquires real power and replaces the objects it originally represented. This process of substitution is analogous to the one that takes place in religion, where the idols replace the god they originally represented. As has already been noted, in de Brosses this stage follows that of fetishism. However, it is not de Brosses's theory that influenced Marx in this case, but Feuerbach's *The Essence of Christianity*.[15] In drawing a parallel between the process of currency substitution and the process of substitution in religion, Marx refers to Christ and his mediating role: "But Christ is God *externalized*, externalized *man*. God has value only insofar as he represents Christ; man has value only insofar as he represents Christ. It is the same with money."[16] Christ and money are the two mediators that assume the power and take the place of what they originally represented. This way of seeing the figure of Christ leads to the idea that Christianity is an evolved form of a substitution process that generally takes place in religion. Christ, the god who becomes man, is the *sensible* form of the divinity; the coming of god to earth represents the refinement of the very same process according to which tangible objects came to replace invisible divinities in acts of religious worship and cults. Religion provides this elaborate answer in order to solve its internal and eternal problem of the mediation between heaven and earth. For Marx Christianity stands to fetishism as classical political economy stands to mercantile economy. The latter focuses on money's tangible attributes, by virtue of its being a metal coin, whereas according to classical political economy, money is a commodity like any other. Nevertheless, neither of these practices has managed to clarify the fact that money is an exchange value. In this sense, they both stop at the appearance of reality, at the processes of projection and transfer, according to which money assumes the dimension of an autonomous power. Within this dimension, men see their will and their activity as if in a deforming mirror and, thus, do not really perceive them. Marx's passage is worth quoting at length:

> Despite all its cleverness, the modern economic order in opposition to the monetary system cannot achieve a decisive victory. The crude economic superstitions of people and their governments hold on to the *perceptible*, *palpable* and *observable* moneybag and believe in the absolute value of precious metals and their possession as the only real form of wealth. The enlightened and knowledgeable economist comes along and proves to them that money is a commodity like any other and that its value, like that of any other commodity, depends on the relationship of the costs of production to demand (competition) and supply, and to the quantity or competition of other commodities. The correct reply to this economist is that the actual value of things, after all, is their *exchange value*, and the exchange value resides in money, just as money exists in precious metals. Money, therefore, is the *true* value of things and hence the most desirable thing.[17]

True, we are still far away from the complexity of Marx's later economic analysis. However, what needs to be underlined here is that the reflections on James Mill already contain an element that is central to his thought and that will play an important part in the theory of commodity fetishism. After all, the "enlightened economist" comes to the same conclusion as he who makes fetishes of metallic coins. Namely, that money is the most desirable thing:

> The economist's doctrines yield the same wisdom, except that he can abstractly recognize the existence of money in all forms of commodities and not believe in the exchange value of its official metallic existence. The metallic existence of money is only the official sensuous expression of the very soul of money existing in all branches of production and in all operations of civil society.[18]

But the enlightened economist does not go beyond the conclusion that money is a commodity like any other. That is to say, he does not go so far as to realize that money, in its capacity as an intermediary, has acquired power over the thing it mediates and that this is the reason why—instead of representing the things produced by man's will and actions—money has turned into the reality represented by things, the revived and autonomous mirror of man's will and activity.

When reflecting upon the notion of property in the third of his *Economic and Philosophic Manuscripts of 1844*, Marx again makes the parallel with religion. This time he explicitly uses the term "fetishist" and applies it to Catholics, whom he sets in opposition to Protestants; analogously, the adherents of the Mercantile System are set in opposition to the "enlightened economists":

> To this enlightened political economy, which has discovered—within private property—the *subjective essence* of wealth, the adherents of the Monetary and Mercantile System, who look upon private property *only as an objective* substance confronting men, seem therefore to be *fetishists, Catholics. Engels* was therefore right to call *Adam Smith* the *Luther of Political Economy* [See *Outlines of a Critique of Political Economy*]. Just as Luther recognized *religion—faith—*as the substance of the external *world* and in consequence stood opposed to Catholic paganism—just as he superseded *external* religiosity by making religiosity the *inner* substance of man—just as he negated the priests outside the layman because he transplanted the priest into laymen's hearts, just so with wealth: wealth as something outside man and independent of him, and therefore as something to be maintained and asserted only in an external fashion, is done away with; that is, this *external, mindless objectivity* of wealth is done away with, with private property being incorporated in man himself and with man himself being recognized as its

essence. But as a result man is brought within the orbit of private property, just as with Luther he is brought within the orbit of religion.[19]

Marx persists, therefore, in drawing an explicative parallel between the development of economic theory and the development of the Christian religion. Here he uses the term "fetishist" in a theoretical context that resembles the previous one at least in one respect: that of the relationship between two economic theories. But should we examine both the observations on James Mill and the latter ones, it becomes apparent that, in actual fact, there are two different discourses overlapping, albeit in a different way, with the concept of fetishism. From the point of view of a theory of the observer, Marx's reflections concern, on the one hand, the social function of money in capitalist society and the way in which the relation between men and things is inverted, as a fetishized process of social self-representation; on the other hand, his reflections deal with economic theories attempting to explain the notion of money. Ultimately, what is analyzed in the first case is the social system as such; whereas, in the second case, the focus is on two of its modes of observation. In this typical situation theoretical reflections overlap with meta-theoretical critique within a scenario characterized by historical phases in which two theoretical modes of observation progressively follow on each other. The parallel with religion, the passage from Catholicism to Protestantism, contributes to strengthening the meaning of the passage from mercantile to classical theory, seen as moments, as figures of the observing conscience which, in a Hegelian manner, prefigure a third mode of observation. This is the very same mode which, in point of fact, criticizes the two previous theories and offers a new way of observing and explaining the phenomenon of money: namely, as a process of the inversion of men's relationship with their self-representation.

The analysis of the inversion process—caused by the fact that money is a particular commodity—overlaps with the critique of previous economic theories in which the inversion is grounded, leading to something like a short circuit. As a matter of fact, Marx situates his analysis of money within the history of progress of economic knowledge, a knowledge that develops by increasing the level of abstraction. In other words, he situates it within a scheme of *continuity*. But for him it is impossible to understand the form of money without observing the phenomenon of inversion it produces in men. The conclusion Marx comes to goes far beyond economic knowledge and its abstractions, since it is grounded in the inquiry about the possible conditions for grasping the phenomenon. In this sense he represents a *break* in the history of economic knowledge. If money is not just the metal it is made of, nor a commodity like any other; if money is a particular commodity that no longer represents other commodities, but is rather something that allows commodities to show their exchange value; and if this process produces an inversion, so that men project and transmit their will and their activities onto it, then this world that has been overturned is not brought into existence by the growing capacity for abstraction shown by economic knowledge. It is brought about by a process that allows the internal observer to see the unconscious phenomenon of inversion as if from the outside. This process is a condition for scientific knowledge, although it does not represent a stage of its "natural" growth. In itself, this condition lies outside the boundaries of economic knowledge, while at the same time becoming the linchpin of its connection. In the capitalist mode of production, money implies and is associated with an inversion process that takes place in other forms of social and human self-representation, such as religion. The reason this process also occurs in the economic field depends on the fact that this field has incorporated all the elements governing society's symbolic and self-representational functions. The discovery of the inversion process produced by money reveals the *social* nature of these economic relations. Similarly, the discovery of the inversion process produced by religion reveals the *social* nature of the human relationship with god. Yet, all this shows the result of the discovery, not the way for achieving it. So how is it possible to observe a process that is produced unconsciously and which the conscience gives a distorted image of when one finds oneself within that very same process? That is to say, when one is subject to the very same conditions leading to the inversion?

Over a short period of time Marx and Engels would produce their theory of history and ideologies, a theory based on this very discovery that, in order to provide an explanation of social relations, one must go beyond the awareness men have of themselves. As can already be seen in the *Manuscripts*, Marx keeps attempting to arrive at an answer:

> The nations which are still dazzled by the *sensuous* glitter of precious metals, and are therefore still fetish-worshippers of metal money, are not yet fully developed money-nations. The contrast of France and England. The extent to which the solution of theoretical riddles is the task of practice and effected through practice, the extent to which true practice is the condition of a real and positive theory, is shown, for example, in *fetishism*. The sensuous consciousness of the fetish-worshipper is different from that of the Greek, because his sensuous existence is different. The abstract enmity between sense and spirit is necessary so long as the human feeling for nature, the human sense of nature, and therefore also the *natural* sense of *man*, are not yet produced by man's own labor.[20]

In this case, the notion of fetishism is applied to nations that are not yet fully capitalist. In *Capital*, as is known, (commodity) fetishism pertains to the stage of fully developed capitalism. This is due to the fact that the concept of fetishism is a general one and indicates the attribution of human qualities and products to things, whereas the objects of fetishism vary with the varying of the practical and historical conditions. Not fully capitalist nations fetishize metal money, while a fully developed capitalist system fetishizes commodities: what this step indicates, in actual fact, is the growing power of the inversion and, thus, the growth of the capitalist mode of production. This means that the process of inversion that masks or distorts real relations between people depends on what society itself *makes visible*, on the point of development society has arrived at and, therefore, on the point people find themselves at, as far as their effective social practices are concerned. Marx establishes a connection between sensuous consciousness and practice and, analogously, between sensuous consciousness and the possibility of developing a theory. It is the analysis and the observation of practice that provide the means for looking beyond consciousness, while the possibility of analysis and observation are provided by *history*, and the specific forms in which history occurs and realizes itself. The possibility, by means of history, of observing the difference between the sensuous consciousness of the fetish worshipper and the sensuous conscience of the Greek (by focusing on their different sensuous existences) depends on the fact that in this case the observer stands outside of time. He is not subjected to the inversion processes that occur in the respective symbolic-social worlds of the fetish worshipper and the Greek. Thus, it is possible to look beyond their sensuous consciousness. But this can be achieved only because the observer belongs to another symbolic-social world. He looks through the prism of his own world at the world of the "others" and—by looking in a certain way, with a certain exactitude—he brings that world to himself. The eighteenth-century philosophers had already achieved this outcome. When Hume explained polytheism, starting from the primitive's fear provoked by the inability to understand nature's irregular phenomena, and when he attributed this inability to the pressure of the needs the primitives were subjected to (since they were reduced to the level of subsistence), he did nothing more than affirm that their limited universe derived from their limited existence. The same can be said of de Brosses's theory of fetishism. But Marx faced a problem of a different kind: he wanted to explain the relationship between sensuous consciousness and sensuous existence with regard to the world he belonged to. So, how is it possible to look beyond one's own sensuous consciousness and one's own historical world? Marx attempted to find a solution to this dilemma by coming up with a different answer to the issue of what, past and present, constituted "other" worlds. This answer is not to be found in the *Manuscripts*, where the problem is left unsolved. But in a short time Marx would seek the solution by theorizing a materialistic conception of history in *The German Ideology*.

The Observed Conscience:
History, Determinacies, and Contradictions

Feuerbach touches on fetishism in *The Essence of Religion*, which was published in 1846. In October of the same year, Engels mentions this work in a letter to Marx.[21] This period coincides with the drafting of *The German Ideology* and, thus, with the theoretical definition of the materialistic conception of history. In referring to Feuerbach's text, Engels asserts that there is no need to examine it, since, without adding any substantial novelty, it merely rephrases previously discussed theses. After transcribing some excerpts from Feuerbach and including some comments on them, Engels states:

> Of the historical development of the various religions one learns nothing. At most they provide examples to support the above trivialities. The main bulk of the article consists in polemic against God and the Christians, altogether in his previous manner, except that now he's run dry, and despite all his repetitions of the old drivel, dependence on the materialists is much more blatantly apparent. If one were to make any comment on the trivialities concerning natural religion, polytheism, and monotheism, one would have to compare them with the true development of these forms of religion, which means they would first have to be studied. But so far as our work is concerned, this is as irrelevant to us as his explanation of Christianity.[22]

What we find here is an outline of the criticism of Feuerbach's views, as expressed later in *The German Ideology*: the abstractness of materialism and the idealism of history. Moreover, while on the one hand Engels states that Feuerbach needs to be checked against the "true" development of the forms of religion; on the other, he maintains that this issue does not concern the object of his and Marx's theoretical reflection. But what does this really mean? This much was already clear in the *Theses on Feuerbach* written by Marx in the spring of 1845. It is worth recalling the seventh thesis: "Feuerbach, consequently, does not see that the 'religious sentiment' is itself a social product, and that the abstract individual whom he analyses belongs to a particular form of society."[23]

A "particular form of society." For Marx, both the societies of the past and the society of the present belong to a particular form of society. This apparently simple theoretical fact plays an important role in paving the way for the Marxian solution to the dilemma. The idea that "religious sentiment" is a social construct is not, in itself, either a novelty or a discovery. For instance, although Benjamin Constant was convinced that "religious sentiment" was a distinguishing aspect of human nature, and although he rejected the idea that religion had its origin in an individual's state of need,[24] he nevertheless established a relation between social conditions and the historical forms of religion under consideration. Constant's comment on the passage from fetishism to polytheism did not escape Marx's notice when in 1842 he read *De la Religion*.

> This revolution corresponds in a certain sense to the division of labour, a division that gives rise to the development of society. In the savage state, everyone provides for the collective needs. Instead in civilized society, everybody concentrates on a specific occupation. In this way the individual provides not only for his own needs, but also for the needs of others. The same thing occurs in the case of fetishism: the fetish takes upon itself the totality of meaning, as far as the individual human being is concerned. As soon as polytheism supplants fetishism, each god takes upon himself an individual meaning. And this meaning is valid for everyone.[25]

Besides the Robinsonadian attitude of the savage, who provides for his needs by himself, Constant distinguishes here between two forms of religion—fetishist and polytheistic—in accordance with the division of social labor. Marx's theoretical extremism (he refutes the idea that "religious sentiment" is a distinguishing aspect of human nature and attributes it tout court to social forms) could thus be rooted in an explanatory context that was not new to theoretical thought, and which had in point of fact already contributed to it. For Marx, the act of attributing "religious sentiment" to social forms means that the central problem is posed by the analysis of these very same forms and their historical determinacy. And yet, from the point of view of a theory of the observer, the fact remains that these determinacies—despite being capable of bringing to the fore the relationship between forms of consciousness and forms of social life—still run the risk of falling into a teleological type of discourse, and thus blending past forms and the conceptual universe, that is, the "sensuous consciousness" of the world the observer belongs to. This is due to the fact that the observer is subjected to the inversion produced by his own world. It is at this stage that one is confronted with the problem of a current society's historical determinacy, as well as the capitalist mode of production, since this very same determinacy makes it possible to *shift the observer*, as though he were outside, even if he is inside the system he is observing. Let us see in what sense this is so.

The idea that it is not possible to explain a social system in terms of the consciousness it has of itself is grounded, in *The German Ideology*, in an implicit assumption. There is, in fact, a strong correspondence between the forms of material production and the consciousness one has of them, but this correspondence is *based on an inversion*. And the form of this inversion is determined historically. Every epoch is defined by its own culture and its own specific forms of expression, by its own consciousness and its own specific ideological forms. *This correspondence is unstable.* The balance of the system is altered by internal social drives. According to Marx, this is due to the fact that a social system is constituted of forms of intercourse, of production relations and of productive forces. The balance between these elements is continuously upset by contradictions that tend to break the connections enabling the system to preserve itself. In turn, these contradictions indicate that, at a certain point, the instability of the correspondence between the primary elements increases and grows until it determines a *noncorrespondence*. That is to say, until it determines the historical conditions of the system's breakdown, and consequently a transition toward new relations and new social connections. These notions are, thus far, well known and relatively simple. *But the central idea of the Marxian scheme is that the observer is in a position to make his observation by starting from the noncorrespondence between the system's internal elements. It is precisely this factor that enables him to observe as if from the outside, notwithstanding the fact that he is located within the observed phenomenon.* The central idea is that the historical process and the historical knowledge are produced, according to Marx, by the noncorrespondences; that is to say, by the possibility, inherent in the system, of its disconnection. This is the reason why Marx explains a society's consciousness by means of the sociomaterial conditions of production. The premise is that the noncorrespondence enables both the explanation and the observation. Moreover, the endorsement of the historical determinacy of the capitalist mode of production depends on the endorsement of the noncorrespondence between its primary elements. Ultimately, the question Marx starts out with is not how a system preserves and reproduces itself, but why a system tends to dissolve and lose its ability to reproduce itself. This is also the reason why Marx's idea of the noncorrespondences is related to historical processes and not to the issue of their politicalcontrol.[26]

This is the horizon opened up by Marx and, from a theoretical point of view, it is crucial that it not be lost sight of. Having said this, however, it is undeniable that once placed within this horizon of meaning, Marx's analysis displays its limits. As we shall see in the next chapter, in this context he gives primacy to the relationship between man and nature over the relationship between man and society. Moreover, as early as *The German*

Ideology, he establishes a connection between the notion of noncorrespondence and the history of the origin of the diverse elements constituting society. Among these, consciousness and language come last.[27] Basically, he smoothes over the method for analyzing a specific mode of production and turns it into a hypothetical history of the origins. The method is thus embedded in a general conception that tends to relate everything to the link between man and nature. Ultimately, Marx enables one to catch sight of an alternative social system as though it was the actual world of correspondences, as though it was the aim of consciousness inversion, determined by real and definitive social mastery over nature. Once the social contradictions have been overcome in a society, that is, once it is constituted of transparent relationships, it appears that one may devote oneself to the relation with nature. But at this point we inadvertently move from the problems that the Marxian paradigm has left unsolved to the history of Marxism. As soon as it became a doctrine, Marxism presumed that it would be possible, especially in its so-called realized forms, to overcome the process of consciousness inversion, merely by dint—which is typical of inversion—of imposing an ideology.

It may be useful to cite a passage from *The German Ideology* where Marx and Engels criticize Stirner's philosophy. They first accuse him of imitating Hegel's notion of stages of consciousness, albeit without either his complexity or his historical knowledge. Then, they comment on the absurdity attached to the identification of the "negro" with the "infant" and see this as a downright deformation of the Hegelian analysis of Africa as a land of childhood (this is where Hegel refers, with utter contempt, to negroes' fetishes).[28] Eventually, after drawing attention to the "figures" of man and underlining the transition from the Mongolians to the Chinese, up as far as the Western world, they observe that:

> [In ancient times] the ideas and thoughts of people were, of course, ideas and thoughts about themselves and their relationships, their consciousness of *themselves* and of people *in general*—for it was the consciousness not merely of a single individual but of the individual in his interconnection with the whole of society and about the whole of the society in which they live.
>
> The conditions, independent of them, in which they produce their life, the necessary forms of intercourse connected herewith, and the personal and social relations thereby given, had to take the form — insofar as they were expressed in thoughts — of ideal conditions and necessary relations, i.e., they had to be expressed in consciousness as determinations arising from the concept of man *as such*, from human essence, from the nature of man, from man *as such*. What people were, what their relations were, appeared in consciousness as ideas of man *as such*, of his modes of existence or of his immediate conceptual determinations.

So, after the ideologists had assumed that ideas and thoughts had dominated history up to now, that the history of these ideas and thoughts constitutes all history up to now, after they had imagined that real conditions had conformed to man *as such* and his ideal conditions, i.e., to conceptual determinations, after they had made the history of people's consciousness of themselves the basis of their actual history, after all this, nothing was easier than to call the history of consciousness, of ideas, of the holy, of established concepts — the history of "man" and to put it in the place of real history. (198)[29]

Since the conditions in which human beings produce their material existence do not depend on their will, they are subjected to the inversion, inasmuch as they are translated into thoughts and ideas. This is the horizon opened up by Marx and, at the same time, its limit: is it really possible to imagine a society in which the conditions of existence depend on man's will and in which, consequently, man's thoughts and ideas are not subject to inversion? This issue concerns the image of a transparent society, hypothetically built on the assumption according to which the ending of social relations based on dependence and subordination means the end of contradictions, and not, instead, their *repositioning*. In a situation like this, we might reach the paradox of the internal observer. He would find himself in the very same situation as an eye whose pupil does not move: he would be blind. Without the movement of the pupil, without the ability to perceive differences, the eye would be unable to see.[30] Similarly, the observer would not be able to see anything without the contradictions and the differences. That is to say, he would neither be subject to inversion, nor capable of freeing himself from it. In fact, how would it be possible for him to see beyond the fixed forms of consciousness if he cannot make comparisons? How would it be possible for him to explore what is not seen in what is made visible, if the visibility is complete? Absolute light has the same effect as absolute darkness.

The Theory of Commodity Fetishism and the Problem of the Observer

Taking into consideration this problematical framework of reference, this chapter aims at examining the analogy drawn by Marx in *Capital* between the image of fetishism and the world of goods. In the first place, it is worth quoting the passage in which Marx explains the mysterious character of the commodity form and then examining it closely:

> The mysterious character of the commodity-form consists therefore simply in the fact that the commodity reflects the social characteristics of men's

own labour as objective characteristics of the products of labour themselves, as the socionatural properties of these things. Hence it also reflects the social relation of the producers to the sum total of labour as a social relation between objects, a relation which exists apart from and outside the producers.

Through this substitution, the products of labour become commodities, sensuous things which are at the same time suprasensible or social.[31]

Marx's analysis here aims at demonstrating the way an inversion is produced: similarly to a mirror, the commodity-form duplicates the social characteristics of men's labor; it modifies and reflects them as natural social characteristics of things. Therefore, the inversion consists of two phases: the first one concerns the act of reflecting the social characteristics of men's labor; the second one implies the fact that this reflected image is modified with regard to the reality it reflects. It is important to underline and distinguish between these two phases, so as to avoid making simplifications that might give rise to misunderstandings such as considering the inversion as a moment of alienation; as a moment, that is, when it is enough to place things in the right order to make the relationships transparent.[32]

It is crucial to devote a little more space to the topic. Obviously, it leads us to the wider issue of ideology in Marx, to the link between structure and superstructure, to the relationship between material life and ideological forms. To this end, it may be useful to cite Lucien Sebag's reflection on the matter and, in particular, on the link between thought and external reality in Marx:

> The fact is that thought is never reflected; through thought, the object undergoes a series of transformations. In this manner, its filtering power and its own logical productivity are displayed at the same time. Once the initial contents have undergone a complex reworking, thought is able to overcome the real contradictions and develop that which had only been sketched in by what exists.
>
> In this perspective there is nothing more ambiguous than the notion of intellectual reification that Marx uses for designating the phenomena of inversion. In the various doctrines, these phenomena transform social reality into a mere appendage of the religious, metaphysical or local Idea. So, one discovers here the sense of Marx's critique of Hegelianism and in particular of the philosophy of law. Now, it is essential to observe the way this inversion, at least in some of its aspects, *is directly linked to the very same practice of symbolic activity*. This activity subjects what-is to a series of operations, by means of which the real is integrated within a system; in this system, the real is defined by its relation to a multiplicity of possibilities to which it is both linked and opposed at the same time, although some of these possibilities will never subsequently be realized.[33]

It is thus possible to assume that the mechanism of inversion concerns men's active attitude toward reality, an active attitude that implies symbolic production. If one starts from this assumption—if, that is, one admits that far from being a mere reflection, thought is actually an active part of the reality it confronts itself with, an element of the real, a way of modifying and transforming the real; and if, at the same time, one takes into consideration the two phases of the inversion, then it becomes necessary to see Marx's analysis of the mysterious character of the commodity form from a different perspective. In fact, the problem one is confronted with in this case is not inversion in itself, but the *type* of modification—a phenomenon peculiar to fetishism—produced in that specific context. In order to clarify this point, it is necessary to go back to Marx's conception of ideology and examine the notion of the relationship between observer and observation. It is undeniable that this conception encounters a basic contradiction, which can be schematized as follows: an analysis of society's material life—by means of which it is possible to grasp the filter-like value ideologies take on—cannot itself be filtered. If this were not so, then we would have to presume that there exists a form of thought that does not filter reality, but grasps it as it is. This is a very tricky presupposition, since in its turn it presupposes an element of *self-description* in this form of thought—a type of self-description capable of maintaining that the thought finds itself in an external theoretical space, yet independent from the observed object. That is to say, within a neutral theoretical space. It is not possible for this form of thought to coincide with *science*,[34] as opposed merely to ideology, since in this case the manifest opposition and the self-description of a science proclaiming itself as such are purely ideological postulates. Neither is it possible to conceive of science as a *direct* vision of reality as opposed to, in this case as well, the *indirect* vision characterizing ideology, since this would confine the discussion to the field of ideological debate. And yet, Marxism has frequently dwelt on these distinctions. This is probably due to the fact that Marx's concept of *inversion* remains theoretically ambiguous, even more so when it is *not* presented *only as a critique*. In all likelihood, this is where Marx's richest and most profound reflection reaches its limit. When we underline the necessity of distinguishing between the two different phases of inversion, we focus, on the one hand, on the way this distinction is articulated in Marx's analysis, while, on the other hand, we realize that this distinction is veiled. It tends to remain only hinted at precisely by reason of the comparative method used by Marx to achieve a penetrating reading and critical explanation of the phenomenon of inversion in relation to the specific field of societies predicated on the supremacy of commodity production. Let us see in what sense this is so by going back to Marx's text. On the one hand, there is the fact that the commodity form reflects, as if in a mirror, the social character of men's labor and the social relationship between producers and overall labor. On the other hand, this image presents that very same character and relationship as socionatural properties of things. As has been noted by a scholar who has strongly emphasized the role played by commodity fetishism in Marx's theory of value, "The given thing, in addition to serving as a use value, as a material object with certain properties which make it a consumer item or a means of production, i.e., in addition to performing a *technical function* in the process of material production, it also performs the *social function* of connecting people."[35] This means that in the capitalist mode of production, things assume a social form insofar as they assume the character of commodity. Commodities are a crystallization of social labor and, therefore, they *really* reflect the image of its social character. The inversion is produced by the peculiar social properties of commodities, which incorporate men's social relationships and, as a consequence, start creating mirror images. The first stage of the inversion is contained in the things themselves, inasmuch as they are products of human social labor, which stand at a remove from the subjects who produce that labor: since inversion is a part of the symbolical activity of human beings, it depends on the way they mirror themselves in the produced things. This is not to be understood in the monadic sense of a single individual facing a single thing, but rather in the structural sense pertaining to the representation of relations, whose reality is different from the sum of individuals. The mirroring of the image, insofar as it is a process in which human beings are actively involved, is necessarily also a modification. The fact that Marx invests this process with the properties of the fetish means that the modification of the image assumes a dimension capable of concealing or making people forget a crucial moment of the mirroring: that is to say, the moment of *self-observation*. It not only enables subjects to engage in symbolic activity, but allows them to conceive of this very same symbolic activity as an object. Basically, subjects split themselves up, double themselves in the representation of their relationships, and are able to observe this splitting.[36] Once again, the issue goes back to the topic of observation and observer. But for the moment we must simply note that the fetish character of the commodity can be considered as the absence of this moment of self-observation. Under this aspect, the analogy used by Marx closely follows de Brosses's definition. In fact, de Brosses insists throughout his work on the idea of fetishism as a form of religion in which animals or inanimate objects are *directly* endowed with divine features. That is to say, animals or inanimate objects themselves are considered to be divinities and not symbols or representations of some abstract god. In the same way, the fetish character of the commodity means that the social form of things is endowed with *naturalness*. More explicitly, the social form of things appears as a *natural* property of commodities and, as a consequence, the link that makes self-observation possible is broken. What is broken is the consciousness of the link between the truly social character of commodities and the social relations of commodity production. By means of this consciousness it is possible, in turn, to *control* the necessary modification produced during the process of image reflection; that is, in the inversion of two realities (the social character of commodities and the social relations of commodity production) that are equivalent but not symmetrical.

The manner in which Marx proceeds with his reflection seems to confirm the possibility of using the natural/social dichotomy in order to read his analysis of commodity fetishism as an absence of the moment of self-observation. After characterizing the commodity as a "sensuous supersensible" thing and after speaking about the inversion of relationship between people and things, he illustrates his point by juxtaposing the act of seeing with fetishism:

> In the same way the light from an object is perceived by us not as the subjective excitation of our optic nerve, but as the objective form of something outside the eye itself. But, in the act of seeing, there is at all events an actual passage of light from one thing to another, from the external object to the eye. There is a physical relation between physical things. But it is different with commodities. There, the existence of the things *quâ* commodities, and the value relation between the products of labour which stamps them as commodities, have absolutely no connection with their physical properties and with the material relations arising therefrom. There it is a definite social relation between men that assumes, in their eyes, the fantastic form of a relation between things. In order, therefore, to find an analogy, we must have recourse to the mist-enveloped regions of the religious world. In that world the productions of the human brain appear as independent beings endowed with life, and enter into relation both with one another and the human race. So it is in the world of commodities with the products of men's hands. This I call the Fetishism which attaches itself to the products of labour, so soon as they are produced as commodities, and which is therefore inseparable from the production of commodities.[37]

The juxtaposition between the act of seeing and the phenomenon of fetishism is quite significant from the point of view of the naturalness/sociality dichotomy. In fact, Marx juxtaposes the first phenomenon—a phenomenon of physical nature—with the second one, which has "absolutely no connection with their [referring to the commodity-form and to the value relation between the products of labour] physical properties and with the material relations arising therefrom." The character of fetishism can therefore be seen as the attribution of naturalness to relations that are social. This is done in accordance with the process of inversion, but without self-observation. If it were not so, it would be impossible to understand why Marx considered fetishism to be inseparable from the production of commodities. The inseparability pertains only to laborers who are involved in the production of commodities and who, therefore, are subject to the phenomenon. But only an observer is able to become conscious of this inseparability and, hence, assert it.

Let us now turn to the analogies with Cuban "savages" uncovered through the comparative process in the essay on wood theft and compare them with the comparative process present in *Capital*.

In the 1842 essay, the comparison was based, as has already been mentioned, on the hypothesis that the Cubans were the observers of the Spaniards and that they considered gold as the Spaniards' fetish, by virtue of the fact that they saw the Spaniards' attitude toward the precious metal through the prism of their conceptual and cultural universe. In *Capital* the analogy drawn between "primitive" religion and the world of commodities implies the overturning of the comparison and the repositioning of the observer. It is the observer himself that uses the analogical value of the concept of fetishism (extrapolated from the observation of the savages' universe) in order to include it in the universe of the world of commodities. This, so to say, internal/external role played by the concept of fetishism, enables the observer to shed light on what is unconsciously endured by the observed subjects in certain relationships.

This fact, the peculiarity of the analysis made by Marx in *Capital*, opens up the question of what the observer's place is. In the 1842 essay, where the observation concerned the Rhenish provincial orders, this place coincided with the "savages'" conceptual universe. In *Capital*, conversely, the conceptual universe of the observer is the same as that of the observed subjects: namely, a society predicated on the supremacy of commodity production. Therefore, the issue remains open.

So, on an initial level, we may suppose that Marx attempts to solve this problem—without, however, conceptualizing it—by using a critical comparison of the capitalist mode of production; a comparison based, so to speak, on "simple," "transparent," "direct" models such as, on the one hand, the image of "use value" as opposed to that of "exchange value" and, on the other, the imaginary models of Robinson Crusoe and the association of free men. In the commodity fetishism chapter of *Capital*, Marx juxtaposes the latter with the opacity of the commodity system. The use of these models stands at the origin of an ambiguity, which is already inherent in Marx (since he does not conceptualize the problem of the observer) and which has brought forth a series of interpretations, conceptions, and critiques in the field of the history of Marxism. In their analysis of Marx, scholars such as Baudrillard and Sahlins have, for instance, pointed out that the limits of his theory are most clearly revealed when he employs comparative references rooted in naturalistic and utilitarian images.[38] But it may well be that the issue ought to be examined in relation to the link between these models and the observer. Behind the ambiguity of this link lies the unsolved problem existing between the central moment of the *critique*[39] and the programmatic-propositive moment that was realized historically.

We have tried so far to examine the first phase of the comparative moment, where it appears clear that the concept of fetishism, drawn from de Brosses, was developed by Marx in a direction that diverged significantly from the main nineteenth-century current headed by Comte. The comparison does not develop within a context of stages in line with Hume's scheme, which—as it involves a passage from the concrete to the abstract—conceives of humanity's progress in terms of a broadening of the knowledge of natural phenomena. We can, therefore, establish the first value of Marx's concept of commodity fetishism.

It is based on the primary role played by *synchronicity* in the comparison of models and lies outside the rigid scheme of the diachronic development of social systems, derived from the evolutionary idea that was predominant in the nineteenth century. What is now required is an evaluation of the *extent to which* Marx pushed himself conceptually in this direction.

Two Historical Examples and Two Imaginary Models

In the paragraph on "The Fetishism of the Commodity and its Secret," Marx examines four social situations in which this feature of the commodity is absent. Two of them are of a historical nature and refer to medieval socioeconomic relationships and to the patriarchal rural industry of a peasant family. The other two are imaginary and refer to Robinson Crusoe's famous island and the equally famous association of free men.[40] The traits that these historical examples and imaginary models have in common have been pointed out by Godelier, who adds another historical case—that of primitive communities—which Marx analyzes in other contexts and mentions only briefly in the paragraph on the fetishism of the commodity. For the moment, we will not investigate this example further. Godelier states:

> The common element in these real or imaginary examples analysed by Marx is that relations of production are, or should be, simpler in structure and more transparent to the consciousness (both spontaneous and scientific)

than market relations of production and above all capitalist market relations of production. And these non-capitalist relations of production above all offer no basis for making social relations as relationships between things. At the same time Marx speaks of the 'masks' worn by men in feudal society and, more generally, of the 'mystical clouds' which obscure social life in pre-capitalist societies.[41]

The historical examples and the imaginary models chosen by Marx show some cases where the process that disguises social relations as relations between things does not occur, cases, that is, that do not provide the basis for this process. In them, the relations seem "simpler'" and "more transparent" and are juxtaposed with the system characterized by commodity fetishism. What we find here is a *comparative* framework, which has as its subject matter a phenomenon belonging to a certain social system: that of capitalist relations of production. This framework is realized by placing side by side various systems that, while *differing from each other*, nevertheless have one trait in common: the absence of the commodity fetishism phenomenon.

But is this enough? We need to ask ourselves whether, at this point, it might not be possible to stop examining the Marxian manner of proceeding. Is it possible to limit the effect of the comparison to the feature of homogenization emerging from the examples and the models described by Marx? Can we limit this effect to a feature rooted in the absence of an element which, in actual fact, is a specific trait of the capitalist system and is emphasized under the name of commodity fetishism?

Absolutely not, and for a variety of reasons. One of the first objections that tends to arise is: what guarantees do we have that the comparison has not been created ad hoc? That the comparison has not been manipulated ab initio? Might it not be possible that the description of the historical examples and the imaginary models has been altered to just the right point? If the comparison is functional to highlighting a specific element (the fetish character of commodities in the capitalist system), is it not possible that this functionality has got the better of the differing characteristics relevant to the various social (historical or imaginary) situations?

Let us admit that this operation is legitimate, that the historical examples and the imaginary models are depicted, so to speak, in a stylized way, so as to make only those aspects showing an absence of the commodity fetishism phenomenon prominent. Shouldn't we ask ourselves in this case what the logical and theoretical assumptions are upon which the descriptions of historical or imaginary systems are based? In fact, the comparison of systems necessarily implies (and this is also true of the case under examination) that the descriptive force deriving from it and grounded in the juxtaposition of nearly *but not quite* homogeneous systems, depends on how these very same systems are approached, described, and observed. Ultimately, the descriptive force of the comparison depends in its turn on the kind of description we use and the way we describe the juxtaposed objects.

If this is so, or, more prudently, if we accept for the moment this methodological admonition, then we should see the effects of the comparison right from the description of the systems. This might enable us to grasp the value and meaning of the fetish character of commodity in the capitalist system, once we have attempted to understand the effective points of comparison, whose function is to measure its specificity.

This is the reason why, going back to our starting point—namely, the fact that all we know for now is that historical examples and imaginary models are both devoid of the fetishism phenomenon and that they are characterized by "simpler" and "more transparent" relations compared to those in the capitalist mode of production—we must see whether the greater simplicity and transparency are expressed in a diversified manner. Or, putting it in another way, we must see whether the description of these systems appears as the description of the totality of their being or just as the description of the aspects that acquire a sense only in a comparative relation to the commodity system.

The question seems to be a very abstract one if posed in this way. Nevertheless, if we take a series of factors into account, it has a very specific raison d'être. This set of issues clearly brings us back to the thorny issue of reductionism in Marx; to the way he examines the relation between consciousness and material life; to the reiterated evocation of images drawn from the "nebulous and bewitched world" in order to explain the forms through which consciousness represents (by sublimating it) material life to itself; and to the concept of production mode and the importance attached to economic factors in the analysis of society.[42]

Undoubtedly, the issue of commodity fetishism and the effect of comparison produced by historical examples and imaginary models immediately poses the problem of reductionism. In fact, the question we have addressed before regarding the *way* Marx describes the historical examples and the imaginary models contains in itself this more generalized problem. Since this description is to be found in *Capital*, it also generates a specific kind of technical interest. Here, the discussion has moved beyond a general outline of the method of historical materialism previously provided by crucial works such as *German Ideology* and examined within the specific framework of the socioeconomical analysis of the capitalist mode of production.

MARX'S THEORY OF FETISHISM / 125

If we now take into consideration the two historical examples and the two imaginary models used by Marx for showing the absence of fetishism in other forms of production, as well as illustrating the historical determinateness of the mode of production based on commodities, it becomes evident that the comparison is organized around the following terms:

(a) The historical case of the feudal mode of production is characterized by the absence of fetishism since the relations of material production are determined by *relations of personal dependence*.[43]
(b) The example of the patriarchal rural industry of a peasant family is also characterized by personal relations presupposed by the structure of the family.[44]
(c) The imaginary model of Robinson Crusoe quite obviously presupposes the absence of any relation, since, in this case, it is an isolated man who relates to objects.[45]
(d) The imaginary model of the association of free men presupposes *direct* social relations between human beings, who control the production in full self-awareness.[46]

In these four cases the absence of commodity fetishism depends on the fact that the objects do not reflect the social characteristics of men's own labor in such a way as to make them seem like the natural properties of the objects themselves. In its turn, this depends on the fact that in the four cases in question commodities are not invested with the social function of regulating personal relations. Yet, there is an essential difference between the historical examples and the imaginary models. In the former, the process of image reflection (the phenomenon of disguise) is seen as a process that occurs outside and prior to any effectively productive activity: in fact, familial relationships and the personal relations between lords and serfs represent the assumption of production and the production bond. Production relations are therefore determined by rigid and noneconomic structures such as those of a familial nature and those between lords and serfs. The process of inversion and image crystallization reflects these structures, which in turn are a prerequisite for the production process. Consequently, it does not concern the commodity objects.

On the other hand, no image reflection occurs in the two imaginary models. It is assumed that the process of inversion does not take place, as though the absence of commodity fetishism implies, in itself, the possibility that the inversion process might end (that the images related to social relationships might stop being reflected), thus engendering social models based *only* on the direct and self-aware activity toward things. As Marx states:

> Let us finally imagine, for a change, an association of free men, working with the means of production held in common, and expending their many different forms of labour-power in full self-awareness as one single social labour force. All the determinacies of Robinson's labour are repeated here, but with the difference that they are *social* instead of *individual*. All Robinson's products were exclusively the result of his own personal labour and they were therefore directly objects of utility for him personally. The total product of our imagined association is a *social* product.[47]

What Robinson's island and the association of free men have in common is the direct and self-aware relationship with things. There are no commodities to regulate social relations and, therefore, the images of those relations are not projected onto them. Nevertheless, there is a specific point only briefly mentioned by Marx, even though it plays a substantial role: the difference between Robinson and the association of free men lies in the fact that, in the first case, the characteristics are *individual*, whereas, in the second, they are *social*. This means that, as far as the association of free men is concerned, the regulation of social relations occurs before the production. From a conceptual point of view, this is exactly what happens in the feudal system of lords and serfs and in the patriarchal rural industry of a peasant family based on familial hierarchy. But, unlike these two historical examples, where the relations of dependence and subordination produce an inversion of the images in the consciousness one has of oneself, in the imaginary ones the relations are not based on dependence. What can be deduced from this? Is it likely that all phenomena of inversion would cease once the relationships of dependence and commodity fetishism have ceased? Even without being based on subordination and dependence, social relationships cannot be reduced to the actions of a self-aware individual. This is precisely the conceptual element that Marx leaves unresolved. That is to say, what is left open to questioning is the meaning of the passage from "individual" to "social" in the passage from Robinson's island to the association of free men. This point marks the limit of Marx's reflection on the relation man-nature/man-society. It almost seems that the history of social relations must ultimately dissolve into their conscious regulation, so as to ensure nature's organic renewal process.[48] The absence of this passage indicates the persistence of theoretical ambiguity in the imaginary models, which take on a regulative, as well as ontological, value.

If the imaginary models' comparative effect is seen only as a regulative occurrence, it will be valid only for as long as one regards the theory of commodity fetishism as a particular case (i.e., the analysis of a historically determined form), which is part of a more general theory concerning the structure of nonintentional relations. But Marx never conceptualized such a theory. Otherwise, the comparative effect assumes an ontological value along the lines of the models. In this case, one would be obliged to suppose that the ideal place of the observer coincides with the very aim of social development: that is to say, a system in which, according to the classical linear theory of progress, everything occurs by means of men's conscious activity. This is, indeed, the case in which the observer cannot be observed, since he presumes and professes that he "sees the world as it really is" and denies the necessity of self-observation. Or, if one prefers, the case in which critical theory cannot be criticized, once it has institutionalized itself in a structure of power and once it has become, in the Marxist sense of the term, an ideology, a fixity of the consciousness of oneself and a concealment of the unconscious process of inversion.

After examining the historical examples and the imaginary models, Marx illustrates the relation—insofar as they are phenomena of inversion—between social forms and religious reflections:

> For a society of commodity producers, whose general social relation of production consists in the fact that they treat their products as *commodities*, hence as *values*, and in this *material [sachlich]* form bring their individual, private labours into relation with each other as *homogeneous human labour*, Christianity with its religious cult of man in the abstract, more particularly in its bourgeois development, i.e. in Protestantism, Deism, etc., is the most fitting *form of religion*.[49]

Human beings project the products of their minds onto a determinate religious form, which depends on a determinate form of society. And this projection is particularly complex in a world dominated by the production of commodities. Societies in which the production of commodities plays a subordinate role, as is the case, for instance, with the ancient Asiatic and Classical-Ancient modes of production, are characterized by "much more simple and transparent" social relations. What is it, then, that produces the phenomenon of inversion in these modes of production? Marx argues:

> They are founded either on the immaturity of man as an individual, when he has not yet torn himself loose from the umbilical cord of his natural species-connection with other men, or on direct relations of dominance and servitude. They are conditioned by a low stage of development of the productive powers of labour and correspondingly limited relations between men within the process of creating and reproducing their material life, hence also limited relations between man and nature. These real limitations

are reflected in the ancient worship of nature, and in other elements of tribalr eligions.[50]

In ancient communities (that is to say, in more simple and transparent societies), the permanence of religious reflection depends on the immaturity of the individual, who—by virtue of still being connected to his species and to his community—is still immersed in natural communal relations. These relations are, therefore, *independent* of the individual's will. But this independence can also derive from relations of subordination. The lack of dependence between social connections and the individual's will is seen by Marx as a trait pertaining to societies which are based either on the supremacy of a natural community (where individuality has not yet fully emerged) or on relations of subordination. It is this lack of dependence (the independence of social connections from the individuals producing them) that generates the phenomenon of inversion in the various forms of religion: the connections are either still immersed in nature or structured according to supremacy principles. The ambiguity of Marx's discourse lies in the conclusion that this independence may break down once both the bonds of nature and those of subordination have been overcome, even though, in actual fact, the issue revolves around a problem that is conceptually different to the problem of these bonds.

This is why he is able to conclude as follows:

> The religious reflections of the real world can, in any case, vanish only when the practical relations of everyday life between man and man, and man and nature, generally present themselves to him in a transparent and rational form. The veil is not removed from the countenance of the social life-process, i.e. the process of material production, until it becomes production by freely associated men, and stands under their conscious and planned control. This, however, requires that society possess a material foundation, or a series of material conditions of existence, which in their turn are the natural and spontaneous product of a long and tormented historicald evelopment.[51]

However, there remains a major unresolved problem: conscious control over processes, exercised according to a plan, will never manage—once it has established itself—to cancel the dimension where social relations between human beings become an entity that differs from the single individual. In order to be able to represent these relations to themselves, individuals will still feel the need for symbolic processes and inversions. At the same time, individuals will still feel the need to critically observe—from the inside, but as though looking from the outside—those processes and thosei nversions.

The Relation between Observer and Observation

There is still one last point to be explained: the analogical function of the concept of fetishism as a means enabling observers—who are inside the phenomenon—to observe the phenomenon itself, even though it is an unconscious one. This analogical function consists in applying a term—extrapolated from the so-called primitive religion—to a process of symbolic inversion, which is typical of a society of commodities. In actual fact, from the point of view of the relationship between observer and observation, this analogical function already contains in itself a comparative effect. This is what makes this concept so specific, if compared, for instance, with that of alienation. Indeed, the act of applying the notion of fetishism to the world of commodities means positioning oneself ideally outside the observed object, which is thus defined and delimited in relation to the transposition from the world of primitive religion to that of capitalism. Once it has been shifted into the world of commodities, the term fetishism must still refer back to its original meaning, the one attributed to the cults of the "savages." The comparative effect depends on this reference:[52] the analogy presupposes the difference between the compared worlds. By means of this transposition it becomes possible to reveal what occurs unconsciously to one's consciousness. Namely, the fact that what appears as a relation between things is instead a social relationship. By means of the concept of fetishism, the observation is performed as if from an external point of view, but without teleological elements: the observer does not stand a step higher than the observed object. He simply transposes it.

The operational concept of fetishism enables the observer to stand contemporaneously both inside and out. Only in such a way can he show the object he observes and is a part of. Fetishism's critical and descriptive function depends directly on its analogical value. In this case, the primacy of the synchronic procedure is obvious. Marx does not need any genetic procedure to solve the problems posed by comparison. Even though, in general terms, the issue of the inversion processes remains unresolved, it is nevertheless undeniable that Marx has drawn attention to a specific condition and opened up a vaster horizon. It is within this horizon that we still look for answers and attempt to orient ourselves.

Chapter Five
History, Nature, and System: Marx's Anthropological Conception

Time and Survival

When referring to so-called primitive societies in his analysis of the historical development of civilization, Bukharin argued:

> In the former society, all activities are devoted to the immediate securing of foodstuffs, hunting, fishing, the gathering of roots, primitive agriculture; of "ideas," of "mental culture," etc, there is very little; we are dealing here with men that are hardly more than monkeys, tribal animals. [...] The growth of *material production*, the increase in the power of man over nature, the increase in the *productivity of human labor*. For, when not all the available time is consumed in exhausting material labor, people are free a portion of the time, which affords them an opportunity to think, reason, work with a plan, create a "mental culture."[1]

This description contains all the anthropological prejudices of utilitarian-instrumental reasoning.[2] In the first place, there is the prejudice of *time*; in the second, the image of *survival*, which is part of that prejudice. In fact, the idea that primitive people are forced to spend all their time seeking their means for survival derives from a paradigm where the measuring of time and the bourgeois organization of time are placed at the origin.

The English historian E. P. Thompson has explored the relationship between the evolution of this notion of time and the development of the capitalistic organization of work. In juxtaposing the noncapitalist systems' conception of working time with that of industrial capitalism, he argues that the former can be described as task orientated.[3] After mentioning the measurement of time among primitive peoples, he calls attention to contemporary peasant societies and asserts:

> Three points may be proposed about task-orientation. First, there is a sense in which it is more humanly comprehensible than timed labour. The

peasant or labourer appears to attend upon what is an observed necessity. Second, a community in which task-orientation is common appears to show least demarcation between "work" and "life." Social intercourse and labour are intermingled—the working day lengthens or contracts according to the task—and there is no great sense of conflict between labour and "passing the time of day." Third, to men accustomed to labour timed by the clock, this attitude appears to be wasteful and lacking in urgency.[4]

Exactly the opposite occurs in the case of hired labor, whose historical development goes hand in hand with the introduction of new working practices, regulated by time: "As soon as actual hands are employed the shift from task-orientation to timed labor is marked.[5] [...] And the employer must *use* the time of his labor, and see it is not wasted: not the task but the value of time when reduced to money is dominant. Time is now currency: it is not passed but spent."[6] Time tends now to be deprived of any concrete determination. Its determination becomes time, which in turn is acquired as a commodity. The abstract dimension that envelops time, labor, and money structures the way of life: in a society dominated by the market, the economy separates itself from and becomes independent of other social spheres;[7] concurrently, labor—which has become time that can be sold—separates itself from other forms of social activity. Working time is opposed to free time because it is a necessary time: since it is spent by the employer, it forces the employee to spend his *own* time only outside work. Furthermore, with the development of the division of labor, the abstract dimension of labor makes the field of *survival* shift: since the necessary products can be purchased only at the market and since independent production within the family unit has ceased to exist, survival becomes an *economic* problem. It ceases to be at one with life and becomes a condition that precedes any other activity. Likewise, working time is a primary condition in relation to which every leisure is deferred.

This way of organizing time becomes a *system* within which the imaginary production of identity is governed by survival. The centrality of the topic of survival brings us, from *Robinson Crusoe* up to modern science fiction stories, to the ultimate sense of our way of life. Allowing the crisis to run its full downward course, to the most extreme conditions of survival, imagination makes the bourgeois individual's primary qualities visible, especially his ability to use scarce resources rationally. Separating itself from other forms of social activity, the economy goes as far as to demand that its autonomy become a tendency of social life itself; while survival—which has become an economic problem—consequently evokes and projects images of ourselves, thus repeating the myth of our origin and our identity. But, quite ironically, if survival provides us with the elements we need for seeing our way of life as if in a mirror, it is because our way life tends to reduce itself to survival.

In this game of mirrors, the time for surviving is juxtaposed with the time for living and this is so because it is none other than the transposition of working time into a naturalistic key. This explains why Bucharin persists in repeating that so-called primitive people devote all their time to providing themselves with the means for survival. If the paradigmatic measure is bourgeois time, then it becomes obvious that the idea of social development translates into a contraction of the working time necessary for surviving and into an expansion of the time necessary for "spiritual culture." Consequently, situations where working time cannot be contracted—because there are no appropriate means for rapidly producing the necessary material goods—generate ancient images of savage, wandering, and anxious hunters; as anxious as we are when we are afraid of being unable to earn our livelihood in time. Indeed, the contraction of working time that fosters the development of civilization is supported by the rational use of scarce resources. This idea is found as early as Defoe: "Man is the worst of all God's creatures to shift for himself; no other animal is ever starved to death; nature without has provided them both food and clothes, and nature within has placed an instinct that never fails to direct them to proper means for a supply; but man must either work or starve, slave or die. He has indeed reason given him to direct him, and few who follow the dictates of that reason come to such unhappy exigencies."[8]

These dictates are provided, if I may repeat it, by the canny ability to use scarce resources. Nevertheless, this scarcity has to be related to something, for instance, to needs. The hunter who spends all his time in the attempt to secure his livelihood tries to satisfy his physical needs. Since the resources he uses are scarce, he cannot do other than this: he identifies his way of life with the organization of his survival.

In this case, as in the former, the idea concerning the use of scarce resources, which supposedly prevents the so-called primitive man from crossing the limit of his naturalness, is none other than a projection of the dialectic of scarcity and abundance characterizing the capitalist mode of production. Time and money become scarce in the abstract world of infinite needs, in a system that—since production is aimed at exchange—places the satisfaction of needs at a median point and not at the final point of the cycle. The satisfaction of needs is only the means that leads us to exchange and not the end of exchange itself. Baudrillard argues:

> The truth is not that "needs are the fruits of production," but that the system of needs is the product of the system of production.[9] [...] Needs as a system are also radically different from enjoyment and satisfaction. They

are produced as *system elements*, not as *a relationship of an individual to an object* (just as labour power no longer has anything to do with—and even denies—the worker's relation to the product of his labour, and just as exchange-value no longer has anything to do with concrete, personal exchange, or the commodity form with real goods, etc.).[10]

In a market society, the dominance of the abstract force of money leads us to identify freedom, thus following Hobbes, with what has not been realized yet and the universal with what precedes the particular choice.[11] But at the moment of choice, of purchase, of buying, money disperses its potential universality. As is the case with Balzac's "Magic Skin," it gradually shrinks and consumes a portion of its energy as it turns bit by bit into particular goods. As is known, one can obtain anything with money, but there are limits to its purchasing power. It reveals itself as *scarce* when faced with the systematic condition of its abstractness; that is to say, when faced with the fact that it is universal only if it does not—or precisely because it does not—take on concrete and specific features. When this happens, then money assumes the form of a *deprivation* of what it might have been before it was exchanged with a specific commodity. This systematic condition of *scarcity*[12] is projected outside the market system and introduced into the relationship between the individual and the object. This projection, on the basis of which we imagine the savage as an individual fighting for survival and the bourgeois as someone who is torn between consumption and abstinence, marks a fundamental theoretical step. To be more precise, the point is *the subsuming of the systems nonintentional processes*[13] under the category of the subject's intentional acting. When this act of subsuming is set in *absolute* and *linear* terms, it ceases to be related to the system's historicity and contradictions and becomes a kind of "egomorphism." That is to say, it transmutes into the reduction of social relationships—of the relationships with *others*—to the level of ego and to the way the ego imagines its social supremacy over nature: an ensemble of many egos, who have the same intentions and the same conscience. Finally free from the "disturbances" of the social system they lived in, they can devote themselves to the relationship with nature, within whose practical and inert horizon they can locate the *Other*. Therefore, the systematic and prevailing relationship that comes to the fore is that between many egos and nature, even though this is the consequence of the abolition of the individuals as *others*: the systematicity of unintentional social processes disappears when faced with the fact that the subject's intentional acting has become a delirium of the self. In this way the many egos are, in reality, only one; the individuals are not social because there is only one individual who multiplies himself, as in magic mirrors. This individual pushes to the limit the bourgeois world's hidden desire: to find oneself alone face to face with the object, face to face with his *own* object, in relation to which the others are either a tool or a disturbance to be eliminated. This desire transcends history in the same way the idea of an absolute degree of intentional action with a zero degree of unintentional processes does. There is no difference between these many egos, which establish a transparent relationship with nature outside history, and President Schreber's delusion regarding the end of the world.[14] Both have eliminated *others* so as to keep the self stable.

In order to clarify this point and return to the problematicity of the initial approach—that is to say, to the anthropological prejudices inherent in the image of the savage who is oppressed by the time of survival— it is opportune to start from the fact that "modern ideology," as Louis Dumont defines it,[15] is characterized by the idea that the reason people live in society is the satisfaction of material needs or, more generally, that the relationships between human beings and society—seen as a tool for the individual's private ends[16]—are structured according to a sequence where the man/object relation governs the man/society relation.

This predominance gives rise to some consequences:

1. that the *relationship*—since it develops in the first place between the human being and the object—is the result of individuals' intentional acting, aimed at satisfying their material needs or at pursuing theirw ellbeing;
2. that the secondary man/society relation is purely instrumental and merely orientated toward the possibility of a fuller and more profitable realization of the former relation;
3. consequently, that the man/society relation derives from the intentional acting of individuals, who can make more or less advantageous deals with regard to the development of the man/object relation;
4. finally, that the man/society relationship presents itself as a *mediation* between the human being and the object. Through this mediation, the artificial world becomes progressively more complex and marks a symbolic transition from the dimension of "naturalness" to culturea ndc ivilization.

As is known, these consequences stand at the origin of political economy, which provides the basis for the anthropological conception of the individual as a being intent on pursuing his own interests—a conception that was to become a universal criterion for any system under investigation.[17] Be that as it may, the issue to be raised here concerns not so much the critique of an ideology which imposes its universality, but another—less clear and to some extent more unsettling—feature: the fact that the notion of the primacy of the man/object relationship over the man/society relationship becomes the formal structure of thinking, capable of subsuming the categories in question; it becomes, in other words, a *system*, whose consistency goes above and beyond what in the past has—erroneously—been defined as a "false conscience."

This points to a fundamental issue: the critique of the universality claims of a determinate ideology might well remain *inside* the same system of thought and thus reproduce the same results, despite its best intentions to the contrary. Therefore, some inconsistencies are likely to occur if one stays, as Bucharin does, within the systemic framework which presupposes the primacy of the man/object relationship over the man/society relationship. These inconsistencies render the theoretical practice difficult and contradictory and weaken its claim to be grounded in a basis which differs from that of the criticized and rejected practice. Should one, for instance, relate the critique of society to the fact that society *distorts* the "correct" and "transparent" relationship between man and object, between the individual and his use value, one would have done nothing more than associate this critique with a system's dissonances and call the system back to its ultimate consistency of *sense*. Similarly, should one see exchange value as something that conceals the "correct" and "transparent" relationship between the individual and his use value, or as the historical form that "embodies" the "natural" relationship between the individual and his use value, one would have done nothing more than refer to the "naturalness" of the primacy of the man/object relationship over the historicity of the man/society relationship. This is not an easy problem since, in the end, all analyses and all social critiques find themselves having to relate any element seen as being variable throughout the historical processes to an invariable feature. In the long run, this invariable feature presents itself as the metaphysical nucleus, as a result and not as the starting point of the construction. In this way, the moment of verification of the critique of a specific thought system does not consist, so to speak, in what this moment thinks of itself (that is to say, its own assertions concerning the opposition to and the exit from that system), but in the practical use of that very same invariable feature and, therefore, of its systematic procedure.

If we return to Bucharin's description, it is easy to see that the image of the savage, who spends all his time in hunting and seeking his means of subsistence, is nothing more than the commodity society's projection of time into the "primitive" world. The separation between working time and leisure time as it manifests structurally in the bourgeois way of life (deprived of its abstract dimension, which constitutes its nonintentional systematic feature) is collocated in a history that is subsumed into the man/

object relationship. Within this relationship, time indeed measures the transition from scarcity to abundance, from survival to life: a measurement that reproduces, from era to era, the anxiety aroused by the need to reduce work time and extend leisure time. This reduction pulsates only insofar as it is enclosed within a specific life system. Once the systematic links scarcity/abundance, survival/life are broken, once they are deprived of their historicity—a historicity that consists in delimiting the pulsation fields of opposed but complementary elements—they become projections, they are projected into the world under the teleological vestiges of history. In the end, it is the primacy of the man/object relationship that supplies analysis with its ultimate sense and brings back unintentional processes within the scheme asserting the primacy of individual action over objects.

But there is more. In this framework, time and survival assume a *semiotic* dimension through which it is possible to trace the actual procedure behind what the analysis and the critique think of themselves. Take, for instance, *time*: according to Bucharin, time finds itself, as already mentioned, between the hunter and his game, thus occupying—within the scheme assigning priority to the man/object relationship—the place of social relationships. In doing so, it represents and simultaneously deforms social relationships. The time of the hunter is at once similar to and yet different from bourgeois time, that is to say, from the abstract time social relationships contribute to identifying as a system. The similarity lies in the connotations of scarcity and in the separation between work and "leisure," whereas the difference is reflected in its concreteness, in the fact that it is internally saturated by the anxiety of a job that offers no opportunity for leisure. This is what makes it comprehensible to the Western viewer, who looks upon a world unlike his own (recalling in this regard the archaic mind, which is allegedly incapable of distinguishing between footprints and the person that left them).[18]

The same can be said of *survival*: the similarity lies in the fact that—insofar as it concerns material and economic survival—the codes of the bourgeois world assign a symbolic value to it. At the same time (and this is where the difference comes in), it plays the role of the whole with respect to the parts; therefore, when its representation is set in a different world, survival becomes a sign of the bourgeois world.

Let us now return to the issue posed above. The primacy of the man/object relationship indicates the subsumption of the system's unintentional processes under the primacy of the subject's intentional acting, thus attributing a universal meaning to the way of life and providing an explanation for everything. Should we take this man/object relationship and situate it in the world of man's origin, there would not be much to say, because in this case the "object" would coincide with the elements purely and simply offered by nature to the abilities, the intelligence, and the instruments of the "primitive" mind. But should we examine the description process, we may notice that it avails itself of categories whose semiotic value reveals a system of thought bound to an assumption that is characteristic of bourgeois life. If, subsequently, we analyze this man/object relationship in connection with the world we live in (that is to say, the world of complexity and exchange), we would perceive that the "object" is a *commodity*, that is, the result of social work: it is no longer connected with nature, but with history, and its *sense* is to be sought not in its natural content, but in its social form.[19] It is thanks to this form that the commodity evokes the systematic relationships established by human beings. Instead, in those cases where the primacy of the connection between man and object is endorsed, these very same relationships emerge *afterwards*, as a mere mediation of this primary and originary dynamic. It is precisely the concealment of the object as the product of social processes—with the consequent inclusion of social relations in the sphere covered by the man/object relationship—that enables the relationship to become so generalized as to turn the object commodity into a natural object when referring to the difficult world of the "primitives." Therefore, we attribute a universal meaning to what appears as universal only in the bourgeois world: the primary importance of material interests within the sphere of action undertaken by individuals. Once again, our society's pursuit of wellbeing becomes the procurement of the means of subsistence, since both actions are subject to the same symbolical universe.

Social relationships appear therefore as the *form* of a content that remains natural; that is to say, they appear as historically changeable when compared to the permanence of the "natural" purpose and sense of human action. As a matter of fact, social relationships are often reduced to historically different ways for pursuing individual wellbeing. It is exactly this process that sanctions the primacy of the economic realm, to which the social reduces itself or from which the social supposedly originates. If an individual's "natural" sense is mainly produced by the pursuit of material subsistence, by the satisfaction of material needs, and by the search for wellbeing, then a "natural" action is an economic one—an action that constitutes itself as a basis (an originary one, if seen from a historical and ideal perspective and a foundational one if seen from a theoretical and operative perspective) for any other action and any other social relationship.

These reasons contribute to explaining the similarity drawn, at least from the eighteenth century onwards, between the image of the "primitive" hunter—to whom we trace our origins—and the paradigm of the "isolated man" intent on explaining and simplifying the dynamics of the market system.[20] Both of them derive from the metaphysics of the economic subject, who is placed at the beginning of the analysis—an analysis focused on his behavior and conduct.[21] This is the metaphysics of the free and conscious subject, based on the illusion that it is the subject who determines the system of nonintentional relations, subordinating those relations to his material needs and to his power to satisfy them. Social relationships thus appear as mere historically changeable modes for realizing this power—whose foundation remains "natural"and meta-historical—in a more or less good way.

Historical Forms and Theoretical Procedure

Thus far we have tried to foreground a form of representation based on the metaphysics of the economic subject, who freely and consciously relates himself to the object. This form of representation turns into a system when it is able to subsume elements that are not immediately part of the primary relationship. So, if in following Louis Dumont we identify "modern ideology" with the idea that the man/object relationship is primary with respect to the man/society relationship, then we should add that *one moves from ideology to system when the determination of this primacy implies the reconstruction of the man/society relationship within the man/object relationship, and, thus, the subsumption of the relationships between human beings under the conceptual system of the man/object relationship.* This systematic dimension allows us to explain how it is possible that, when we oppose an ideology, the form or representation stays the same if the system of thought supporting it stays the same, as happens in the case of Bucharin.[22] When an analysis crosses the limits of the determinate forms of the object under examination and presses on into fields that imply a *generalization* of the concepts supporting it, it becomes possible to oppose the metaphysics of the free and conscious economic subject and surreptitiously reintroduce it under the guise of an out-and-out "spontaneous philosophy." This is probably the reason behind Marx's attempt to make clear, especially in the last stage of his reflections and his life, that his analysis of the formation of the capitalist mode of production was limited to the history of Western Europe. Marx insists on this point by making a reference to *Capital* when, in the drafts to the *Letter to Vera Zasulich*, he engages in a controversy against those who thought that Russia would evolve by following the historical stages of Western capitalism. As far as the analysis of the genesis of capitalist production is concerned (a production based on the separation of the producer from the means of production), he states that "the 'historical inevitability' of this course is therefore *expressly* restricted to *the countries of Western Europe.*"[23] This means that the *historical* analysis of what has happened in the formation process of capitalist production cannot be used for deducing the future evolution of systems which have not yet gone through the same process. Therefore, a theoretical analysis based on specific historical changes, which are limited in space and time, should not be turned into *a conceptual generalization*. In the *Letter to the Editor of Otecestvenniye Zapisky*, Marx once again underlines the fact that, from a historical point of view:

> events strikingly analogous but taking place in different historic surroundings led to totally different results. By studying each of these forms of evolution separately and then comparing them one can easily find the clue to this phenomenon, but one will never arrive there by the universal passport of a general historico-philosophical theory, the supreme virtue of which consists in being super-historical.[24]

Marx's refusal of super-historical generalizations—that is to say, of a philosophy of history capable of explaining historical movements in general terms and in the register of a determination of sense within which to inscribe them—is directly related, in the last period of his research, to historical and anthropological studies.[25] Here, attention is theoretically focused on *separation* processes[26] that transform or extinguish a socioeconomic system, without *any* tolerance for the pursuit of a unique trace capable of metaphysically explaining the mechanisms of social evolution.[27] Staying anchored to history—seen by Marx as a field of manifold possibilities that open up from analogous conditions—is a caution against historical-philosophical generalizations, where by historical-philosophical generalizations he means the transposition of an analysis limited to a specific historical context to other contexts, before analyzing their dynamics and specific contradictions. From the theoretical point of view, the analysis of the different historical contexts is conceptually based on the processes through which the connecting elements of a specific system are *separated*. For Marx, what counts in the first place is the effect of differentiation, not that of a system's homogenization—not the features that contribute to its reproduction or to the preservation of its identity, but those that tend to destroy them,[28] thus creating the conditions for the transition to another system. From this perspective, Marx therefore attempts, on the one hand, to find in history the determination and the delimitation of the analysis. On the other hand, he bases this analysis on the features related to the system's transformation (not on the conditions contributing to its preservation, but on the specific possibilities of its disruption).

If we return to this strand of Marxian thought and relate it to the issue of representative forms and their tendency to turn into a system, it becomes quite apparent that staying anchored to history is a clear expression of

Marx's acknowledgment of the need to avoid a generalizing perspective and to stay within what is historically analyzable. It is, therefore, a clear expression of his *tendency* to reject giving a "naturalistic" content (an assumption common to all forms) to the variation of historical forms.[29] Nevertheless, it still does not say much about another element of the issue: namely, the fact that the association of a historical form with "something else"—that is to say, with an element which contrapuntally reveals the historicity of this form—*presupposes in turn that this "something else" be historically determinate, unless we wish to provide a naturalistic foundation.*

The issue must be addressed within the framework of the systematic counterpoint generated by the relationship between man and object and between man and society. It is known that Marx gave prominence to the social character of the individual—a feature he saw as constitutive of the individual's identity and specificity—and to the social character of production, which expresses itself as a system of relations. More precisely, the critique of the primacy of the man/object relationship as constitutive of the representative form is based on the fact that this representation is the result of certain *social* relationships and that the "object" is the result of *social* production: not a primordial element, but—in and of itself—the removal of the historical social relationship that produces it. The key for understanding the conceptual genealogy which has led "modern ideology" to assume as primary the man/object relation is provided by the section on commodity fetishism. The commodity's fetish character is examined starting from the social relationships between human beings in a system dominated by commodities. The point of departure is the *relationships* which, by means of commodity exchange, turn into a *system* within the determinate mode of production. What Marx foregrounds is the fact that these relationships, since they turn into a system, structure themselves in a way that determines both men's consciousness and their intentionality. Social relations appear to men's consciousness "as what they are," that is, as "thing-like [sachliche] relations between persons, and social relations between things [Sachen]." Were the elimination attempted, together with this fetish character, of the *systemic* character as well within which the fetish manifests itself, *were the elimination attempted of something which is intrinsically related to what, in the social context, cannot be reduced either to the sum of single individuals, or to the transparent relationships determined by conscience*, then one would arrive again at the spontaneous theoretical solution based on the metaphysics of the free and conscious subject. In the case where social relationships "appear as they are," the starting point becomes the primacy of the man-object relation, because the assumption of the metaphysics of the free and conscious subject translates itself in the way in which this subject "sees" social relations: namely, as a consequence of the private problem posed by the urge to satisfy needs through the appropriation of "objects." And yet, the metaphysics of the free and conscious subject can reintroduce itself in an operative way even in the case where one distinctly perceives the fetish character of commodity and acknowledges the fact that the man-object relationship is the result of determinate sociohistorical relations. This might occur when, in the process of determining their historicity, the critique of the social relations fetishized by commodities bases itself on the assumption that the removal of the fetish opens up the possibility of eliminating *tout court* every nonintentional systemic character of these relations and, therefore, characterizes this liberation as a transition toward the pure and simple transparency of conscious relations. The *social* character of individuals is affirmed only in a metaphysical way every time the critical assumption of the primacy of the man/society relationship over the man/object relationship results in the removal of the systemic character of social relations. It is affirmed as a point around which sociohistorical forms revolve and rotate, as is exactly the case with the assumption of the primacy of the man/object relationship. The fact, for instance, that the relationship with the objects is established by many people and not only by a single person does not change the issue. This remains so if we say nothing about the *social way* in which these many people relate to objects. It has, however, to be borne in mind that the systematicity of this social way cannot be reduced to the manner of appropriating objects. As an alternative, the act of relating the historical forms to the relationship between men and nature would lead us once again to see these forms as "disturbances," as something that prevents the human being from realizing the transparency of this relationship so that it no longer be alienated.[30]

As it is possible to observe, the problem emerges when conceptual generalization faces the need to have a firm point from which to capture the historicity of the forms under analysis. Seeking out a firm point, overlooking the permanence of the systemic character of historically determined social relations, and referring to the metaphysics of the free and conscious subject, this generalization reaches a point where it has to relate, once again, the historicity of social forms to a naturalistic presupposition. But the question cannot be solved—even if it opposes "modern ideology" or steps away from both it and its ahistoricity—if the theorization is based on the same presuppositions. The reason lies in the fact that the systemic logic which guides the forms of representation goes beyond the ideology of the person who makes the generalization.

Indeed, we might argue, in general, that these contradictions are typical of presymbolic thought. This type of thought does not take account of the unintentional systematic dimension that determines social relationships and makes them concrete. So, it might seem reasonable to hypothesize that it consequently produces the need to relate the analysis of historical forms to a general condition of a naturalistic kind, because it is grounded in the assumption that the only dimension which characterizes the human animal is individual conscience. In an enlightened way, this conscience has to free itself of every obscurity, attempting thus to free itself from all those aspects of social and individual actions and life which are, and are bound to remain, systematically unconscious. It is as if, in wishing to free ourselves from a neurosis, we claim to have dispensed with our unconscious forever.

A "Genealogy of Marx's Conceptual Thought"

It is universally known that Marx brought the primacy of being over conscience to the fore.[31] Yet, this does not exclude the possibility of revising his theorization, which attempted, on the one hand, to establish the systematicity of social relations and, on the other, to determine their historicity. This historicity was also based on a critique of political economy (which Marx saw as the point of departure for the free and conscious economic subject). There are, however, a series of generalizations and assumptions in his theoretical framework which go against his own critical presuppositions and lead toward the idea of a naturalistic transparency of the very same relations that were supposed to play the role of reference points, as well as showing the variation of the historically determined social forms.

For instance, at times use value is seen, together with needs,[32] as historically determined, while at other times it is contrasted with the opacity deriving from relationships that are based on exchange value, as happens in the chapter on commodity fetishism.[33] But then, the description we find in *Kapital* of a communist society eliminates every unintentional systemic element of the relationships (viewed as clear and transparent) between human beings. It does so through a descriptive procedure in which the association of free producers is composed of individuals who reiterate Robinson's determinations; that is to say, of a man who, despite possessing things, is "socially" isolated.[34] It is as if the primary relation were still that between man and object, and as if human beings developed social structures under a pact, without anything to disturb their conscience. Obviously, Marx made various statements on this subject. One might also assert that the ambiguity was created in some cases by the simplifying features of the exposition. But what matters for the analysis is neither this idea nor the fact that, at the most, we might profitably pinpoint the less ambiguous (at least from the perspective of this discussion) passages. What interests us here, on the contrary, is the contradictions inherent in Marx's theoretical procedure; they are crucial in order that the threads may be drawn together on contemporary Marxian reflection. Only in this way can we give prominence to the actuality and vitality of his thought.

In relation to this, it has been observed that the discussion contained in the "Marginal Notes on Adolph Wagner"—a text published in 1879–1880—plays a relevant role. In his *The Concept of Nature in Marx*, Alfred Schmidt argued that this work contained a kind of "genealogy of conceptual thought"[35] and formulated, in opposition to Adolph Wagner, a concept that was important for a restatement of the philosophical position Marx developed since the *Theses on Feuerbach*: the relationship between human beings and nature cannot be established in an abstract way; its fundamental characteristic is not theoretically contemplative but practical and transformational. He goes on to argue that no other passage in Marx's writings offers such a neat formulation of concepts, and schematizes this "genealogy"a sf ollows:

1. productiond erivesf roms ensiblen eeds;
2. the recurrent "trade" with nature—an attitude common to both animals and human beings—sets a process in motion that leads to a first division of objects according to the criterion of pain or pleasure;
3. the human group, which is economically more developed and, therefore, better organized, bearing in mind the level of conflict it experiences, performs a theoretical act; this act surpasses the nominalist classification of natural objects since, in this case, it is based on real supremacy.

Schmidt continues by asserting that originally the spirit is a *tabula rasa*; the concepts it formulates are produced through the accumulation of practical experience and their value lies directly in their instrumental features.

Seen in this framework, the moments of knowledge turn out to be diversely determined products of history, says Schmidt; it follows, he asserts, that a formal analysis of consciousness in the Kantian sense, that is, knowledge about knowledge, isolated from problems of fact and content, is no longer possible. Only on the basis of its concrete historical application is it possible to establish what purpose the instrument of knowledge serves.

The determination of the primacy of practical-transformative characteristics over theoretical-contemplative ones leads Marx's materialism to associate the analysis of knowledge forms with the historical substance of the man-nature relationship. The "genealogy of Marx's conceptual thought" is therefore characterized, according to Alfred Schmidt, by three phases:

1. the assertion of the primacy of practical activity, seen as a concrete and dynamic element of the man-nature relationship;
2. this relationship is associated with the historical forms within which it emerges and within which we become aware of it;
3. knowledge forms are related to the historical forms within which the transformative relationship between man and nature develops.

Yet, should we accept this, a problem immediately arises: what is the connection between the general statement which assigns priority to the practical-transformational features of the man-nature relationship and the obvious fact that this relationship manifests itself within the historical concreteness under determinate forms? Doesn't this mean that we should come up against the problem of a *generalization* grounded in a "naturalistic" presupposition—the man-nature relationship—to which we must correlate the variable sociohistorical forms? In this case, the *primal* relationship risks becoming the element that produces the sense of the explanation. Furthermore, are the practical-transformational features of the man-nature relationship sufficient to distinguish Marx's materialism from the utilitarian materialism of instrumental reason? Are they sufficient to distinguish it from the metaphysics of the free and conscious economic subject, even when this subject is seen as an active agent (as in the case of Robinson Crusoe)? Unquestionably, what must be verified is whether in Marx's text this generalization eliminates—to the complete benefit of materialistic metaphysics—the systemic features of the relations between human beings.

More recently, the anthropologist Marshall Sahlins has drawn attention to Marx's writing and made a comparison between Marx's generalizations on the stages in human development (seen from the perspective of the practical-transformational relationship to nature) and some passages on totemism written by Malinowski.[36] In fact, Malinowski is a very interesting author, especially when considering the difference between ideology and forms of representation, since, as Sahlins argues: "it is true that Malinowski was the first anthropologist to deny the generality of 'economic man'. But was this not simply to give the same concept even greater scope"?[37] What is noticeable in his work—and was criticized by Lévi-Strauss[38]—is the analysis of totemism. In *Magic, Science and Religion* there is an explanation of the totemic phenomenon:

> From the survival point of view, it is vital that man's interest in the practically indispensable species should never abate, that his belief in his capacity

to control them should give him strength and endurance in his pursuits and stimulate his observation and knowledge of the habits and natures of animals and plants. Totemism appears thus as a blessing bestowed by religion on primitive man's efforts in dealing with his useful surroundings, upon his "struggle for existence."[39]

Here, as Sahlins has stressed, the issue of totemism is related to the classical terms of instrumental and utilitarian reason: *survival*, the utilitarian relationship with nature; religion as a form of opacity versus a transparent and scientific relationship between man and nature; and, more generally, the reduction of the culture and knowledge question to data related to material and biological subsistence. So here again may be found a naturalistic conception that projects the *time* dimension of the bourgeois system—whose symbolic model is constituted precisely by the figure of economic man—back to the origins. Furthermore, whereas in the case of totemism the dimension that constitutes the core of awareness is alienated, in this case it is biological and instinctual. What moves the awareness is the practical end of the satisfaction of needs. This is the theoretical sphere where its core dissolves.

At this point we must closely examine Marx's text, starting from a sentence by Adolph Wagner that he calls attention to. According to Wagner, "It is a *natural* striving of man to arrive at a *clear awareness* and *understanding* of the *relationship* which inner and outer *goods* bear to his *needs*. This is done through *appreciation, (valuation)* by which *value is attributed* to goods or things of the outside world and this value is *measured*."[40] In this sentence, Wagner forms a hypothesis about the psychology of the individual who arrives, in a "natural" way, at a "clear awareness" of the relationship between goods and his needs. As we see, Marx's critique is directed at statements grounded in the metaphysics of the free and conscious economic subject—at statements based on an anthropological conception where the subject uses the external world for satisfying his needs in accordance with the relationship between object (the goods) and needs. Accordingly, the presupposition of this anthropology is the subject's level of awareness, which is also the central point of Marxist philosophy.

Let us now examine Marx's comment:

> '*Man*'? If the category "man" is meant here, then he has "no" needs at all; if man in isolated juxtaposition with nature, then each individual must be considered a nongregarious animal; if a man already existing in some kind of society—and this is what Mr. Wagner implies, since his "man" does have a language, even though he lacks a university education—then as a starting-point the specific character of this social man must be presented,

i.e. the specific character of the community in which he lives, since in that case production, i.e. *the process by which he makes his living*, already has some kind of social character.⁴¹

Marx's observations are directed here against the idea of starting from an isolated man who, in the first place, is aware of his means and possibilities. In particular, he criticizes that form of generalization which dissolves the *determinate* character of this awareness. Marx argues that the figure of "man" conceived by Wagner cannot but be the result of a determinate society ("i.e. the specific character of the community in which he lives"). He therefore relates man's consciousness to man's social and historical being and, consequently, to the social *relations* through which the human being poses himself the problem of goods and needs. Furthermore, Marx underlines the fact that, in assuming a determinate society, the relationship between man and object presupposes language. This means that the behavior conceived by Adolph Wagner erroneously disregards two essential components.

Marx asserts two things here. In the first place, he argues that one cannot make generalizations outside the scope of specific historical conditions. Thus, the act of referring to history critically renders the generalization problematical. Secondly, he states that the primacy goes to social man, to the social relationships determining the form in which the individual becomes aware of his needs. As a result, the primacy of man-object over the man-society relationship is allegedly subverted here by Marx and subjected to a direct critique. Nevertheless, two problems remain open. The first lies in the fact that it is not clear the extent to which Marx considers the reference to what is socially and historically determined as a mutation of the forms versus the permanence of content (i.e., the relationship between human beings and nature). The second lies in the fact that the affirmation of the primacy of the man-society relationship is still indefinite when compared to the characterizing point (i.e., the relationship's tendency to form systems without being reduced either to the sum of individuals or to the ultimate sense, which is still that of the man-nature relation). Actually, these two problems can be considered together, if we bear in mind that in the end the basic question remains open: *if the historicity of social relationships is responsible for reducing their systemic character to variable forms through which human beings undertake a constant material exchange with nature, then this exchange will become, once again, the firm point around which the analysis revolves.*

If this is so, then the problem is not that of eliminating historicity in favor of the systemic character of relationships,⁴² but, rather of eliminating a meta-historical assumption: namely, eliminating a generalization that claims to presuppose the substantial immutability of the content (the material exchange between human beings and nature) versus a variation of the forms in which it supposedly realizes itself. This would represent some sort of materialistic metaphysics, not materialistic philosophy, because the generalization would attach a greater value to the generic element and underestimate the element that *differentiates* human beings from other animals; that is to say, it would minimize the fact that human beings are social animals endowed with symbolic abilities. Social codes—which cannot be reduced to man's level of awareness—are determined precisely by these abilities.

Marx goes on to argue:

> But for a professorial schoolmaster the relations between men and nature are a priori not *practical*, that is, relations rooted in action, but *theoretical*, and two relations of this kind are packed up together in the first sentence. [...] But men do not by any means begin by "finding themselves in this theoretical relationship to the *things of the outside world.*" They begin, like every animal, by *eating, drinking,* etc., that is not by "finding themselves" in a relationship, but *actively behaving*, availing themselves of certain things of the outside world by action, and thus satisfying their needs. (They start, then, with production.) By the repetition of this process the capacity of these things to "satisfy their needs" becomes imprinted on their brains; men, like animals, also learn "theoretically" to distinguish the outer things which serve to satisfy their needs from all other. At a certain stage of evolution, after their needs, and the activities by which they are satisfied, have, in the meanwhile, increased and further developed, they will linguistically christen entire classes of these things which they distinguished by experience from the rest of the outside world. This is bound to occur, as in the production process—i.e. the process of appropriating these things—they are continually engaged in active contact amongst themselves and with these things, and will soon also have to struggle against others for these things. [...] Thus: human beings actually started by appropriating certain things of the outside world as a means of satisfying their own needs, etc. etc.; later they reached a point where they *also* denoted *them linguistically* as what they are for them in their practical experience, namely as a *means of satisfying their needs*, as things which "satisfy" them.[43]

The following conceptual scheme may be drawn up:

(a) human beings appropriate—or, rather, they start by appropriating—objects belonging to the outside world;
(b) at a later stage, human beings give a verbal designation to these objects on the basis of their practical usefulness as a means of satisfyingt heirn eeds.

What we have here, in contrast to Wagner, is the idea that the relationship of human beings with nature is active and practical and that the process of humanization—that is, the process of differentiation and characterization of human beings as such, compared to other animals—ideally originates and delineates itself from this activity. In the course of this process society and language[44] are viewed as resulting from natural evolution, as the outcomes, that is, of practical-transformative activities and of the experience gained through material exchange with nature. Apparently, there is nothing more obvious than this, except—as noticed by Sahlins[45]—that we are faced with a theoretical incongruence. If, from a theoretical point of view, we follow the thread of this natural evolution, then the specifically human social aspect must necessarily be seen as originating from the natural process. But this occurs in tandem with the very same human social aspect constituting the starting point of the analysis. We are thus faced with the fact that on the one hand Marx asserts the primacy of the man-society relationship over the generic relationship with nature and recognizes as fundamental its systemic character and differentiating condition; while on the other, he once again correlates the man-society relationship and its historical forms with the general datum of the man-nature material exchange. In the first case human beings differentiate themselves from other animals and from nature through their social character. Exactly the opposite happens in the second case, since what prevails is the generic character, the act of including the human being in the animal reign.

Obviously, here the problem concerns the logical procedure and not the level of animality in humans. As far as the logical reasoning is concerned, there is no doubt that the exposition provided by Marx in his *Marginal Notes on Wagner* entails the danger of what he himself feared in the method of the political economy critique. That is to say: "The elements which are not general and common, must be separated out from the determinations valid for production as such, so that in their unity—which arises already from the identity of the subject, humanity, and of the object, nature—their essential difference is not forgotten."[46] And yet, this is what happens in the *Marginal Notes on Wagner*. What is lost sight of is precisely this essential difference: that is, the historical modes of the man-nature relationship and also the more general fact that the logical procedure cannot metaphysically presuppose the man-nature relationship as a foundation for the historical variation of the man-society relationship. In this case the act of correlating the subject, who is free and conscious in relation to nature, with the sociohistorical forms that determine his origin and his limits (that is to say, his being), leads us to the vicious circle of having once again to relate—at a later stage—the sociohistorical forms to the man-nature relationship. This, probably, is the reason that lies behind the fact that Marx's fundamental contribution to the critique of the metaphysics of the free and conscious subject (seen as the starting point of the analysis and of the assumption concerning the primacy of relationships that tend to form a system) in a certain sense comes to a standstill at the moment when it was possible to draw from it the most extreme consequences. We can apply to this "genealogy of Marx's conceptual thought" what Marx himself asserted about the thought pattern that provides economic categories with an organic structure:

> It would therefore be unfeasible and wrong to let the economic categories follow one another in the same sequence as that in which they were historically decisive. Their sequence is determined, rather, by their relation to one another in modern bourgeois society, which is precisely the opposite of that which seems to be their natural order or which corresponds to historical development. The point is not the historic position of the economic relations in the succession of different forms of society. Even less is their sequence 'in the idea' (Proudhon) (a muddy notion of historic movement). Rather, their order within modern bourgeois society.[47]

If this can be done within the field of economic analysis, then surely—and to an even greater extent—it can be done within the more general field of the distinction between the man-society and man-nature relationship. Shouldn't we follow the reverse course of the evolutionary scheme (from nature to society to culture) delineated by Marx in the *Marginal Notes on Wagner*? Isn't it more important to start from the differential factor rather than from the generic one? In the end, the contradictions of Marx's conceptual thought arise from the fact that he assigns priority to the man-nature relationship and does not extricate himself from the general philosophy he dreaded so much precisely when it was possible to broaden the scope of his theorizations and bring to the fore the theoretically irreversible elements of his analysis of the capitalist mode of production, that is, the attempt to view the *historicity* of social forms as separation and difference within the systematic dimension of the relationship between human beings.[48]

Notes

Introduction

1. Voltaire, *Candide and Other Stories*, translated by Roger Pearson, Oxford World Classics, Oxford University Press, 2006, p. 48.
2. D.Hume, *Treatise of Human Nature*, Book I, Part III, section VIII.
3. D. Hume, *The Natural History of Religion*, with an Introduction by John M. Robertson, Freethought Publishing Company, London, 1889.
4. E. B. Tylor, *Primitive Culture* (1871), New York, Brentano, 1924, vol. I, p. 477 ff.; S. Freud, *Totem and Taboo*, translated by A. A. Brill, New York, Moffat,1 918.
5. D. Freedberg, *The Power of Images*, University of Chicago, Chicago, 1989. See also D. Freedberg and V. Gallese, "Motion, Emotion and Empathy in Aesthetic Experience," *Trends in Cognitive Sciences*, 11, 2007, pp. 197–203; V. Gallese and D. Freedberg, "Mirror and Canonical Neurons Are Crucial Elements in Aesthetic Response," *Trends in Cognitive Sciences*, 11, 2007, p. 411.
6. On this see my *Paura e meraviglia. Storie filosofiche del XVIII secolo* (Fear and Wonder. Philosophical Stories of the Eighteenth Century) Rubbettino, Catanzaro1 998.
7. On the notions of "formal connections" and "perspicuous representation," see L. Wittgenstein, "Remarks on Frazer's *Golden Bough*," in *Philosophical Occasions* (1912–1951), edited by J. Klagge and A. Nordmann, Hackett, Indianapolis, 1993. See also L. Wittgenstein, *Philosophical Remarks*, edited by Rush Rhees, translated by Raymond Hargreaves and Roger White, Oxford, Blackwell, 1975. These concepts have also been examined in A. G. Gargani, *Wittgenstein. Musica, parola, gesto,* Cortina, Milan, 2008, p. 68 ff. and in A. M. Iacono, "Attorno al concetto di rappresentazione perspicua. Spengler e Wittgenstein," in *Goethe, Schopenhauer, Nietzsche. Saggi in memoria di Sandro Barbera*, ETS, Pisa, 2012.
8. K.M arx, *Capital*,I .4.
9. See J. Lacan, *Le séminaire de Jacques Lacan, Livre IV: La relation d'objet* (1956–1957), edited by J. A. Miller, Seuil, Paris, 1994. For a detailed discussion of fetishism in the context of the modern world, starting from Marx, Freud, and Lacan, see S. Zizek's *The Plague of Fantasies*, Verso, London–New York, 1997. See also *Figure del feticismo*, a cura di S. Mistura, Einaudi, Turin, 2001; U. Fadini, "Attraverso il feticismo radicale," *Millepiani*, no. 21, 2002, pp. 63–77, where Baudrillard's theorization is also discussed.

10. B.B ettelheim, *The Uses of Enchantment*, Vintage Books, New York, 2010.
11. Camille Tarot, *De Durkheim à Mauss. L'invention du symbolique*, La Découverte, Paris, 1999, pp. 507–508. Tarot notices that my *Le fétichisme. Histoire d'un concept*, PUF, Paris, 1992 does not mention another consideration, besides that of Mauss's "misunderstanding," which is quite pithy in itself. Namely that this "misunderstanding" constituted a "necessary mistake" for social sciences. Apart from the fact that Mauss does not explain his claim, as Tarot rightly notes—whatever the meaning he attributed to it may have been—the risk posed by this ambiguous concept of "inevitability" is that it can become a historical justification. In any case, I would distinguish between what is irreversible and what is inevitable.
12. W. Pietz, "The Problem of the Fetish," *Res*, no. 9, 1985, pp. 5–17; no. 13, 1987, pp. 23–45; no. 16, 1988, pp. 105–123. See Ch. Antenhofer (ed.), *Fetisch als euristiche Kategorie*, Transcript Verlag, Bielefeld, 2011 for a recent debate on the notion of fetish.
13. W. Pietz, *Le fétiche. Généalogie d'un problème*, Kargo & L'Éclat, Paris, 2005.
14. B. Latour, *Petite réflexion sur le culte moderne des dieux faitiches*, Synthékabo, Paris, 1996, p. 23 ff.
15. Latour considers the interpretation made both by me and by Pietz to be still insidet hisi llusion.

One The Theoretical and Historical Assumptions Underpinning the Concept of Fetishism

1. See D. Vieira, *Grande Diccionario Portuguez ou Thesouro da Lingua Portugueza*, edited by Ernesto Chardron and Bartholomeu H. De Moraes, vol. III, Porto, 1873, p. 623. The word "feitiço" is to be found in J. Barros's 1552 Década I (liv. 3, Chapter 10; liv. 8, Chapter 4, liv. 10, Chapter 1).
2. Ibid. See also V. Valeri, *Feticcio*, Enciclopedia, vol. VI, Einaudi, Torino 1979, p.1 00.
3. Charles de Brosses, *Du Culte des Dieux fétiches ou Parallèle de l'ancienne Religion de l'Egypte avec la Religion actuelle de la Nigritie*, Genève, 1760. van der Leeuw argues that the term "fetishism" had already been used by G. Carolinus in his 1661 *Het hedendaagsche Heidendom of Beschrijving van der Godtienst der Heidenen* (a work cited by Balthazar Bekker in *The World Bewitch'd* where, as we shall see, a comparison is made between practices associated with the "Fetisso" and practices bound to other ancient and modern religions). But van der Leeuw also adds: "It is certain that de Brosses used the word for the first time as a scientific and phenomenological expression. He used fetishism as a general term for the religion of the Negroes. He was also the first to write on the psychological origin of fetishism," G. van der Leeuw, *Phänomenologie der Religion*, Mohr Siebeck, Tübingen, 1956 (2nd edition), *Religion in Essence and Manifestation*, translated by J. E. Turner, Peter Smith, Gloucester (MA), 1967 [1963], 2 vols. with appendices to the Torchbook edition incorporating the additions of the second German edition by Hans H. Penner. As far as the origin of the word "feitiço" is

concerned, de Brosses—albeit using it in the sense of "artificial," "fictitious" (see Valeri, op. cit., p. 100)—attributes it to the Latin root "fatum," "fanum," "fari" (Brosses, op. cit., p. 18). Meiners and Böttiger add to de Brosses's explanation the one given by Th. Winterbotton in his *Account of the Native Africans in the Neighborhood of Sierra Leone*, printed by C. Whittingham, London, 1803, p. 99. According to Winterbotton the word "feitiço" derives from "feticeira" (sorceress, witch) or "faticaria" (witchcraft, magical power). See Ch. Meiners, *Allgemeine kritische Geschichte der Religionen*, Hannover, 1806–1807, I Bd., pp. 142–143; C. A. Böttiger, *Ideen zur Kunst-Mythologie*, Dresden und Leipzig, 1826–1836, I Bd., p. 6. In 1888 Alfred Binet also accepted the thesis of the Latin root "fatum" (A. Binet, *Le fétichisme dans l'amour*, in *Étudesd eP sychologiee xpérimentale*, Paris, 1888, p. 2).

4. One of the fundamental essays on the history of the word "civilization" is L. Febvre's essay "Civilisation: évolution d'un mot et d'un group d'idées" ("Civilisation, le mot, l'idée"), *I Semaine Internationale de Synthèse*, vol. 2, Octave Doin, Paris, 1930, now in *Pour une histoire à part entière*, Service d'édition et de vente des publications de l'Éducation nationale. Abbeville, impr. F. Paillart, Paris, 1962. See also E. Benveniste, *Civilisation. Contribution à l'histoire du mot,* in *Hommage a Lucien Febvre*, Paris, 1954, now in *Problèmes de Linguistique générale*, Gallimard, Paris, 1971. On the complex relationship between "culture" and "civilization," see Pietro Rossi, "'Cultura' e civiltà come modelli descrittivi," now in *Cultura e antropologia*, Einaudi, Turin, 1983.

5. B. Bekker, *Le Monde Enchanté ou examen des communs sentiments touchant les Esprits, leur nature, leur pouvour, leur administration, et leurs opération*, vol. 4, Librarie fur le Vygendam, Amsterdam, 1694 (the original Dutch edition, entitled *Die Betoverde Weereld*, Andries van Damme, Leuwarden, 1691, was translated into German in 1693 in Amsterdam and into English (only the first volume) in 1695 in London. See F. Manuel, *The Eighteenth Century Confronts the Gods*, Harvard University Press, Cambridge, MA, 1959, p. 313). The edition I am referring to is the one that circulated in de Brosses's cultural context, and was prepared under the author's supervision.

On Bekker's comparative methodology, see F. Manuel, op. cit., in particular, pp. 28–29. See also P. Hazard, *The Crisis of the European Mind, 1680–1715*, New York Review Books Classics, New York, 2013.

6. B. Bekker, *The World Bewitch'd or, An Examination of the Common Opinions Concerning Spirits: Their Nature, Power, Administration, and Operations. As, Also, The Effects Men Are Able to Produce by their Communication*, translated from a French Copy, approved of and subscribed by the Author's own Hand, printed for R. Baldwin, 1695, vol., I. p. 28, Cornell University Library, The Division of Rare and Manuscript Collections, Digital Witchcraft Collection.

7. Ibid.,p .2 9.
8. Ibid.
9. Thomas Hobbes, *Leviathan* (1651), *English Works*, printed for Andrew Crooke at the Green Deagon in St. Paul's Churchyard, London, 1831 (reprint Aalen 1962), vol. III; B. Spinoza, *Tractatus theologico-politicus* (1670), *Opera*, Carl Winter, Heidelberg s.d. (1924), vol. III; *Ethica ordine geometrico demonstrata*

(1677). In addition to the topic of "fear" examined in Chapter XII of the *Leviathan*, and the idea expressed in *Propositio LI* of Spinoza's *Ethics*, according to which superstition originates in the relationship between fear and hope, as well as the discussion on miracles contained in *The Leviathan*, Chapter XXXVII, and *Tractatus*, Chapter VI, it is worth quoting at length the following reflections by Hobbes and Spinoza. Reflecting on the relationship between *sight, imagination, memory, and dream*, Hobbes says: "This nature of sight having never been discovered by the ancient pretenders to natural knowledge, much less by those that consider not things so remote (as that knowledge is) from their present use, it was hard for men to conceive of those images in the fancy and in the sense otherwise than of things really without us: which some, because they vanish away, they know not whither nor how, will have to be absolutely incorporeal, that is to say, immaterial, or forms without matter (colour and figure, without any coloured or figured body), and that they can put on airy bodies, as a garment, to make them visible when they will to our bodily eyes; and others say, are bodies and living creatures, but made of air, or other more subtle and ethereal matter, which is, then, when they will be seen, condensed. But both of them agree on one general appellation of them, demons," *Leviathan*, printed for Andrew Crooke, 1651, Chapter XLV, "Of Demonology and Other Relics of the Religion of the Gentiles," p. 399. The author asserts, on the one hand, that demons have no active involvement in the historical acting of people, while, on the other hand, considering them to be exteriorizations of the human brain. This is a central topic in what is to become the concept of "fetishism."

Reflecting on the introduction of ceremonial laws in Judaism and Christianity, Spinoza affirms: "This, then, was the object of the ceremonial law, that men should do nothing of their own free will, but should always act under external authority, and should continually confess by their actions and thoughts that they were not their own masters, but were entirely under the control of others" (*The Chief Works of Benedict de Spinoza*, translated from the Latin with an Introduction by R. H. M. Elwes, *Tractatus Theologico-Politicus*, Chapter V, vol. I, London, George Bell and Sons, 1891, p. 76). The complexity of the historical and conceptual processes is proven by the fact that the Spinozian analysis of the *external* forms of religion as a means for exercising control over people becomes—when transposed into the world of "savages"—a means for justifying colonization. The discovery of the "fetishes" as a central aspect of a religion based on exterior practices became the proof of their primitiveness. This idea was to be endorsed, in particular, by the Dutchman Bosman.

10. A. van Dale, *De Oraculis Veterum Ethnicorum Dissertationes Duae*, Apud Henricum, Amsterdam, 1700 (2nd edition). The first edition (1683) was favorably reviewed by Pierre Bayle (*Nouvelles de la République des Letters*, mars 1684, Amsterdam, 1715, vol. I, pp. 1–18).

11. B. de Fontenelle, *Histoire des Oracles* (1686), in *Oeuvres*, Académies Françaises des Sciences, vol. II, Paris, 1767, p. 201. Some years after the publication of the second edition of van Dale's *De Oraculis*, and thus after the publication of Fontenelle's work, Jean Leclerc examined both the Dutchman's theory of oracles and his other work entitled *Dissertationes de Origine et Progressu*

Idolatriae, Apud Henricum, Amsterdam, 1696. Leclerc disagreed with van Dale's (and Fontenelle's) radical assumption that oracles must be *tout court* the result of priests' mendacity. Falsehood, argued Leclerc, is merged with truth, at least in the sense that there must have been a truthful origin in what has subsequently become an object of mendacity: "It is also possible to affirm that Mendacity would never have found a place among men if Truth had not, against its nature, frequently paved the way for it" (J. Leclerc, *Bibliothéque choisie, pour servir de suite à la Bibliothèque universelle*, Henri Schelte, Amsterdam, 1704, vol. III, p. 115; my translation). In 1707 Baltus confuted van Dale in a piece of writing directed at Fontenelle (J. F. Baltus, *Résponse à l'Histoire des oracles...dans laquelle on réfute le systeme de M. Van D.*, Jean Regnauld Doulssecker, Paris, 1707). In 1685, in the third edition of his *Tractatus philologico-theologicus*, Leipzig, 1657, Moebius had already added a *Cum vindiciis adversus A. van Dale*. Bernard (J. Bernard, *Nouvelles de la République des Lettres*, juin, 1707, David Mortier, Amsterdam, 1716) and Leclerc (J. Leclerc, *Bibliothèque choisie*, cit., vol. XVII, pp. 309–312) replied to Baltus in their funeral oration after van Dale's death. On the relationship between van Dale and Fontenelle, see Manuel, op. cit., pp. 48–52 and Hazard, op. cit., vol. I, p. 203.
12. Ivi,p .2 05.
13. A. van Dale, *Lettre, Nouvelles de la République des Lettres*, mai, 1687, article I, Amsterdam, 1687, pp. 459–487.
14. Following the theorization of Hobbes and Spinoza, Bekker excludes "diabolic mimesis" from the field of inquiry and does not consider it to be at the origin of idolatry. In actual fact, this topic is of crucial importance in the influential anthropological treatise by the Jesuit José de Acosta, *Historia Natural y Moral de las Indias*, Sevilla, 1590, Book V, p. 303 (anastatic copy, Valencia, 1977) and also in Ahanasius Kircher's complex reflections (see D. Pastine, *La nascita dell'idolatria*, la Nuova Italia, Florence, 1979, pp. 136–158). Nevertheless, and even before the theorization developed by Hobbes, as may be seen for instance in the case of the Neapolitan G. B. Della Porta, "the demonic aspects occupy a marginal place and are similar to those emerging in other contemporaries, such as Campanella" (N. Badaloni, "I fratelli Della Porta e la cultura magica e astrologica a Napoli nel '500," in *Studi Storici*, no. 4, 1959–1960, p. 31).
15. B. Bekker, op. cit., Book I, Chapter X, p. 115.
16. Ivi,p .1 02.O nC arolinus,s eef ootnote3 .
17. Ivi,p .1 04.
18. W. Bosman, *Voyage de Guinée contenant une Descrition nouvelle et trés exacte de cette Côte où l'on trouve et où l'on trafique l'or, les dents d'Elephant, et les Esclaves*, Marchand Libraire, Utrecht, 1705. This translation into French is quoted by both Bayle and de Brosses. The Dutch edition is entitled W. Bosman, *Nauwkeurige beschryving van de Guinese Good-, Tand- en Slave-Kust*, Isaak Stockman, Utrecht, 1704. The quotations are taken from the English edition: William Bosman, *A New and Accurate Description of the Coast of Guinea. Divided Into The Gold, The Slave, and the Ivory Coasts*, a new edition with an introduction by John Ralph Willis and notes by J. D. Fage and R. E. Bradbury, Frank Cass, 1967.

19. Ivi, pp. 147–165. In Letter VI he had already mentioned fetishes made of gold or black earth and gold, or silver, copper, and gold. The European observer's interest in these fetishes is clearly expressed in the following passage: "There are also Fetiche's cast of unalloyed Mountain Gold; which very seldom come to our Hands, because they keep them to adorn themselves: So that if ever we meet with them, those who part with them are obliged to it by necessity, or they are filled with the mentioned black heavy Earth; with which the unskillful are liable to be basely cheated, receiving instead of Gold frequently half the weight in this sort of Earth," William Bosman, op. cit., p. 74.
20. Ivi,p .1 46.
21. Ivi,p .1 46.
22. Ivi,p .1 48.
23. Ivi,p .1 56.
24. Ivi,p p.1 55–156.
25. J. Lubbock, *The Origin of Civilization and the Primitive Condition of Man*, Longmans, London, 1870. Marx would quote Lubbock's observations in his ethnological notebooks. See *The Ethnological Notebooks* of Karl Marx, by L. Krader, Van Gorcum, Assen, 1974, pp. 342–343. As far as the absence of idols is concerned, the source is Lafitau.
26. W. Wundt, *Völkerpsychologie. Eine Untersuchung der Entwicklungsgesetze von Sprache, Mythus und Sitte*, Verlag von Wilhelm Engelmann Leipzich, 1904; *Elements of Folk Psychology: Outlines of a Psychological History of the Development of Mankind*, translated by Edward Leroy Schaub, George Allen & Unwin, London, 1916.
27. J. F. McLennan, *The Worship of Animals and Plants* (1869), in *Studies in Ancient History: The Second Series*, Macmillan, London, 1896.
28. The problematic aspects inherent in the definition of the terms fetish and fetishism are examined in V. Valeri, *Feticcio*, pp. 111–113; J. Pouillon, "Fétiches sans Fétichisme," in *Objects du fétichisme, Nouvelle Revue de Psychanalyse*, no. 2, 1970, pp. 135–147; A. Adler, *L'ethnologue et les Fétiches*, ivi, pp. 149–158; B. Bonafré, *Object magique, sorcellerie et fétichisme?*, ivi, pp.1 59–192.
29. P. Bayle, *Résponses aux questions d'un provincial* (1704–1706), in *Oeuvres diverses*, La Haye 1737, t. III, I Partie, pp. 970–971 (my translation).
30. Ivi,p .9 71.
31. I. Kant, *Die Religion innerhalb der Grenzen der blossen Vernunft*, in *Werke*, Berlin, 1907, VIB d., pp. 177–180. *Religion within the Boundaries of Mere Reason and Other Writings*, translated and edited by Allen Wood, Cambridge University Press, Cambridge, 1998.
32. J. F. Lafitau, *Moeurs des sauvages américains comparées aux moeurs des premiers temps*, Paris, 1724, vol. 1, p. 264, footnote b. The author borrows the notion of the fetish from G. Loyer, *Relation du Royaume d'Issini, Côte d'Or, païs de Guinée, en Afrique*, Charles Estienne Hochereau, Paris, 1714, in particular the description of the purification rite of Guinean women and those of the Gold Coast, p. 168. Like Bosman, Lafitau underlines the similarities between African fetishes and those of the natives of Formosa.
33. J. F. Lafitau, *Customs of the American Indians Compared with the Customs of Primitive Times*, edited by W. N. Fenton and E. L. Moore, 2 volumes, Toronto 1974, vol. I, p. 243.

34. J.F.L afitau, *Moeurs*, volume I, p. 383.
35. M. Mauss, *L'art et le mythe d'àprès M. Wundt* (1908), in *Oeuvres*, vol. II, Éditions de Minuit, Paris, 1969, p. 217.
36. J. B. Labat, *Voyage du Chevalier des Marchais en Guinée, Isles voisines et Cayenne*, 4 volumes, Aux dépens de la Compagnie, Amsterdam, 1731 (first edition in 1730, Sangrain, Paris, volume I, p. 296; my translation). In the *Préface* Father Labat affirms that he is quoting from des Marchais's travelogue, who at the time was captaining the expedition on his return trip from Guinea and Cayenne. Involved in the slave trade, des Marchais was well acquainted with indigenous languages (*Préface*, vol. I, p. IV). The peoples he established a relationship with accepted and respected him. This was, according to Labat, crucial in order to obtain substantial commercial advantages. This is how Labat describes the capable and shrewd captain's relationship with the natives: "As is expected of a Captain on these occasions, he was always vigilant and prudent. He could never be taken by surprise and kept his eyes wide open, although pretending to fully trust the people he met. No matter how essential these two features might seem in a captain, they are very difficult to find in the same subject and even more so if the subject is French. The indigenous peoples are naturally sly and cunning, they dissimulate and are greedy, cruel and not restrained at all by honour or religion" (pp. V–VI; my translation). The apologia of the European's dissimulation is based on the assumption that the tendency to dissimulate is natural for indigenous people: the real and principal exchange of communication is the trade of human beings and things. Less pathetically than Labat (as P. Rossi argues in his *I segni del tempo*, Feltrinelli, Milan, 1979, p. 263), Mandeville considers dissimulation to be an inborn quality of language. Reflecting on how much there is of Labat and how much of Captain des Marchais in the account, Prévost observes: "Whatever judgment anyone may form on the accuracy and trustworthiness of his observations, it does not seem that the mistrust should be extended to the works he is editing; or, at least, only the observations he could not help himself from including are of a nature to arouse our doubts. But this mistrust must dissolve every time it becomes possible to glimpse someone else's work in his comments. This is much more true for the comments in which his firsthand evidence coincides with that of other travellers," A. F. Prévost, *Histoire générale des voyages, ou nouvelle collection de toutes les relations de voyages*, vol. IV, Book VIII, La Haye 1747, pp. 500–501, footnote (a) (my translation).
37. *Voyage du Chevalier des Marchais en Guinée, Isles voisines et Cayenne*, 4 volumes, Amsterdam, 1731 (first edition in 1730, Paris, volume I, p. 297 (my translation).
38. Ibid.
39. Ivi,p p.2 97–298.
40. Ivi,p .3 05.
41. Voltaire, *Essai sur les moeurs et l'esprit des nations*, edited by R. Pomeau, Garnier frères, Paris, 1963, vol. I, p. 7; *An Essay on Universal History, the Manners, and Spirit of Nations*, translated into English by Mr. Nugent.
42. On polygenism and monogenism, see G. Gliozzi, *Adamo e il Nuovo Mondo*, La nuova Italia, Florence, 1977. On Voltaire, see pp. 602–603; P. Rossi, *I segni del tempo*, cit., p. 150 ff. D. Pastine, *Le origini del poligenismo e Isaac Lapeyrére*, Miscellanea Seicento, I, Le Monnier, Florence, 1971.

43. On the concept of secularization, see G. Marramao, *Potere e secolarizzazione. Le categorie del tempo*, Editori Riuniti, Rome, 1983.
44. On Lafitau see G. Chinard, *L'Amérique et le rêve exotique dans la littérature française au XVII et au XVIII siècle*, Hachette, Paris, 1913; A. van Gennep, *Religions, Moeurs et Légendes. Essais dethnographie et de linguistique*, V série, Mercure de France, Paris, 1914, pp. 111–113; see also "*Pro Ethnographie*," in *Réligions, Moeurs et Légendes*, III série, Société du Mercure de France, Paris, 1911; A. Métraux, "*Précurseurs de l'ethnologie en France du XVI au XVIII siècle*," in *Cahiers d'histoire mondiale*, vol. VII (1963), no. 3, pp. 721–738; G. Hervé, "Débuts de l'Ethnographie au XVIII siècle (1701–1765) ," in *Revue de l'Ecole d'anthropologie*, November 1909, pp. 360–363; M. Duchet, *Anthropologie et histoire au siècle des lumières*, Flammarion, Paris, 1971 and "Discours ethnologique et Discours historique: le texte de Lafitau," in *Studies on Voltaire and XVIIIth Century*, vol. VLII (1976), pp. 607–623; E. Lemay, "Histoire de l'Antiquité et Découverte du Nouveau Monde chez le auteurs du XVIII siècle," in *Studies on Voltaire*, vol. CLI-CLV, 1976, pp. 1313–1328; M. T. Hodgen, *Early Anthropology in the Sixteenth and Seventeenth Century*, University of Pennsylvania Press, Philadelphia, 1964, pp. 348–349; P. Vidal Naquet, *Le Cru, l'Enfant grec et le Cuit*, in *Faire de l'histoire*, vol. II, Gallimard, Paris, 1974, pp. 137–168; S. Landucci, *I filosofi e i selvaggi (1580–1780)*, Laterza, Bari, 1972, pp. 247–262; W. N. Fenton—E. L. Moore's "Introduction" to *Customs of the American Indians*, op. cit., vol. I; Detienne, *L'invention de la mythologie*, Gallimard, Paris, 1981; S. Moravia, *La scienza dell'uomo nel Settecento*, Laterza, Bari, 1978, pp. 146–148. See also F. Meinecke, *Die Entstehung des Historismus*.
45. On the relationship between Lafitau and de Brosses, see A. Radcliffe-Brown, *Method in Social Anthropology*, University of Chicago Press, Chicago, 1958 and J. P. Vernant, *Mythe et société en Grèce ancienne*, Maspero, Paris, 1974, in addition to some of the texts cited above such as van Gennep, 1914, op. cit., pp. 161–178, Hervé, op. cit., pp. 394–401, Landucci, op. cit., pp. 255–261 (who underlines the differences between them), Fenton-Moore, op. cit., pp. CI–CII, Moravia, op. cit., pp. 149–150.
46. Voltaire, *Essai sur le moeurs*, op. cit., vol. I, pp. 29–30.
47. C. De Pauw, *Recherches philosophiques sur les Américains*, J.M. Place, Londres, 1774, .t. II, pp. 54–55.
48. A. Y. Goguet, *De l'Origine des Lois, des Arts et des Sciences; et de leurs progrès chez les anciens Peuples*, 3 volumes, L. Hausmann, Paris, 1758. On the relationship between Goguet and Lafitau, see S. Landucci, op. cit., p. 255; Fenton-Moore, op. cit., pp. C–CI; A. Van Gennep, *Religions...*, V série, 1914, cit., pp. 154–160; G. Hervé, op. cit., pp. 363–366; J. C. Herder, *Ideen zur Philosophie der Geschichte der Menschheit* (1784–1791); J. Ferguson, *An Essay on the History of Civil Society* (1767), H. Home (Lord Kames), *Sketches of the History of Man* (1774), Basil, 1796; A. Smith, *Lectures on Jurisprudence* (Report 1762–1763), by R. L. Meek, D. D. Raphael, P. G. Stein, Oxford 1978, vol. V, *The Glasgow Edition of the Works and Correspondence of Adam Smith*; J. Millar, *The Origin of the Distinction of Ranks* (1771), in W. C. Lehmann, *John Millar of Glasgow*, Cambridge University Press, Cambridge, 1960 (reprint of the third 1779 edition, pp. 175–322); W. Robertson, *History*

of America (1777), in *Works*, vol. VI, Cadel, London, 1827 (Robertson notes that *Lafitau's* section on religion "extends to 347 tedious pages in quarto," p. 470). On Lafitau's influence see Fenton-Moore's, "Introduction," cit., pp. LXXXIII ff.; E. Lemay, "Introduction," Lafitau, *Moeurs des sauvages américains* (textes choisis), 2 volumes, Saugrain et Charles-Estienne Hochereau, Paris, 1983, pp. 17 ff. This selection of writings excludes the chapter on religion and the "Design and Plan of the Work," although it is not clear why. On the relationship between Lafitau and the Scotsmen, see R. L. Meek, *Social science and the ignoble savage*, Cambridge University Press, Cambridge, 1976.

49. Cf. Fenton-Moore, op. cit., p. CVII; F. Remotti, "Lewis H. Morgan e lo studio della società antica," *Sociologia del diritto*, X/1982/3, pp. 92–93.
50. Fenton-Moore,o p.c it.,p p.C X–CXI.
51. A.V anG ennep, *Pro Ethnographie*, cit., p. 12.
52. G.C hinard,o p.c it.,p .3 19f f.
53. F.M einecke,o p.c it.,p .5 3.
54. As well as the aforementioned writings of Vernant, Detienne, and Vidal-Naquet, see A. Momigliano, "The Place of Herodotus in the History of Historiography," in *Secondo contributo alla storia degli studi classici*, Edizioni di storia e letteratura, Rome, 1960, p. 43.
55. P. Vidal-Naquet, op. cit., p. 139. Michèle Duchet criticizes Vidal-Naquet for restricting the concept of "premiers temps" to the past of the Greeks, Egyptians, and Phoenicians. The "premiers temps" of Lafitau's title indicate all that precedes "historical time." "The dissonance in the title is only apparent: speaking about American savages or primitive times does not only mean comparing two objects that have a homologous structure. It means the implication in its entirety, through this homology, of the functioning of historical discourse" (M. Duchet, *Discourse ethnologique*, cit., p. 615, my translation).
56. P. Bayle, *Continuations de Pensées diverses, in Oeuvres diverses*, cit., III, p.3 11.
57. M.D uchet, *Discours ethnologique*, cit., p. 607.
58. Father Joseph François Lafitau, *Customs of the American Indians Compared with the Customs of Primitive Times*, edited and translated by William N. Fenton and Elizabeth L. Moore, in two volumes, The Champlain Society, Toronto, 1974, p. 27.
59. A.M omigliano,o p.c it.
60. Thucydides, I, 6. See P. Vidal-Naquet, op. cit., p. 138.
61. Lafitau,M oeurs,o p.c it.,v ol.I ,p .4 .
62. Ivi,p .4 8.
63. Ivi,v ol.I ,p p.1 04–105.
64. See C. B. Macpherson, *The Political Theory of Possessive Individualism: Hobbes to Locke*, Oxford University Press, Oxford, 1962.
65. It is in this sense that Duchet's interpretation of the "Discours historique" in Lafitau should be seen (see footnote 55). Organized in a system, the Jesuit's comparative method implies the assimilation of what precedes historical times into a general historical discourse.
66. Lafitau, op. cit., vol. I, pp. 105–106.

67. Ivi,v ol.I ,p .1 07.
68. B. Malinowski, "The Primitive Economics of the Trobriand Islanders," *The Economic Journal*, March 1921, pp. 1–16; and *Argonauts of the Western Pacific*, George Routledge, London, 1922.
69. K. Polanyi, *The Livelihood of Man*, Academic Press, New York, 1977, by H. W.P earson.
70. See M. Duchet, *Anthropologie et histoire*, cit. (Italian translation vol. I, p. XIX). On the use of categories such as "primitive" and "savage" in anthropology and, more generally, in the cultural sphere, see M. Godelier, "Primitive," in *Enciclopedia*, vol. X, Einaudi, Turin, 1981 and I. Sachs, "Selvaggio, barbaro, civilizzato," in *Enciclopedia*, vol. XII, Einaudi, Turin, 1981. On the history of the complex problem of the New World in Western culture, see G. Gliozzi, *Adamo e il nuovo mondo*, cit., and also *La scoperta dei selvaggi*, Principato, Milan, 1971; A. Gerbi, *La disputa del Nuovo Mondo. Storia di una polemica 1750–1900*, Ricciardi, Milano-Napoli, 1983; M. T. Hodgen, op. cit.; S. Landucci, op. cit., G. Atkinson, *Les relations de voyages du XVIIe siècle et l'évolution des idées*, Paris, 1924; G. Gliozzi, "Il 'Nuovo Mondo' nella cultura del Seicento," in multiple authors, *L'Europa cristiana nel rapporto con le altre culture nel secolo XVII*, La Nuova Italia, Florence, 1978. On the notion of the savage as "other," see G. Cocchiara, *Il mito del buon selvaggio*, D'Anna, Messina-Florence, 1948; E. Garin, "Alla scoperta del 'diverso': i selvaggi americani e saggi cinesi," in *Rinascite e rivoluzioni. Movimenti culturali dal XIV al XVIII secolo*, Laterza, Bari, 1976; Multiple authors, "Il buon selvaggio nella cultura francese ed europea del settecento," in *Studi di letteratura francese*, VII, 1981. On the "non-contemporaneity of the contemporaries" in the XVIII century, see R. Koselleck, "Il secolo XVIII come inizio dell'età moderna," in *Studi Settecenteschi*, no. 3–4, 1982–1983, pp. 9–23.
71. Lafitau, *Moeurs*, cit., "Americans. The Origin of the Peoples of America," vol. I, pp. 27–102.
72. P. D. Huet, *Demonstratio Evangelica ad serenissimum Delphini*, Parisiis, 1679.
73. Lafitau, *Moeurs*, cit., vol. I, p. 13.
74. Ivi,p p.1 4–15.
75. Ivi,p .1 6.
76. Ivi,p .1 7.
77. B.M alinowski, *The Primitive Economics*, cit., and *Argonauts*,c it.
78. M. Mauss, "Essay sur le don," in *Sociologie et Anthropologie*, Presses Universitaires de France, Paris, 1950; *The Gift*, English edition first published in 1954 by Cohen & West.
79. E. Durkheim, *Leçons de sociologie*, Presses Universitaires de France, Paris, 1950.
80. Lafitau, *Moeurs*, cit., p. 123.
81. W. Warburton, *The Divine Legation of Moses Demonstrated*, vol. II, London, 1741, p. 81, footnote (a). The reference is to Diodorus Siculus, I, 8 and to Vitruvius, II, 1. On Warburton, see Paolo Rossi, *I segni del tempo*, cit., pp. 270–281; M. V. David, *Le debat sur les écritures et l'hiéroglyphe aux XVII et XVIII siècles*, Bibliothèque générale de l'École pratique des Hautes Études,

Paris, 1965, pp. 95–103; M. G. Lombardo, "La filosofia della religione di William Warburton," in *Studi Settecenteschi* , cit., pp. 119–127.
82. W. Warburton, *Essai sur les hiéroglyphes des Egyptiens*, translated by L. de Malpeines, Paris, 1744.
83. E. Bonnot de Condillac, *Essai sur l'origine des connaissances humaines*, 1746. The Italian translation may be found in *Opere*, Utet, Turin, 1976, pp. 207–208, footnote (a). See also C. A. Viano's "Introduction," p. 37.
84. E. Bonnot de Condillac, *Traité des systèmes* (1749). *Philosophical Writings of Etienne Bonnot, Abbé de Condillac*, translated by Franklin Philip, 2 volumes, Lawrence Erlbaum, Hillsdale, NJ, 1982–1987. Volume I (1982) contains *A Treatise on Systems, A Treatise on Sensations*, and *Logic, or the First Developments of the Art of Thinking.*
85. The *Treatise on Systems* was of crucial importance to Enlightenment thought. On this topic see E. Garin's, "Introduction" to the Italian edition, cit.; E. McNiven Hine, *A Critical Study of Condillac's Traité des systems*, The Hague–Boston–London, 1979. As Garin notes (p. ix, footnote 3), the entries on "Système" and "Divination" in the *Encyclopédie* draw heavily on Condillac's work. D'Alembert's *Discours préliminaire* is also influenced by the *Traité des systèmes* (on "Discours" [1751] see *Encyclopédie ou Dictionnaire raisonné des Sciences, des Arts et des Mètiers*, Impr. des Editeurs, Livourne, 1770, vol. I. D'Alembert–Diderot, *La filosofia dell'Encyclopédie*, edited by P. Casini, Laterza, Bari, 1966; "Divination," ivi, 1772, vol. IV, pp. 978–981; "Système," ivi, 1775, vol. V, pp. 745–749. On Condillac and on the concept of system, see W. Tega, *Arbor Scientiarum*, il Mulino, Bologna, 1984, Chapters I and II, pp. 13–111.
86. Condillac, *A Treatise on Systems,* cit., p. 3.
87. Ivi,p .3 .
88. Ivi,p .1 23.
89. Ivi,p .1 33.
90. Ibid.
91. Lucretius, V, 924–1240. See also *Primitivism and Related Ideas in Antiquity*, by A. O. Lovejoy and G. Boas, Baltimore, 1955.
92. Lucretius,V ,1 029.
93. Lucretius,V ,1 218–1221.
94. ThomasH obbes, *Leviathan*,p .6 7.
95. G. B. Vico, *Principii di Scienza Nuova* (1744), edited by Fausto Nicolini, Bari, Laterza, 1928; *Scienza nuova seconda*, 1730/1744; *The New Science of Giambattista Vico*, revised translation of the third edition by Thomas Goddard Bergin and Max Harold Fisch, Cornell University Press, Ithaca, 1948; Cornell Paperbacks, 1976. Vico quotes a passage from Statius's *Thebaid*, III, 661: "Primos in orbe deos fecit timor" [Fear first created gods in the world], the same passage cited by Hobbes, op. cit., p. 67. In examining the concept of fear, Vico states that "false religions were not born of imposture but of credulity" (ibid.). In a footnote Nicolini refers to Vico's polemics against van Dale and Fontenelle. Nevertheless, it is worth pointing out that in his *History of the Oracles* Fontenelle sees imposture as a consequence of the easy credulity of primitive minds, of the link between ignorance and

a sense of wonder, which produce "fables," myths, stories, and false beliefs (*Histoire des Oracles*, cit., p. 226). On the topic of fear, see A. Minerbi Belgrado, *Materialismo e origine della religione nel '700*, Sansoni, Florence, 1977, pp. 1–29.

96. Condillac, *A Treatise on Systems*, cit., p. 23.
97. On Fontenelle's comparative method and on the theory of the "fables," see the section "Lafitau and Fontenelle: Two Hypotheses for Comparison."
98. Lafitau, *Moeurs*, cit., vol. I, pp. 355–356. But as far as comparison is concerned, he rejects the thesis of "diabolic mimesis," see ivi, vol. I, pp. 10, 124.
99. In the chapter on divination, Condillac cites Fontenelle's *Histoire des Oracles* (*A Treatise on Systems*, p p.3 0–31).
100. J. Le Rond D'Alembert, *Discourse préliminaire*, cit., Italian translation, see in particular, pp. 126–127.
101. On Fontenelle and Hume, see also P. Bayle, *Pensée écrites à un docteur de Sorbonne, à l'occasion de la comète qui paruit au mois de Décembre 1680*, in *Oeuvres diverses*, La Haye (Trévoux), 1737, 2nd edition, vol. III, paragraph 65 (Italian translation, pp. 120–121; on the issue concerning the several editions of the work, see the Editor's note, vol. I, pp. VII–XVI). On Bayle and his influence, see E. Cassirer, *La filosofia dell'illuminismo*, La Nuova Italia, Florence, 1973, p. 283. Spinoza and Toland associate fear with hope. On Spinoza, see footnote 8; J. Toland, *Letters to Serena* (1704), Italian translation by E. Lecaldano, Laterza, Bari, 1977, p. 79; *Adeisidaemon e Origines Judicae* (1709), Italian translation by A. Sabetti, Liguori, Naples, 1984. On Toland and Leclerc and the relationship between a "primitive mentality" and the origins of religion, see M. Iofrida, *La filosofia di J. Toland*, Angeli, Milan, 1983, p. 74; B. de Mandeville, *The Fable of the Bees: or, Private Vices, Public Benefits*, edited by F. B. Kaye, Oxford, 1966, vol. II, p. 207. See also M. E. Scribano, *Natura umana e società competitiva. Studio su Mandeville*, Feltrinelli, Milan, 1980, p. 21.
102. G. B. Vico, op. cit., pp. 84 ff., 138 ff. On the relationship between "lightning" and the primitive mentality in Vico, see N. Badaloni, *Vico*, Laterza, Bari, 1984, p. 77 ff. Another element that must be stressed, as far as the issue of a theory of the primitive mind is concerned, is the relationship between Fontenelle and Vico, who share the same view, in particular of the role played by "wonder" and "ignorance." Vico states, "Wonder is the daughter of ignorance; and the greater the object of wonder, the more the wonder grows" (184), p. 63. On the same topic, see the *Histoire des Oracles*, cit., p. 226 ff. In his analysis of *De l'Origine des Fables*, S. Moravia, op. cit., pp. 146–147, has drawn attention to the relationship between Fontenelle and Vico in connection with the link between the theory of the myths and the theory of a primitive mind. See also Manuel, op. cit.
103. Condillac, *A Treatise on Systems* cit., pp. 22–23.
104. B. de Fontenelle, *De l'Origine des Fables* (1724), edited by J. R. Carré, Paris, 1932, p. 40.
105. It is in this context of the autonomization of human history from revealed history (at least as far as the idea is concerned that it is possible to retrace this history without resorting to God and his truth) that the eighteenth-century

debate against diffusionism can be inserted. For an overview of the issue in relation to the New World, see G. Gliozzi, *Adamo e il Nuovo Mondo*, cit.; A. Gerbi, op. cit. A theory of primitive mentality in which the uniformity of peoples is explained in relation to their degree of civilization tends to break the link between revealed history and diffusionism. Already present in Fontenelle (see Manuel, op. cit., p. 46), this idea would gain ground with Hume and de Brosses. Vico also states: "Uniform ideas originating among entire peoples unknown to each other must have a common ground of truth," op. cit., XIII, 144, p. 57. In his *Scienza Nuova Seconda* (1730) he referred to Lafitau's diffusionism as follows: "Someone recounted to me, since I have not personally seen the book, that Father Lafitau, a Jesuit missionary in America, has written a very erudite work entitled *Customs of the American Indians Compared with the Customs of Primitive Times*. In this work he argues that the Amerindians bear a striking resemblance to the ancients from Asia and undertakes to prove that they migrated to America from Asia. But this is very hard to prove. He might have taken the right direction, had my work preceded his," G. B. Vico, *La Scienza Nuova l'edizione del 1744 con le varianti dell'edizione del 1730 e di due redazioni inedite e corredata di note storiche*, a cura di F. Nicolini, vol. III, Laterza, Bari, 1916, p. 1031.

See also A. Momigliano, now in *Sui fondamenti della storia antica*, Einaudi, Turin, 1984, p. 235 and S. Landucci, op. cit., pp. 309–310. For an interpretation of the Vichian theory of primitive mind, see N. Badaloni, *Vico*, cit.

106. A. R. J. Turgot, *Plan de deux discours sur l'histoire universelle* (1751), *Oeuvres*, edited by G. Schelle, vol. I, Paris, 1913, pp. 303–304; in "On Universal History," *Turgot on Progress, Sociology and Economics*, translated and edited by Ronald L. Meek, Cambridge University Press, Cambridge, 1973, p. 89.
107. On Turgot's stages theory, see R. I. Meek, translation quoted, pp. 52–57. R. Finzi, "The Theory of Historical stages in Turgot and Quesnay," *The Economic Review*, vol. 33, no. 2, April 1982, pp. 109–118. On the relationship between Fontenelle and Turgot, see S. Bartolomei, "Analisi di una similitudine: 'età dell'uomo' ed 'età del genere umano' in Fontenelle e Turgot," *Studi Settecenteschi*, cit., pp. 84–106.
108. For some background to this issue, see Chapter III.
109. See *Autopoiesis*, edited by M. Zeleny, North Holland, New York, 1978; H. R. Maturana and F. J. Varela, *Autopoiesis and Cognition. The Realization of Living*, D. Reidel Publishing Company, Dordrecht, 1980.
110. See R .L .M eek,t ranslationq uoted,p p.4 3–48.
111. Bernard Fontenelle, *On the Origin of Fables*, in Burton Feldman and Robert D. Richardson, *The Rise of Modern Mythology*, Indiana University Press, Bloomington, Indianapolis, 1972, p. 16. For the important role played by Fontenelle in the comparative method, see Andrew Lang, *Myth, Ritual and Religion*, London, 1887, 2 vol. edition, especially Appendix A in the second volume, "Fontenelle's Forgotten Common Sense." On the relationship between myth and history in Fontenelle, see G. Cantelli, "Mito e storia in J. Leclerc, Tournemine e Fontenelle," in *Rivista critica di storia della filosofia*, no. 3 and 4, 1972, especially pp. 391–399 of no. 4. On the concepts of history and system, see A. Pizzorusso, "Fontenelle e l'idea del progresso," *Belfagor*, no. 2, 1962, pp. 150–180.

112. It is true that Fontenelle speaks about the Kaffirs, the Laplanders, and Iroquois as "already ancient" peoples, who have achieved some level of knowledge ("who have come to a degree of knowledge and manners that the earliest men did not have," p. 11). In this sense, they are ancient with respect to the men of primitive times.
113. Ivi,p .1 7.
114. Ivi,p .1 7.
115. Ivi,p .1 7.
116. Lafitau discovers matriarchy among the Iroquois and compares it with that of the Lycians described by Herodotus (I, ii, 173). As a proof of his diffusionist assumption, see op. cit., vol. I, pp. 69–70. Lafitau hypothesizes that this Iroquoian system derives from the Lycian people. As we can see, this subject fits into a *genetic* determination, thus anticipating McLennan's and Bachofen's theories: matriarchy passes from the Lycian people to the Iroquois. The biblical dispersal of humankind and the ensuing diffusionist idea impart a genetic, and thus temporal structure to the comparison of peoples with similar customs. Adam Ferguson would take a strong stand against the hypothesis of matriarchy. See A. Ferguson, *An Essay on the History of Civil Society* (1767), cit., p. 95.
117. SeeM .D uchet, *Discourse ethnologique*, cit., p. 607.
118. On the relationship between the fragment *Sur l'Histoire* and *De l'Origine des Fables*, see the already quoted critical edition of the latter, edited by J. Carré, where a comparison between the corresponding passages can be found. The fragment was published for the first time in 1758, after Fontenelle's death. On the dating of the fragment, see G. Cantelli, pp. 392–394, footnote 41.
119. SeeM .D etienne,o p.c it.,p .1 7.
120. *Histoire des Oracles*, cit., p. 226. *De l'Origine des Fables*, cit., pp. 12–14.
121. *Histoire des Oracles*, cit., p. 227.
122. *De l'Origine des Fables*, cit., p. 15.
123. G. Canguilhem, "Histoire des religions et histoire des sciences dans la théorie du fétichisme chez Auguste Comte," in *Études d'Histoire et de Philosophie des Sciences*, Vrin, Paris, 1968, pp. 88–89.
124. Ibid.
125. See *De l'Origine*, cit., p. 16.
126. *The Rise of Modern Mythology*, cit., p. 12.
127. *The Rise of Modern Mythology*, pp. 11, 13.
128. Ivi,p .1 2.
129. Ivi,p .1 3.
130. Ivi,p p.1 2–13.
131. Ivi,p p.1 2–13.
132. Ivi,p p.1 2–13.
133. Ibid.
134. Ibid.
135. On the relationship between the notion of antiquity and the conceptual organization of time between the seventeenth and eighteenth centuries, see P. Rossi, *Sterminate antichità. Studi vichiani*, Nistri Lischi, Pisa, 1969; see also *I segni del tempo*,c it.
136. Lafitau, *Moeurs*, cit., vol. I, p. 126.

137. Ivi,p .1 24f f.
138. David Hume, *Natural History of Religion* (1757), with an Introduction by John M. Robertson (London, A. and H. Bradlaugh Bonner, 1889), p. 20. See Manuel, op. cit., for Fontenelle's influence on Hume.
139. "Mankind are so much the same, in all Times and Places, that History informs us of nothing new or strange in this particular. Its chief Use is only to discover the constant and universal Principles of human Nature, by shewing Men in all Varieties of Circumstances and Situations, and furnishing us with Materials, from which we may form our Observations, and become acquainted with the regular Springs of human Action and Behaviour," David Hume, *Philosophical Essays Concerning Human Understanding* (1748), London, A. Millar, p. 134, Essay VIII.
140. D.H ume, *Natural History*, cit., p. 23.
141. A. Smith, "The Principles which Lead and Direct Philosophical Enquiries," in *The Early Writings of Adam Smith*, edited by J. R. Lindgren, New York, 1967 (published posthumously in 1795), p. 50. Philosophy does not arise from an expectation of advantage, but from wonder, once the stage of mere subsistence is outgrown and law has established order and security. The date of publication is uncertain. See P. Berlanda's "Introduction" to the Italian edition (*Saggi filosofici*, edited by P. Berlanda, Angeli, Milan, 1984, p. 68). On Adam Smith's essay, see also S. Moscovici, "A propos de quelques travaux d'Adam Smith sur l'histoire et la philosophie des sciences," in *Revue d'Histoire des Sciences et de leur applications*, no. 9, 1956, pp. 1–20 and H. F. Thomson, "Adam Smith's Philosophy of Science," *Quarterly Journal of Economics*, no. 79, 1965, pp. 212–233.
142. D.H ume, *Natural History*, cit., p. 25.
143. Ivi,p .2 6.
144. Hume disagrees with Fontenelle (and so does Brumoy in *Théâtre des Grecs*, Paris, 1730) on an important point. Referring to a passage of the *Histoire des Oracles*, where Fontenelle speaks about the impieties of Aristophanes, which were applauded by the very same Athenians who put to death the incredulous Socrates (*Histoire des Oracles*, cit., pp. 270–271), he observes: "These writers consider not that the ludicrous, familiar images, under which the Gods are represented by that comic poet, instead of appearing impious, were the genuine lights in which the ancients conceived their divinities" (*Natural History*, p. 30). Hume therefore underlines, for the observer, the problem concerning the relationship between the historical determinacy of a people and the way they imagine themselves by means of the way they imagine their deities.
145. D.H ume, *Natural History of Religion*,p .1 8.
146. Ibid.
147. Ibid.,p .1 8.
148. Ivi,p .1 8.
149. Ivi,p .1 9.
150. Ibid.,p .1 9.
151. Ivi,p .1 9.
152. Ivi,p .2 0.
153. Ibid.,p .2 0.

154. D. Stewart, "Account of the Life and Writings of Adam Smith," in A. Smith, *The Theory of Moral Sentiments*, London, 1853, vol. I, p. xxxv. On "conjectural history," see G. Gusdorf, *De l'histoire des sciences à l'histoire de la pensée*, Payot, Paris, 1966, p. 79.
155. *Natural History*, p.2 6.
156. See R. L. Meek, op. cit., pp. 52–57, 67–72.
157. A. Smith, op. cit. See in particular pp. 48–49.
158. A. Smith, Lectures on Jurisprudence, cit., p. 14. See also Meek, op. cit., p. 84 ff.
159. See the already quoted essay by Meek, op. cit., pp. 73–123.
160. According to Smith, the North American Indians are an "exception." Even though they have no conception of sheep farming, they have nevertheless some notions of agriculture. See A. Smith, *Lectures on Justice, Police, Revenue and Arms*, edited by E. Cannan, London, 1896 (reprint New York 1964), p. 108. In the 1762–1763 Lectures Smith had already observed: "The whole of the savage nations which subsist by flocks have no notion of cultivating the ground. The only instance that has the appearance of an objection to this rule is the state of the North American Indians. They, tho' they have no conception of flocks and herds, have nevertheless some notion of agriculture. Their women plant a few stalks of Indian corn at the back of their huts. But this can hardly be called agriculture. This corn does not make any considerable part of their food; it serves only as a seasoning or something to give a relish to their common food; the flesh of those animals they have caught in the chase.—Flocks and herds therefore are the first resource men would take themselves to when they found difficulty in subsisting by the chase." *Lectures on Jurisprudence* (Report of 1762–1763), edited by R. L. Meek, D. D. Raphael, and P. G. Stein, in *The Glasgow Edition of the Works and Correspondence of Adam Smith*, Oxford University Press, Oxford, 1978, p. 15. A noteworthy element is Adam Smith's attempt to minimize the exception of the North American Indians when compared to the "natural" course of the stages theorized by the conjectural method.

Two   Charles de Brosses's Theory of Fetishism

1. See footnotes 44 and 45 in the previous chapter.
2. F. E. Manuel, *The Prophets of Paris,* Harvard University Press, Cambridge, MA, 1962, p. 32.
3. Ch. de Brosses, *Lettres familières sur l'Italie*, edited by Y. Bezard, Paris, 1931, 2 volumes. On the history of the *Lettres*, see E. Kanceff, *Notes sur l'histoire des Lettres familières sur l'Italie,* in *Charles de Brosses 1777–1977*, Actes du Colloque de Dijon, 3–7 mai 1977, Textes recueillis par J.-C. Garreta, Genève, 1981, pp. 35–46; on the issues regarding the editions, see E. Cagiano, *Les éditions des "Lettres familières": analyse et perspectives,* ivi, pp. 15–34.
4. Ch. de Brosses, *Traité de la formation mécanique des langues et des principes physiques de l'étymologie,* Paris, 1765, 2 volumes. On Turgot and the entry *Etymologie,* see Manuel, *The Eighteenth Century,* cit., p. 184. On de Brosses's works, see the essays by S. Auroux (pp. 187–200), D. Droixhe (pp. 201–208),

C. Porset (pp. 209–218) contained in *Ch. de Brosses, 1777–1977*, cit.; see also G. Gusdorf, *Les principes de la pensée au siècle des Lumières*, Payot, Paris, 1971. On the connections between the *Traité* and de Brosses's theory of fetishism, see P. P. Gossiaux, *De Brosses: le fétichisme, de la démonologie à la linguistique*, in *Ch. de Brosses, 1777–1977*, cit., pp. 167–185.

5. Ch. de Brosses, *Histoire des navigations aux Terres Australes, contenant cé que l'on sçait des moeurs et des productions des Contrées découvertes jusqu'à ce jour; et où il est traité de l'utilité d'y faire de plus amples découvertes, et des moyens d'y former un établissement*, 2 tomes, Paris, 1756, t. II, p. 372 ff. (translated and edited by John Callander, *Terra Australis Cognita: or, Voyages to the Terra Australis, or Southern hemisphere, during the sixteenth, seventeenth, and eighteenth centuries*, Donaldson, Edinburgh, 1766–1768).
6. Ivi, t. II, p. 377 (my translation). Cf. M. David, "Histoire des religions et philosophie au XVIII siècle: le président de Brosses, David Hume et Diderot," *Revue Philosophique*, no. 2, April–June 1974, p. 156 and "Le président de Brosses historien des religions et philosophe, in Ch. de Brosses," 1777–1977, cit., p. 130.
7. Ibid. (my translation). On "Baetyles," see p. 110 ff.
8. Ibid.(myt ranslation).
9. On this, cf. the two articles by M. David, cit., p. 146 and p. 123 ff., respectively.
10. Ch. de Brosses, *Du Culte*, cit., p. 10 (partly translated by B. Feldman and R. Richardson, *The Rise of Modern Mythology 1680–1860*, Indiana University Press, Bloomington, 1972, p. 171).
11. Ivi, pp. 10–11 (trans. cit., p. 171). It has been pointed out that the inappropriate use of the word "fetish" singles out the African practices from similar ones in the rest of the world. In 1760 de Brosses had already done away with this divisive tendency, yet with him, as we shall see, the "misunderstanding" began! Cf. G. Parrinder, *African Traditional Religion*, Hutchinson, London, 1954.
12. Ch.d eB rosses, *Du Culte*, cit., p. 12 (trans. cit., p. 172).
13. Ivi,p p.1 4–15(trans.c it.,p .1 72).
14. Ivi,p .1 4(trans.c it.,p .1 72).
15. Ivi,p .1 5(trans.c it.,p .1 72).
16. Ibid.
17. Ivi,p p.1 5–16(trans.c it.,p .1 72).
18. Ivi,p .1 7(trans.c it.,p .1 73).
19. Lafitau, *Moeurs*, vol. I, pp. 39–42.
20. *Du Culte*, cit., p. 46 (my translation).
21. Ivi,p .6 7(myt ranslation).
22. Ivi,p .7 6(myt ranslation).
23. In this category de Brosses includes, like Hume (*Natural History*, cit., p. 310), atheist peoples (p. 199), who are classified as the stage zero of religiousp rogress.
24. Ivi, p. 103. Cf. also p. 64, on the difference between fetishism and idolatry.
25. Eusebius, *Praeparatio Evangelica*, I, pp. 9–10. On Sanchuniaton, cf. L. B. Paton, *Sanchuniaton*, in *Encyclopaedia of Religion and Ethics*, C. Scribner's sons, New York, 1920, vol. XI, pp. 178–181; O. Eissfeldt, *Sanchunjaton von*

Berut und Ilumilku von Ugarit, Max Niemeyer, Halle, 1952; U. Hölscher, *Eredità di concezioni cosmogoniche in Esiodo,* in AA.Vv., *Esiodo,* edited by G. Arrighetti, Mursia, Milan, 1975, pp. 127–135; L. Troiani, *L'opera storiografica di Filone da Byblos,* Goliardica, Pisa, 1974; S. E. Loewenstamm, *Sanchuniaton, Pauly-Wissowa,* Suppl. XIV, München, 1974, pp. 593–598; A. Momigliano, *Interpretazioni minime VII,* in "Annali della Scuola Normale Superiore di Pisa D," serie III, vol. X, 4, Pisa, 1980, pp. 1227–1231 (Momigliano is openly skeptical on the antiquity and authenticity of Sanchuniaton). Cf. also, S. Moscati, *Il mondo dei Fenici,* Mondadori, Milan, 1979, especially pp. 50–63.
26. Cf., for example, Huet, op. cit., Prop. IV, chap. II, 2, pp. 42–43; S. Bochart, *Geographia Sacra seu Phaleg et Canaan* (1646), Ludgurni Batavorum 1707 (4th), lib. II, Chapter II, pp. 703–712; A. van Dale, *Dissertatio super Sanchoniatone,* in *Dissertatio super Aristea,* Amsterdam, 1705, pp. 472–506; W. Warburton, *The Divine Legation,* vol. I, London, 1738, p. 153; E. Fourmont, *Réflexions sur l'Origine, l'Histoire et la Succession des Ancien Peuples,* Paris, 1747 (2nd) (1st ed. 1735), t. I, 2 volumes, pp. 162–165 (in particular on "Baetyles"); Voltaire, *Essai sur les Moeurs,* cit., vol. I, pp. 46–50; Court De Gebelin, *Monde Primitif,* Paris, 1773, p. l ff. (on "Baetyles" p. 58 ff.). For the seventeenth- and eighteenth-century discussion of peoples' antiquity, cf. P. Rossi, *I segni del tempo,* cit., p. 150 ff.
27. Eusebius of Caesarea, I, 10, 23. Cf. Troiani, op. cit., p. 167 ff.
28. Huet,o p.c it.,p .1 23.
29. Bochart,o p.c it.,p .7 07.
30. *Genesis,* XXVII, 10, 22; cf. also XXXI, 13.
31. Bochart,l oc.c it.
32. Fourmont,o p.c it.,t .I ,p .1 65.
33. Op.a ndl oc.c it.(myt ranslation).
34. *Du Culte,* p. 116 (my translation).
35. Ivi,p .1 35f f.
36. Ivi,p .1 61.
37. Ivi,p .1 17.
38. Ibid.
39. Ibid.(myt ranslation).
40. Ivi, p. 150 (my translation).
41. Ivi, p. 158 (my translation).
42. Ivi, p. 161 (my translation).
43. Lafitau, *Moeurs,* cit., p. 130. Badaloni draws attention to the differences between Lafitau and de Brosses when he compares the latter, with reference to the question of the "primitive mentality," to Vico. According to Vico, the peculiar character of the "primitive mentality" is the substitution of substance with an idea or quality. The simplest form of such substitution (which amounts to a conceptual change when compared to Lafitau's theory) is described by de Brosses as "fetishism." It is important to note that for Vico such substitution is due to the unusual natural phenomena. Cf. N. Badaloni, *Vico,* cit., p. 77.
44. Ivi,p .1 51.
45. Ivi,p .1 46.

46. Ivi,p p.1 45–146.
47. In M. David, *Lettres inédites de Diderot et de Hume écrites de1755 à 1763 au président de Brosses,* in "Revue Philosophique," no. 2, April–June, 1966, p. 138 (my translation).
48. Ibid.(myt ranslation).
49. M. David, *Histoire des religions,* cit., p. 155 ff. and *Le pré*sident *de Brosses historien des religions et philosophe,* cit., p. 132 ff. On Hume-de Brosses's relations, cf. A. de Brosses, *Les relations du president de Brosses avec David Hume,* in *Ch. de* Brosses, 1777–1977, cit., pp. 141–148.
50. Ibid.
51. *Du Culte,* cit., p. 182 (translated by B. Feldman and R. Richardson, cit., p.1 74).
52. Ivi,p .1 84(myt ranslation).
53. Ivi,p .1 85.
54. Ivi,p .1 90(myt ranslation).
55. Ivi,p .1 96(myt ranslation).
56. InD avid, *Lettres inédites de Diderot et de Hume,* cit., pp. 140–141.
57. Lafitau, *Moeurs,* cit., pp. 360–361.
58. *Du Culte,* cit., p. 200.
59. On this issue cf. L. Dumont, *Homo aequalis. Genèse et épanouissement de l'idéologie économique,* Gallimard, Paris, 1977 (in English: *From Mandeville to Marx: Genesis and Triumph of Economic Ideology,* University of Chicago Press, Chicago, 1977).
60. I.K ant,o p.c it.
61. C. G. Heyne, *De causis fabularum seu mythorum veterum physicis,* 1764 (partly reproduced in B. Feldman and R. Richardson, op. cit., pp. 215–220). Cf. also: V. Verra, *Mito, rivelazione e filosofia in J.C. Herder e nel suo tempo,* Marzorati, Milan, 1966, pp. 180, 21 ff.; and Landucci, op. cit., p. 243.
62. J.-J. Rousseau, *Émile ou de l'éducation* (1762), Paris 1966, p. 334 (translated by B. Foxley, *Emile,* Dent, London, 1974).
63. C. F. Dupuis, *Origine de tous les cultes,* Paris, 1791 and *Abrégé de l'origine de tous les cultes,* Paris, 1796 (in English: *The Origin of all Religious Worship,* Unknown Publisher, New Orleans, 1872).
64. (Destutt De Tracy), *Analyse raisonnée de l'origine de tous les cultes, ou religion universelle,* Paris, 1804. On Dupuis and de Tracy, see M. David, *La notion de fétichisme chez Auguste Comte et l'oeuvre du président de Brosses "Du culte des dieux fétiches,"* in *Revue de l'Histoire des Religions,* no. 2, April–June, 1967, pp.2 11–212.
65. Ch.-G. Leroy, *Lettres philosophiques sur l'intelligence et la perfectibilité des animaux, avec quelques lettres sur l'homme,* Paris, 1802, p. 305.
66. A. Comte, *Cours de Philosophie positive* (1830), t. V, 52 Leçon, Paris, 1908 (translated and adapted by H. Martineau, *The Positive Philosophy of Auguste Comte,* London, 1853); H. Spencer, *Principles of sociology,* London, 1873, vol. I, Chapter XXI.
67. OnM einers,B öttiger,C onstant,s eeC hapterI Vb elow.
68. G. W. F. Hegel, *Die Vernunft in der Geschichte,* von J. Hoffmeister, Bd. XVIII/A, Meiner, Hamburg, 1955, pp. 213–234 (p. 222) (translated by H. B. Nisbet, *Lectures on the Philosophy of World History,* Cambridge University

Press, Cambridge, 1975, p. 198). See also *Vorlesungen über die Philosophie der Religionen,* Dunker u. Humblott, Berlin, 1840, translated by J. C. Sanderson, *Lectures on the Philosophy of Religion,* K. Paul Trench Trübner, London,1 895).
69. J.F .M cLennan,o p.c it.
70. J.L ubbock,o p.c it.
71. A.B inet,o p.c it.
72. A. Comte, *Considerations philosophiques sur les* sciences *et les savants* (1825), in *Éscrits de jeunesse,* Paris-La Haye, 1970, pp. 324–325 (translated by H. D. Mutton and F. Harrison, *Early Essays on Social Philosophy,* Routledge, London [1911]); *Cours,* cit., vols. IV, pp. 365 e VI, 168. For more details on this, see articles by G. Canguilhem, *Histoire des religions,* cit., and M. David, *La notion de fétichisme,*c it.

Three   The Concept of Fetishism as a Theoretical and Historical Problem

1. M. Mauss, *Oeuvres,* edited by V. Karady, Paris, 1969, vol. II, pp. 244–245 (my translation). Cf. J. Pouillon, *art. cit.,* p. 138. This is not withstanding the fact that Mauss still regards de Brosses's work as "the first scientific work of comparative religions" (*Oeuvres,* Paris, 1969, vol. III, p. 395, my translation). Before Mauss, Max Müller had already leveled charges against both the concept of fetishism and de Brosses's theories. Cf. F. M. Müller, *Natural Religion. The Gifford Lectures* (1888), Longmans, Green & Co., London, 1889, pp. 158–159, 219–220.
2. W.W undt,o p.c it.,t rans.p .2 22f f.
3. M. Mauss, *L'art et le mythe d'après M. Wundt,* in *Oeuvres,* vol. II, cit., p. 216 ff.
4. G. Schmidt, *Manuale di storia comparata delle religioni,* Morcelliana, Brescia, 1934, p. 94. On the theories of a "primordial monotheism," see the critique by R. Pettazzoni, *L'essere supremo nelle religioni primitive,* Einaudi, Torino, 1974, pp. 153–162 and by G. Van Der Leeuw, op. cit.
5. V.V aleri,o p.c it.,p p.1 12–113.
6. J. Goetz, *L'esperienza di Dio nei primitivi,* Morcelliana, Brescia, 1983, p. 20 (myt ranslation).
7. For the concept of "formal connections," cf. L. Wittgenstein, "Bemerkungen über Frazers 'The Golden Bough'," in *Synthese,* edited by R. Rhees, XVII, 1967 (translated by J. Beversluis, "Remarks on Frazer's *Golden Bough,*" in *Wittgenstein: Sources and Pespectives,* edited by C. G. Luckhardt, Cornell University Press and Harvester-Wheatsheaf, 1979, pp. 61–81, reproduced, with minor corrections in *Philosophical Occasions 1912–1951,* edited by J. C. Klagge and A. Nordmann, Hackett, Indianapolis and Cambridge, 1993, pp. 119–155). On the theoretical-critical perspectives opened up by Wittgenstein, cf. A. G. Gargani, *Introduzione a Wittgenstein,* Laterza, Bari, 1973.
8. J.-B.B ossuet, *Discours sur l'histoire universelle* (1681), Paris, 1966.

9. W. Wundt, op. cit., trans. p. 222. The fetish is also "a means for furthering purposes of magic" (translation, p. 223).
10. M.M auss, *Oeuvres,* II, cit., p. 217. Cf. Valeri, op. cit., p. 111.
11. M.F oucault, *Le mots et les choses,* Gallimard, Paris, 1966.
12. C. Lévi-Strauss, *Introduction,* in *Sociologie et anthropologie,* edited by M. Mauss, Presses Universitaires de France, Paris, 1950 (translated by F. Baker, *Introduction to the Work of Marcel Mauss,* Routledge & Kegan Paul, London, 1987). For a discussion of Mauss's essay *The Gift,* cf. M. Sahlins, *Stone Age Economics,* Aldine de Gruyter, New York, 1972, pp. 148–182; L. Dumont, *Essais sur l'individualisme,* Seuil, Paris, 1983, pp. 167–186; R. Guidieri, *L'abondance des pauvres,* Seuil, Paris, 1984, pp. 31–85, 129–156.
13. C.L évi-Strauss, *Introduction,* cit., p. XXVIII (trans. cit., pp. 30–31).
14. G. Bateson, *Mind and Nature. A Necessary Unity,* E. P. Dutton, New York, 1979, p. 8 ff.
15. C.L évi-Strauss,l oc.c it.
16. T. H. Kuhn, *The Structure of Scientific Revolution,* Chicago University Press, Chicago,1 962.
17. Cf.B .B aczko, *Lumièresd el 'Utopie,* Payot, Paris, 1978, on Condorcet.
18. Cf. M. Eliade, *The Quest. History and Meaning in Religion,* Chicago University Press, Chicago and London, [1969] 1984, p. 44; also M. Bloch, *Apologie pour l'histoire ou métier d'historien,* Armand Colin, Paris, 1949 on the confusion between "explanation" and "filiation" in those searching for "origins." In tribal societies, the *myth* of the "origins" is used to provide the reasons for the permanence and stability of the world. Cf. R. Pettazzoni, op. cit., pp. 89–91.
19. L. Wittgenstein, *Philosophische Untersuchungen,* Oxford 1953 (translated by G. E. M. Anscombe, *Philosophical Investigations,* Blackwell, Oxford [1953] 2001, 3rd edition, p. 122) and "Remarks on Frazer's *Golden Bough,*" cit., p.1 33.
20. "Remarkso nF razer's *Golden Bough,*" cit., p. 133.
21. On the observer in anthropology, cf. C. Lévi-Strauss, op. cit.; but also the theory put forward by M. Harris in *The Rise of Anthropological Theory. A History of Theories of Culture,* Routledge and Kegan Paul, London, 1968; and *Cultural Materialism. The Struggle for a Science of Culture,* Random House, New York, 1979. On the epistemology of observation, cf. H. Von Foerster, *Notes pour une épistemologie des objets vivants,* and H. Maturana, *Stratégies cognitives,* both included in *L'unité de l'homme,* edited by E. Morin and M. Piattelli Palmarini, vol. II, Seuil, Paris, 1974. See also H. Maturana and F. J. Varela, *Autopoiesis and Cognition. The Realization of Living,* cit.; F. J. Varela, *Principles of Biological Autonomy,* North Holland, New York, 1979. A.M. Iacono, *L'evento e l'osservatore,* ETS, Pisa, 2013.
22. A. Radcliffe-Brown, op. cit., p. 128. On this, cf. Pietro Rossi, *Antropologia culturale e ricerca storica,* in *Cultura* e *antropologia,* cit., pp. 76–104 (pp. 87–88). On the relationship between history and the comparative method, cf. also R. A. Nisbet, *Social Change and History. Aspects of the Western Theory of Development,* Oxford University Press, New York, 1969.
23. Ivi,p .1 59.

24. M. Mauss, *Les civilisations: élements et formes*, in *Civilisation. Le mot et l'idée*, cit. (I am using here the text in *Essais de sociologie*, Seuil, Paris, 1971.)
25. Cf. G. Gliozzi, *Adamo e il Nuovo Mondo*, cit., on colonialism and ideologies before the eighteenth century.
26. K. Marx, *Das Kapital. Kritik der politischen Oekonomie (1867)*, I Bd., Berlin, 1977, B. I, K. 1,4, pp. 85–98 (translated by B. Fowkes, *Capital. A Critique of Political Economy*, Vol. 1, Penguin in association with New Left Review, London [1976] 1990, pp. 163–177); S. Freud, *Drei Abhandlungen zur Sexualtheorie* (1905), in *Gesammelte Werke*, V Bd., Frankfurt am Main 1972 (5th ed.), pp. 52–54 (translated by A. A. Brill, *Three Contributions to the Theory of Sex*, Nervous and Mental Disease Publishing Co., New York, and Washington 1920, pp. 1–35); S. Freud, *Fetischismus* (1927), in *GW*, XIV Bd., pp. 301–317; S. Freud, *Die Ichspaltung in Abwehrvorgang*, in *GW*, XVII Bd., pp.5 9–62.
27. On the connections between Marx's theory and Freud's theory, cf. Valeri, op. cit., and the essays in *Objets du Fetichisme, Nouvelle Revue de Psycanalyse*, no. 2, 1970.
28. R. Jakobson, "Coup d'oeil sur le développement de la sémiotique," in *A Semiotic Landscape. Proceedings of the First Congress of the International Association of Semiotic Studies*, Milan, June 1974, edited by S. Chatman, U. Eco, and J. M. Klinkenberg, Mouton, The Hague, 1979, pp. 3–19, ivi, p. 16. On this point cf. U. Eco, "The Influence of Roman Jakobson on the Development of Semiotics" (1981), in *Classics of Semiotics*, edited by M. Krampen, K. Oehler et al., Plenum Press, New York and London, 1987, pp.1 09–127.
29. On the concept of "context," cf. G. Bateson, op. cit., p. 14 ff. For a semiotics perspective, cf. J. M. Lotman, *Universe of the Mind. A Semiotic Theory of Culture*, translated by A. Shukman, Tauris, London and New York, [1990] 2001.
30. G. Bateson, *Steps to an Ecology of Mind*, Intertext Books, London, 1972, p. 182 ff.
31. Ivi,p p.1 90–191.
32. Ibid.
33. Ivi,p .1 82f f.
34. S.F reud, *Drei Abhandlungen*, cit., p. 52.
35. Ibid.
36. C. S. Peirce, *Peirce on Signs. Writings on Semiotic*, edited by J. Hoopes, University of North Carolina Press, Chapel Hill, 1991, p. 252 (article originally published in 1906).
37. J.M .L otman, *Universe of the Mind*, op. cit., p. 54.
38. On the concept of "habit" in anthropological epistemology, cf. P. Bourdieu, *Le sens pratique*, Les Éditions de Minuit, Paris, 1980, p. 87 ff.
39. G.B ateson, *Mind and Nature*, op. cit., p. 14.
40. Ivi,p p.1 4–15.
41. Cf., for instance, N. Wiener, *Cybernetics*, MIT Press, Cambridge (MA), 1965.
42. G.B ateson, *Mind and Nature*, op. cit., p. 15.
43. H.M aturanaa ndF .J .V arela, *Autopoiesis*, cit., p. 8.

44. Cf. the questions arising from the concept of "paradigm" in "scientific revolutions" in T. H. Kuhn, op. cit.

Four   Marx's Theory of Fetishism

1. See Marx-Engels, *Gesamtausgabe*, IV/1, Berlin, 1976 (MEGA from now onwards), pp. 320–359. In K. Marx, *Early Political Writings*, Cambridge Texts in the History of Political Thought, edited by Joseph O'Malley, Cambridge University Press, Cambridge, 1994. The excerpts in question are dated to 1841. Furthermore, the excerpts from Benjamin Constant are not indicated.
2. Ivi, pp. 320–329. The translation used by Marx is that of Pystorius, Berlin and Stralsunt, 1785.
3. Ivi,p p.3 35–338.C .M einers,o p.c it.
4. Ivi,p p.3 29–334.C .B öttiger,o p.c it.
5. Ivi, pp. 342–367. B. Constant, *De la Religion considérée dans sa source, ses formes et ses développements*, Bossange, Paris, 1824–1831, 5 volumes.
6. Marx-Engels, *Werke*, Bd. 1, Berlin, 1964 (MEW), in *Early Political Writings*, op.c it.
7. MEW,B d.X III,p p.7 –8.
8. MEW, Bd. I, pp. 147. "Proceedings of the Sixth Rhine Assembly. Debates on the Law on Thefts of Wood," in *Collected Works. Marx K. & F. Engels*, New York, International Publisher, 1. 1975, pp. 224–263.
9. *Du Culte*, cit., pp. 52–53. The story is, in turn, taken from Herrera.
10. *MEW*, Ergänzungsband I Teil, Berlin, 1969.
11. Quotation taken from "Money and Alienated Man," in *Writings of the Young Marx on Philosophy and Society*, translated and edited by D. Easton and Kurt H. Guddat, Hackett Publishing Company, Indianapolis, 1997, p. 266.
12. R. Rosdolsky, *Genesi e struttura del "Capitale" di Marx*, Laterza, Bari, 1975, pp. 161–162, vol. I.
13. Quotation taken from "Money and Alienated Man," in *Writings of the Young Marx on Philosophy and Society*, translated and edited by D. Easton and Kurt H. Guddat, Hackett Publishing Company, Indianapolis, 1997, p. 266.
14. Ibid., pp.2 66–267.
15. L.F euerbach, *Das Wesen des Christenthums*, Berlin, 1956, 2 volumes.
16. Quotation taken from "Money and Alienated Man," p. 267.
17. Ivi,p .2 68.
18. Ibidem.
19. *Economic and Philosophic Manuscripts* of 1844, translated by Martin Milligan from the German text, revised by Dirk J. Struik, contained in *Marx/Engels, Gesamtausgabe*, Abt. 1, Bd. 3, p. xxxvi.
20. *Economic and Philosophic Manuscripts* of 1844. Translated by Martin Milligan from the German text, revised by Dirk J. Struik, contained in *Marx/Engels, Gesamtausgabe*, Abt. 1, Bd. 3, p. xxxvi.
21. MEW, Bd. XXVII, Berlin, 1963, pp. 55–59 (18 October 1846). The reference is to Feuerbach's *Das Wesen der Religion*, in *Die Epigonen*, Leipzig, 1846.

22. MEW, bd. XXVII, cit., pp. 57–58. MECW Volume 38. First published in *Der Briefwechsel zwischen F. Engels und K. Marx*,1 913.
23. MEW, Bd. III, Berlin, 1962, p. 7. Written by Marx in the spring of 1845, but edited slightly by Engels; first published as an appendix to *Ludwig Feuerbach and the End of Classical German Philosophy* in 1888; source: Marx/Engels *Selected Works*, Volume One, pp. 13–15. Note that this version differs from the version in Engels' edition published in MECW Volume 5, pp. 6–8; publisher: Progress Publishers, Moscow, USSR, 1969; translated by W. Lough from the German.
24. B. Constant, op. cit., vol. I, 1824, p. 3 ff.
25. Ivi, vol. II, 1825, p. 7 (Marx, *MEGA*, cit., p. 350), my translation.
26. This, on the contrary, is the line of thought adopted by Luhmann, who establishes a relation between the idea of control and the noncorrespondencies, which are seen as the structural elements of complex societies. See N. Luhmann, *Political Theory in the Welfare State*, de Gruyter, New York, 1990, translated by John Bednarz Jr. In this work, the author uses the idea of observing and self-observing systems.
27. MEW, Bd. III, p. 3; MEO, vol. V, p. 29. On the genealogy of conceptual thought in historical materialism, see M. Sahlins, *Culture and Practical Reason,* University of Chicago Press, Chicago, 1976.
28. Hegel,o p.c it.
29. MEW, cit., Bd. III, pp. 166–167 (MEO, vol. V, p. 177).
30. R. L. Gregory, *Eye and Brain, The Psychology of Seeing* (1966), Oxford University Press, Oxford, 1998.
31. K. Marx, *Das Kapital*, cit., p. 86 (*Capital. A Critique of Political Economy*, Volume One, Introduced by Ernest Mandel, translated by Ben Fowkes, Penguin Books in association with New Left Review, Harmondsworth, pp.1 64–165).
32. On the relationship between commodities, imagination, and symbolism and, in particular, on the notion that commodities are fetishes insofar as they are fixations of the imagination, see W. Benjamin, "Baudelaire in Paris," in *Angelus Novus*, Einaudi, Turin, 1962, pp. 150–151; Selected Writings, translated by Edmund Jephcott et al., Cambridge, MA, 1996–2003, 4 vols. Benjamin's criticism is directed at the *way* the inversion is produced, since, in capitalistic societies, inversion is inevitably bound up with commodities, even when (or, mainly when) commodities are transfigured and hidden in their social role.
33. L.S ebag, *Marxisme et structuralisme*, Payot, Paris 1964 (my translation).
34. The limit of Marx's analysis, the centre of conflict between two opposite conceptions, can be exemplified by this well-known statement: "In studying such transformations it is always necessary to distinguish between the material transformation of the economic conditions of production, which can be determined with the precision of natural science, and the legal, political, religious, artistic or philosophic—in short, ideological forms in which men become conscious of this conflict and fight it out" (MEW, cit., Bd. XIII, p. 9; K. Marx, *A Contribution to the Critique of Political Economy*, Progress Publishers, Moscow, 1977, with some notes by R. Roja). This is the vantage point from which, one moment, the observer can see the transformations as

if from the outside and the next, experience them within ideological forms. In this sense, one either assumes that science can provide guarantees against the filter or ideology, or that the observer is subject to the same conditions as those of the people he observes. The significance of Marx's major discovery that one has to look beyond the ideological forms, cannot be limited to a rigid juxtaposition between right and distorted forms of observation. This is where we are confronted with some of the contemporary problems related to self-observation, meta-descriptions, and the context. By circumscribing and determining the framework of observation, the context itself becomes an observedo bject.

35. I. I. Rubin, *Essays on Marx's Theory of Value*, Aakar Books, Delhi, 2007, pp.2 1–22.
36. "The perceptions of my two alternate lives always remained very clear and distinct. However, there was one phenomenon that was inexplicable: that the consciousness of the same 'I' could exist in two so very different beings. I was unable to account for this anomaly, whether I imagined myself to be village priest of ***, or *il signor Romualdo*, the recognized lover of Clarimonde," Théophile Gautier, "The Dead in Love" (1836), in *Demons of the Night: Tales of the Fantastic, Madness and the Supernatural*, edited by Joan C. Kessler, University of Chicago Press, Chicago, 1995, pp. 111–112. The writer here gives an anguished description of the most crucial problem of human knowledge. On the double see O. Rank, *Der Doppelgänger*, Internationaler Psychoanalytischer Verlag, Leipzig-Wien, 1914.
37. *Das Kapital*, I, cit., pp. 86–87 (p. 88); *Capital*, cit., p. 47, Chapter 1.
38. J. Baudrillard, *Pour une critique de l'"économie politique du signe*, Gallimard, Paris, 1972; M. Sahlins, *Culture and Practical Reason*,c it.
39. See N. Badaloni, "Marx: centralità della "critica" e suo modo d"essere," in *Marx, un secolo*, Editori Riuniti, Rome, 1983, pp. 11–38.
40. The first draft of *Capital's* first chapter, as it appeared in the first edition, contained only the imaginary models. The historical examples were not included in it. In the *Postscript* to the second edition Marx stated that the paragraph on the fetishism of the commodity had been extensively revised (Das Kapital, I, cit., p. 18. See Marx, *L'analisi della forma di valore*, edited by C. Pennavaja, Laterza, Bari, 1976).
41. Maurice Godelier, *Perspectives in Marxist Anthropology* (1973), translated by Robert Brain, Cambridge University Press, Cambridge–New York–Melbourne, 1977, p. 175.
42. In an essay where he examines these topics in relation to the role and concept of history in Marx, Luporini concludes with the following observation: "The question remains open whether this concept—despite taking this final complexity into account—manages to avoid socio-economical reductionism," C. Luporini, "La concezione della storia in Marx," in *Marx, un secolo*, cit., p.2 04.
43. *Das Kapital*, I, cit., p. 91 (English edition p. 170).
44. Ivi.p .9 2(Englishe dition,p .1 71).
45. Ivi,p p.9 0–91(Englishe dition,p p.1 69–170).
46. Ivi,p p.9 2–93(Englishe dition,p p.1 71–172).
47. Ibid.

48. Seet hef ollowingc hapter.
49. Ivi,p .9 3(Englishe dition,p .1 72).
50. Ivi,p p.9 3–94(Englishe dition,p .1 73).
51. Ibid.(p.9 6;E nglishe dition,p .1 73).
52. For the concept of the sign as reference ("renvoi"), see Jakobson, op. cit.

Five   History, Nature, and System: Marx's Anthropological Conception

1. Nikolai Bukharin, *Historical Materialism. A System of Sociology* (first published in English in 1926), Routledge, New York, 2011, pp. 60–61.
2. See M. Sahlins, *Stone Age Economics* (first published in the United Kingdom in 1974), Routledge, London, 2004: "That sentence of 'life at hard labor' was passed uniquely upon us. Scarcity is the judgment decreed by our economy—so also the axiom of our Economics: the application of scarce means against alternative ends to derive the most satisfaction possible under the circumstances. And it is precisely from this anxious vantage that we look upon hunters. But if modern man, with all his technological advantages, still hasn't got the wherewithal, what chance has this naked savage with his puny bow and arrow? Having equipped the hunter with bourgeois impulses and Paleolithic tools, we judge his situation hopeless in advance," "Sources of the Misconception,"c hapter1 .
3. E. P. Thompson, "Time, Work-Discipline, and Industrial Capitalism," in *Past and Present*, no. 38 (December, 1967), pp. 56–97 (p. 60).
4. Ibid.
5. Ivi.
6. p.6 1.
7. For an analysis of the process of separation of economy from other social spheres as a result of the capitalist way of production, see chapter 4 ("Societies and Economic Systems") of K. Polanyi's *The Great Transformation: The Political and Economic Origins of Our Time*, Beacon Press, Boston, 1944. See also the essays edited by G. Dalton, *Primitive, Archaic and Modern Economies: Essays of Karl Polanyi*, Beacon Press, Boston, 1968. For an analysis of Polanyi's thought, see S. C. Humphreys, "History, Economics, and Anthropology: The Work of Karl Polanyi," in *History and Theory*, VIII, 1969, no. 2, pp. 165–212; E. Grendi, *Polanyi*, Etas, Milan, 1978; F. Apergi, "*Karl Polanyi e la fondazione dell'antropologia economica*," in *Intersezioni*, no. 3, 1928, pp. 603–613.
8. Daniel Defoe, *An Essay Upon Projects*, Arc Manor, Rockville, Maryland 2008, p. 27.
9. J. Baudrillard, *The Consumer Society. Myths and Structures* (1970), English translation by Chris Turner, Sage Publications, London 1998, p. 74.
10. Ivi,p .7 5.
11. "This alternate succession of appetite and fear, during all the time the action is in our power to do, or not to do, is that we call DELIBERATION; which name hath been given it for that part of the definition wherein it is said that it lasteth so long, as the action whereof we deliberate, is in our power; for so

long we have liberty to do or not to do: and deliberation signifieth the taking away of our own liberty," T. Hobbes, *Elements of Law Natural and Politic* (1640), Routledge, New York 2013, p. 61.

12. On the relationship between the notion of scarcity and the social system, see, besides the already quoted works by Sahlins and Baudrillard, N. Luhmann's systemic approach in "Knappheit, Geld und die bürgerliche Gesellshaft," *Jahrbuch für Sozialwissenshaft*, 1972. On the role played by "abundance" and "scarcity" in modern reason, see C. A. Viano, "La ragione, l'abbondanza e la credenza," in *Crisi della ragione. Nuovi modelli nel rapporto tra sapere e attivitàu mane*, edited by A. Gargani, Einaudi, Turin 1979, pp. 305–366.

13. For a definition of the notion of "non-intentional" or "unintentional," see M. Godelier, "Objet et méthodes de l'anthropologie économique," *L'Homme*, vol. 5, no. 2, 1965, pp. 31–91. On the one hand, the "non-intentional" is related to Marx's treatment of the relationship between "being" and "conscience," while, on the other, it is connected to an idea that emerged in sociology, linguistics, anthropology, and psychoanalysis. On this topic, grounded in the studies of de Saussure and Durkheim (on the links between them, see W. Doroszewski, "Alcune osservazioni sui rapporti tra la sociologia e la linguistica: E. Durkheim e F. de Saussure," in multiple authors, *Il linguaggio*, Dedalo, Bari, 1976, pp. 221–231), see E. Sapir, "The Unconscious Patterning of Behaviour in Society," in *Selected Writings of Edward Sapir in Language, Culture and Personality*, edited by D. Mandelbaum, University Press of California, 1949, pp. 544–559 and C. Lévi Strauss, "L'analyse structurale en linguistique et en anthropologie," "Langage et société," "Linguistique et anthropologie," "La notion de structure en ethnologie," contained in *Anthropologie structurale* I, Plon, Paris, 1974.

14. See S. Freud, "The Schreber Case. Psychoanalytic Remarks on an Autobiographically Described Case of Paranoia (Dementia Paranoides)," in *The Schreber Case*, translated by Andrew Webber, Penguin, London, 2002. This case has also been addressed by Elias Canetti, who has underlined the relationship between power and the vision in which everyone has perished: "As far as his fellow men are concerned, they have all perished, and he is, as he wishes to be, *the only one*. This is the final and most extreme phase of power. One can work towards it, but it can be fully realized only in delirium," Elias Canetti, *The Conscience of Words*, translated by Joachim Neugroschel, Farrar, Straus and Giroux, New York, 1984, p. 27. In delirium, power is fully realized the moment Schreber becomes the sole one by annulling the *others*, by reducing the *others* to objects. This is an extraordinary example of the most extreme form of desire to entirely subsume unintentional relationships into intentional acting. On the topic of power and survival, see above all Elias Canetti, *Crowds and Power*, translated by Carol Stewart, Continuum, New York, 1978.

15. L.D umont, *Homo aequalis*, cit., p. 115.

16. "It is only in the eighteenth century, in 'civil society', that the different forms of social union confront the individual as a mere means to his private ends, as an external necessity," Karl Marx, *Grundrisse*, Diez Ferlag, Berlin, 1953, p. 6; Karl Marx, *Selected Writings*, edited by David McLellan, Oxford University Press, New York, 2000, p. 380. On the origins of the relationship

between possessive individualism and the seventeenth-century market society, see G. B. Macpherson, op. cit.

17. See on this topic Marx's critique of the economists' Robinsonades (*Grundrisse*, cit., pp. 5–6). The fundamental issue lies in the problem of the relationship between the theoretical procedure of political economy (when it distinguishes between the "transparent" relationship of the isolated individual with objects and the complex relationships of the market system) and the topic of society's origin according to the "four stages" historical theory. Although Meek explored the influence of this theory upon eighteenth-century Scottish and French philosophers, he nevertheless did not address a crucial point: the role played by the "four stages" theory *within* the procedure of economic theory. He briefly touches upon the issue when speaking about analogies and influences (see, for instance, his discussion of the role played by unconscious processes in history and economy alike) and even underlines the fact that the "stages" theory provides economic theory with the idea of an earlier and simpler society; but he fails to grasp, for example, that it was the teleological conception of the "stages" theory that transformed the isolated human being, the hunter and the fisherman—inasmuch as he was seen as the effective historical starting point—into the political economy's operative startingp oint.

18. Juri Lotman, "Painting and the Language of Theater: Notes on the Problem of Ironic Rhetoric" (1978), translated by Alla Yefimov, in *Tekstura: Russian Essays on Visual Culture*, edited by Lev Manovich and Alla Yefimov, Chicago University Press, Chicago, 1993.

19. On the problem of the relationship between the material-natural content of a commodity and its social form, as examined in "The Fetishism of the Commodity" in Chapter 1 of *Capital* Volume 1, see the pages that follow.

20. Good or bad as the "savage" may be—insofar as he is represented as a member of the bourgeoisie living in a world from which social relationships are imagined as having been excluded, because the primal act, the starting point, is the relationship between the individual and the object—he is an ad hoc deformed mirror: the true identity of the bourgeois individual where difference is domesticated even before being established as such. This idea can be traced back to Adam Smith and to Turgot's "Value and Money," but its most effective expression is to be found in Sismondi, where the image of the isolated man is explicitly used for summarizing the development of the whole society. In his *New Principles of Political Economy*, Sismondi dedicates a chapter to the "Formation of Wealth for Solitary Man," where, among other things, this figure ideally crosses the four "stages" of society's development as envisaged by Adam Smith and other eighteenth-century economists and philosophers (hunting, pasturage, farming, and commerce): from the struggle for primary needs to the gradual improvement of his technical and organizational capacities. "The history of this man is the history of humanity itself," J. C. Sismonde de Sismondi, *New Principles of Political Economy, or, Of Wealth in its Relation to Population* (1819), translated and annotated by Richard Hyse, 1991. Hence, it is in Sismondi that the figure of the isolated man fully realizes its semiotic value.

21. "That is to say that Classical Economics can only envisage economic facts as belonging to the homogeneous space of their positivity and measurability on condition that it accepts a *'naïve' anthropology,* which bases all the acts involved in the production, distribution, reception and consumption of economic objects on the economic subjects and their needs. Hegel provided the philosophical concept of the *unity* of this 'naïve' type of anthropology with economic phenomena in his famous expression *'the sphere of needs'*, or 'civil society', as distinct from political society. In the concept of the sphere of needs, economic facts are thought as based in their economic essence on human subjects who are a prey to 'need': on the *homo oeconomicus,* who is a (visible, observable) given, too," Louis Althusser, "The Object of *Capital*," in Louis Althusser, Étienne Balibar, *Reading Capital*, translated by Ben Brewster, New Left Books, London, 1970.

22. As Althusser observes, following Foucault, "The invisible is defined by the visible as *its* invisible, *its* forbidden vision: the invisible is not therefore simply what is outside the visible (to return to the spatial metaphor), the outer darkness of exclusion—but the *inner darkness of exclusion,* inside the visible itself because defined by its structure" (From *Capital* to Marx's Philosophy," in Reading *Capital*, op. cit.). It is precisely for this reason that the structure of the visible and the invisible is determined by the same conceptual system, even when one employs an opposing ideology. Even when we admit that this specific conceptual system derives from an ideology, it nonetheless acquires autonomy and permanence, in the face of which there is not much sense in relinking it to its original ideology (this is true for the individual who supports an opposing ideology, but maintains the same visual field) or placing ourselves in another conceptual system, which we ideologically define as *the* science. In other words, there is not much sense in reducing a conceptual system to the opposition ideology/science, because—although related to both of them—it cannot in any case be reduced to either.

    For an analysis of the juxtaposition (and its role) between different structures of the visible and different conceptual systems, see T. Todorov, who starts from the crisis of communication and failure of comprehension between two worlds, T. Todorov, *La conquête de l'Amerique. La question de l'autre*, Seuil, Paris, 1982.

23. Karl Marx, *MEW*, cit., Bd. 19, 1962, pp. 242–243. "The Reply to Zasulich," in *Marx-Zasulich Correspondence February/March 1881.* Source: *Late Marx and the Russian Road, Marx and the 'peripheries of capitalism'*, edited by Teodor Shanin, Monthy Reivew Press, New York, 1983.

24. Karl Marx, *MEW,* cit., Bd. 19, p. 112. Written in French at the end of November 1877, Source: *Karl Marx and Frederick Engels: Selected Correspondence, 1846–1895,* International Publishers (1942), translated by Donna Torr.

25. *The Ethnological Notebooks of Karl Marx*, by L. Krader, cit. For an analysis of these passages, see L. Krader's and D. R. Kelley's "Introduction" to "The Science of Anthropology: An Essay on the Very Old Marx," *Journal of the History of Ideas,* no. 2, 1984, pp. 245–262.

26. See Marx's critique of Maine in *The Ethnological Notebooks,* p. 329, and the attention he pays to the elaboration of individuality, viewed as a tearing loose from the originally nondespotic chains of the primitive community.

Marx had already addressed the centrality of the concept of separation in his *Formen*: "*The original conditions of production* (or, what amounts to the same, the reproduction of a growing number of human beings through the natural process between the sexes; for this reproduction, although it appears as the appropriation of the objects by the subjects in one respect, in another appears as the formation or subjugation of the objects to a subjective purpose; their transformation into results and repositories of subjective activity) *cannot themselves* originally *be products*—results of production. It is not the *unity* of living and active humanity with the natural, inorganic conditions of their metabolic exchange with nature, and hence their appropriation of nature, which requires explanation or is the result of a historic process, but rather the *separation* between these inorganic conditions of human existence and this active existence, a separation which is completely posited only in the relation of wage labour and capital," K. Marx, "Forms which precede capitalist production," in *Grundrisse*, cit., pp. 388–389; *Grundrisse: Foundations of the Critique of Political Economy*, translated by Martin Nicolaus, Penguin, London, 1973. This passage has been examined by C. Luporini in his "Critica della politica e critica dell'economia politica in Marx," in *Critica marxista*, 1978, no. 1. Nevertheless, it is necessary to observe that—although he lays great emphasis on the concept of separation—Marx tends to consider historical development as a progressive separation of men from nature, as their alienation from naturalness. This is why, if on the one hand the analysis of social forms is focused on the processes of separation which develop within them, on the other, all this seems to be in some way supported by a more general process of separation from nature, which seems to incorporate the forms themselves. But the problematic point here is linked to the following question: does the idea of the latter process take on such a decisive role *within* its theoretical procedure, which is based on separation, as to domesticate the disruptive power of this category?

27. This, on the contrary, is the interpretation proposed by Krader, who attributes a "stages" theory to Marx. See L. Krader, "Evoluzione, rivoluzione e Stato: Marx e il pensiero etnologico," in *Storia del marxismo*, I, *Il Marxismo ai tempi di Marx*, Einaudi, Turin, 1978.

28. It is quite significant, for instance, that whereas Adam Smith needs a simplification for explaining the mechanisms of the capitalist mode of production and refers to an imaginary "rude and primitive stage of society" where he locates the formation of the original accumulation process, Marx shifts his analysis of historical processes that have contributed to the formation of the capitalist mode of production toward the dissolution of feudal production. In the former the problem of the system's *identity* within the theoretical procedure predominates (this does not mean that Smith does not oppose the feudal system), whereas what prevails in Marx's theoretical procedure is the problem of difference and separation.

29. It is the emphasis placed on separation that hinders this attribution of sense, because internal historicity always implies a bringing to the fore of the *specific* conditions through which a determinate *form* moves with its contradictions. See Balibar in *Reading Capital*, cit. On the centrality of concepts

such as "antagonism" and "difference," see Antonio Negri, *Marx oltre Marx. Quaderno di lavoro sui Grundrisse*, Feltrinelli, Milan, 1970.
30. See Baudrillard's *Société de Consommation* (cit., p. 94) for a critique of scholars such as Galbraith, who reduce society's alienation to the problem of consumption.
31. K. Marx, Preface to *A Contribution to the Critique of Political Economy*, MEW, cit., Bd. 13, 1963, p. 9.
32. In the "Marginal Notes on Wagner"—some of whose arguments I would like to call into question—we find the following statement: "But if Rodbertus only wishes to make the trivial statement that use-value which really stands in relation to an individual as an object of utility, relates to him as an individual use-value for him—then this is either a trivial tautology or it is incorrect, since not to mention such things as rice, maize, wheat or meat which does not stand in any relation to a Hindu as food, an individual's need for the title of Professor or Privy Councillor or an order is possible only in quite a definite "social Organisation." "Randglossen zu A. Wagners 'Lehrbuch der politischen Oekonomie'," *MEW*, cit., Bd. 19, pp. 372–373 (English translation in *Theoretical Practice*, no. 5, London, 1972). What we find here is the idea that use value cannot be addressed outside a certain social context.
33. "So far as it is a use-value, there is nothing mysterious about it, whether we consider it from the point of view that by its properties it satisfies human needs; or that it first takes on these properties as the product of human labour. It is absolutely clear that, by his activity, man changes the forms of the materials of nature in such a way as to make them useful to him," *Kapital*, cit., p. 163. This description of use value is contrasted with the fetish form assumed by exchange value. The crucial problem lies in the fact that—since it is contrasted—use value is conceptually *external* to the commodity form and to its exchange value: it assumes a "simple" form of content through which it is possible to fill a determinate form. And yet, at the same time, we are aware of the fact that use value can only be determined within a specific social organization. But the two ways of understanding use value must be seen as two inseparable and opposed moments of the same theoretical procedure. If they are separated and used in a unilateral way, the former case would lead toward the "naturalization" of the category which is both related and juxtaposed with exchange value; in the latter case, the same category dissolves into exchange value, losing its oppositional theoretical effectiveness.
34. K.M arx, *Das Kapital*, Bd. I, cit, p. 92.
35. Alfred Schmidt, *The Concept of Nature in Marx*, Verso Books, London, 2013.
36. M. Sahlins, *Culture and Practical Reason*, The University of Chicago Press, Chicago,1 976.
37. Ivi,p .8 6.
38. C.L éviS trauss, *Totemism*, Beacon Press, Boston, 1963.
39. B. Malinowski, *Magic, Science and Religion and Other Essays* (1948), Doubleday Anchor Books, New York 1954, p. 46.
40. Marx, *Marginal Notes on Adolph Wagner's* "Lehrbuch der politischen Ökonomie," in Vol. 24 (1874–1883) in *The Collected Works of Karl Marx and Frederick Engels*, 50 volumes, International Publishers, New York, 1989.

41. Ibid.
42. From a theoretical point of view, what seems to be placed in the background in Sahlins's analysis is the aspect of historicity. Within systems of relations historicity is seen as a permanently problematic element, as an element that enables us to draw attention to differences and contradictions instead of emphasizing the system's power to reproduce itself.
43. Marx, *MEW*, cit., p. 362; *Marginal Notes on Adolph Wagner's* "Lehrbuch der politischen Ökonomie," in Vol. 24 (1874–1883) in *The Collected Works of Karl Marx and Frederick Engels*, 50 volumes, International Publishers, New York,1 989.
44. On the active and constructive features of language, see Ernst Cassirer's "Die Sprache und die Aufbau ded Gegenstandswelt," reprinted in *Symbol, Technik, Sprache, Aufsätze aus den Jahren 1927–1933*, edited by E. W. Orth and J. M. Krois, Meiner, Hamburg, 1985, pp. 121–151. On the ability of language to transcend experience, see E. Sapir, *Culture, Language and Personality: Selected Essays*, edited by David Goodman Mandelbaum, University of California Press, Berkeley and Los Angeles, 1985.
45. M. Sahlins, *Culture and Practical Reason*, cit.: "What is missed by Marx is that men begin *as men*, in distinction to other animals, precisely when they experience the world as a concept (symbolically)," p. 142. On the symbolic role of society, see also E. De Martino's reflections on Marx and Marxism in *La fine del mondo. Contributo all'analisi delle apocalissi culturali*, edited by Clara Gallino, Einaudi, Turin, 1977, pp. 446–462.
46. Marx, Grundrisse: *Foundations of the Critique of Political Economy*, translated by Martin Nicolaus, Penguin, London, 1973, p. lxxxii.
47. Ivi,c xii.
48. In his *L'anatomia della scimmia. La formazione economica della società prima del capitale* (Einaudi, Turin, 1979, p. 91). A. Carandini argues that by reciprocally laying the foundations for each other, the systematic and historical planes generate a continuous tension, which prevents them from completely merging into one another. If this is so, then the epistemological problem lies precisely in this "continuous tension."

Bibliography

De Acosta, José, *Historia Natural y Moral de las Indias*, Sevilla, 1590, Book V (anastatic copy, Valencia 1977).
Adler, A., "L'ethnologue et les Fétiches," in *"Objects du fétichisme,"* Nouvelle Revue de Psychanalyse, no. 2, 1970, pp. 149–158.
Althusser, L., "The Object of *Capital*," in Louis Althusser, Étienne Balibar, *Reading Capital*, translated by Ben Brewster, New Left Books, London, 1970.
Antenhofer, Ch. (ed.), *Fetisch als euristiche Kategorie*, Transcript Verlag, Bielefeld, 2011.
Apergi, F., "Karl Polanyi e la fondazione dell'antropologia economica," *Intersezioni*, no. 3, 1928, pp. 603–613.
Atkinson, G., *Les relations de voyages du XVIIe siècle et lévolution des idées*, Champion, Paris, 1924.
Baczko, B., *Lumièresd el 'Utopie*, Payot, Paris, 1978.
Badaloni, N., "I fratelli Della Porta e la cultura magica e astrologica a Napoli nel '500," *Studi Storici*, no. 4, 1959–1960, pp. 399–677.
Badaloni, N., "Marx: centralità della 'critica' e suo modo d'essere," in *Marx, un secolo*, Editori Riuniti, Rome, 1983, pp. 11–38.
Baltus, J. F., *Résponse à l'Histoire des oracles...dans laquelle on réfute le systeme de M. Van D.*, Strasbourg, Jean Renauld Doulssecker, 1707.
Bartolomei, S., "Analisi di una similitudine: 'età dell'uomo' ed 'età del genere umano' in Fontenelle e Turgot," *Studi Settecenteschi*, no. 3–4, 1982–1983, pp. 89–106.
Bateson, G., *Steps to an Ecology of Mind*, Intertext Books, London, 1972.
Bateson, G., *Mind and Nature. A Necessary Unity*, E. P. Dutton, New York, 1979.
Baudrillard, J., *Pour une critique de l'économie politique du signe*, Gallimard, Paris, 1972.
Bayle, P., *Résponses aux questions dun provincial (1704–1706)*, in *Oeuvres diverses*, La compagnie des libraires, La Haye, 1737, t. III, I Partie, pp. 970–971.
Bayle, P., *Pensée écrites à un docteur de Sorbonne, à l'occasion de la comète qui paruit au mois de Décembre 1680*, in *Oeuvres diverses*, La compagnie des libraires, La Haye (Trévoux), 1737, 2nd edition, vol. III.
Bekker, B., *Le Monde Enchanté ou examen des communs sentiments touchant les Esprits, leur nature, leur pouvour, leur administration, et leurs opération*, Amsterdam, Pierre Rotterdam, 1694, vol. 4; *The World Bewitch'd or, An Examination of the Common Opinions Concerning Spirits: Their Nature, Power, Administration, and Operations. As, Also, The Effects Men Are Able to Produce by their Communication*, translated from a French Copy, approved of and subscribed by the author's own hand, printed for R. Baldwin, 1695, vol. I.

Benjamin, W., *Selected Writings*, translated by Edmund Jephcott et al., 4 volumes, Harvard University Press, Cambridge, MA, 1996–2003.
Benveniste, E., *Civilisation. Contribution à l'histoire du mot*, in *Hommage à Lucien Febvre*, Armand Colin, Paris, 1953, pp. 47–54 (in *Problèmes de Linguistique générale*, Gallimard, Paris, 1971, pp. 336–345).
Bettelheim, B. *The Uses of Enchantment*, Vintage Books, New York, 2010.
Binet, A., *Le fétichisme dans l'amour*, in *Études de Psychologie expérimentale*, Doin, Paris, 1888.
Bloch. M., *Apologie pour l'histoire ou métier d'historien*, A. Colin, Paris, 1949.
Bochart, S., *Geographia Sacra seu Phaleg et Canaan* (1646), Lugduni Batavorum 1707 (4th), lib. II, Chapter II, pp. 703–712.
Bonafré, B., "Object magique, sorcellerie et fétichisme?," in "*Objects du fétichisme*," *Nouvelle Revue de Psychanalyse*, no. 2, 1970, pp. 159–192.
Bosman, W., *Nauwkeurige beschryving van de Guinese Good-, Tand- en Slave-Kust*, Anthony Schouten, Utrecht, 1704. English edition: *A New and Accurate Description of the Coast of Guinea. Divided into The Gold, The Slave, and the Ivory Coasts*, a new edition with an introduction by John Ralph Willis and Notes by J. D. Fage and R. E. Bradbury, Frank Cass, London, 1967.
Bossuet, J. B., *Discours sur l'histoire universelle* (1681), Flammarion, Paris, 1966.
Böttiger,C .A ., *Ideen zur Kunst-Mythologie*, Dresden und Leipzig, 1826–1836.
Bourdieu, P., *Le sens pratique*, Éditions de Minuit, Paris, 1980.
de Brosses, Ch., *Histoire des navigations aux Terres Australes, contenant ce que l'on sçait des mœurs et des productions des Contrées découvertes jusqu'à ce jour; et où il est traité de l'utilité d'y faire de plus amples découvertes, et des moyens d'y former un établissement*, 2 tomes, Paris, Durant, 1756 (translated and edited by John Callander, *Terra Australis Cognita: or, Voyages to the Terra Australis, or Southern Hemisphere, during the Sixteenth, Seventeenth, and Eighteenth Centuries*, Donaldson, Edinburgh, 1766–1768).
de Brosses, Ch., *Traité de la formation mécanique des langues et des principes physiquesd el 'étymologie*, Saklant, Vincent, Desaint, Paris, 1765, 2 volumes.
de Brosses, Ch., *Lettres familières sur l'Italie*, edited by Y. Bezard, Firmin–Didot, Paris, 1931, 2 volumes.
de Brosses, A., *Les relations du président de Brosses avec David Hume*, in *Charles de Brosses*, 1777–1977, in Actes du Colloque de Dijon, 3–7 mai 1977, Textes recueillis par J.-C. Garreta, Slatkine, Geneva, 1981, pp. 141–148.
de Brosses, Ch., *Du Culte des Dieux fétiches ou Parallèle de l'ancienne Religion de l'Egypte avec la Religion actuelle de la Nigritie* (1970), Geneva, Slatkine, 1981.
de Brosses, Ch., *Du Culte des Dieux fétiches ou Parallèle de l'ancienne Religion de l'Egypte avec la Religion actuelle de la Nigritie* (1970), Fayard, Paris, 1988.
Bukharin, N., *Historical Materialism. A System of Sociology* (first published in English in 1926), Routledge, New York, 2011.
Cagiano, E., *Les éditions des "Lettres familières": analyse et perspectives*, in *Charles de Brosses* 1777–1977, Actes du Colloque de Dijon, 3–7 mai 1977, Textes recueillis par J.-C. Garreta, Slakine, Geneva, 1981, pp. 15–34.
Canetti, E., *Crowds and Power*, translated by Carol Stewart, Continuum, New York, 1978.
Canetti, E., *The Conscience of Words*, translated by Joachim Neugroschel, Farrar, Straus and Giroux, New York, 1984.

Canguilhem, G., "Histoire des religions et histoire des sciences dans la théorie du fétichisme chez Auguste Comte," in *Études d'Histoire et de Philosophie des Sciences*, Urin, Paris, 1968, pp. 81–98.

Cantelli, G., "Mito e storia in J. Leclerc, Tournemine e Fontenelle," in *Rivista critica di storia della filosofia*, no. 3 (pp. 269–286) and 4 (pp. 385–400), 1972.

Carandini, A., *L'anatomia della scimmia. La formazione economica della società prima del capitale*, Einaudi, Turin, 1979.

Cassirer, E., *La filosofia dell'illuminismo*, La Nuova Italia, Florence, 1973.

Cassirer E., "Die Sprache und die Aufbau ded Gegenstandswelt," reprinted in *Symbol, Technik, Sprache, Aufsätze aus den Jahren 1927–1933*, edited by E. W. Orth and J. M. Krois, Meiner, Hamburg, 1985, pp. 121–151.

Chinard, G., *L'Amérique et le rêve exotique dans la littérature française au XVII et auX VIIIs iècle*, Hachette, Paris, 1913.

Cocchiara, G., *Il mito del buon selvaggio*, D'Anna, Messina-Florence, 1948.

Comte, A., *Cours de Philosophie positive* (1830), t. V, 52 Leçon, Schleicher, Paris, 1908 (translated and adapted by H. Martineau: *The Positive Philosophy of Auguste Comte*, Chapman, London, 1853).

Comte, A., *Considérations philosophiques sur les sciences et les savants (1825)*, in *Écrits de jeunesse*, Mouton, Paris-La Haye, 1970, pp. 324–325 (translated by H. D. Mutton and F. Harrison, *Early Essays on Social Philosophy*, Routledge, London [1911]); *Cours vols IV–V*.

de Condillac, E. Bonnot, *Traité des systèmes* (1749). *Philosophical Writings of Etienne Bonnot, Abbé de Condillac*, translated by Franklin Philip, Lawrence Erlbaum, Hillsdale, NJ, 1982–1987, 2 volumes, vol. I (1982).

Constant, B., *De la Religion considérée dans sa source, ses formes et ses développements*, Bossange, Paris, 1824–1831, 5 volumes.

van Dale, A., *Lettre*, in *Nouvelles de la République des Lettres*, mai 1687, article I, Henry Desbordes, Amsterdam, 1687, pp. 459–487.

van Dale, A., *De Oraculis Veterum Ethnicorum Dissertationes Duae*, Apudu Henr cum Vidvam Theodori Boom, Amsterdam, 1700, 2nd edition.

van Dale, A., *Dissertatio super Sanchoniatone*, in *Dissertatio super Aristea*, Joannis Wolters, Amsterdam, 1705, pp. 472–506.

Dalton, G., *Primitive, Archaic and Modern Economies: Essays of Karl Polanyi*, Beacon Press, Boston, 1968.

David, M. V., *Le débat sur les écritures et l'hiéroglyphe aux XVII et XVIII siècles*, Bibliothèqueg énéraled el 'École pratiqued esH autes Études,P aris,1 965.

David, M., "Lettres inédites de Diderot et de Hume écrites de1755 à 1763 au président de Brosses," *Revue Philosophique*, no. 2, April–June, 1966, pp. 135–144.

David, M., "La notion de fétichisme chez Auguste Comte et l'œuvre du président de Brosses 'Du culte des dieux fétiches'," *Revue de l'Histoire des Religions*, no. 2, April–June, 1967, pp. 211–212.

David, M., "Histoire des religions et philosophie au XVIII siècle: le président de Brosses, David Hume et Diderot," *Revue Philosophique* no. 2, April–June, 1974, pp. 145–160.

David, M., *Le président de Brosses historien des religions et philosophe*, in *Charles de Brosses 1777–1977*, Actes du Colloque de Dijon, 3–7 mai 1977, Textes recueillis par J.-C. Garreta, Slatkine, Geneva, 1981, pp. 123–140.

Defoe, D., *An Essay Upon Projects*, Arc Manor, Rockville, MD, 2008.

de Martino, E., *La fine del mondo. Contributo allanalisi delle apocalissi culturali*, edited by Clara Gallino, Einaudi, Turin, 1977.
Detienne, M., *L'invention de la mythologie*, Gallimard, Paris, 1981.
Doroszewski, W., "Alcune osservazioni sui rapporti tra la sociologia e la linguistica: E. Durkheim e F. de Saussure," in multiple authors, *Il linguaggio*, Dedalo, Bari, 1976, pp. 221–231.
Duchet, M., *Anthropologie et histoire au siècle des lumières*, Albin Michel, Paris, 1971.
Duchet, M., "Discours ethnologique et Discours historique: le texte de Lafitau," *Studies on Voltaire and XVIIIth Century*, vol. VLII, 1976, pp. 607–623.
Dumont, L., *Homo aequalis. Genèse et épanouissement de l'idéologie économique*, Gallimard, Paris 1977 (in English: *From Mandeville to Marx: Genesis and Triumph of Economic Ideology*, University of Chicago Press, Chicago, 1977).
Dumont, L., *Essais sur l'individualisme*, Seuil, Paris, 1983.
Dupuis, C. F., *Origine de tous les cultes*, Agasse, Paris, 1791.
Dupuis, C. F., *Abrégéd e l'origined et ous lesc ultes,* Agasse, Paris, 1796 (in English: *The Origin of all Religious Worship*, C.C.W. Müller, New Orleans, 1872).
Durkheim, E., *Leçons des ociologie*, P.U.F., Paris, 1950.
Easton, D. and Guddat, Kurt H. (ed.), *Writings of the Young Marx on Philosophy and Society*, Hackett Publishing Company, Indianapolis, 1997.
Eco, U., "The influence of Roman Jakobson on the development of Semiotics" (1981), in *Classics of Semiotics*, edited by M. Krampen, K. Oehler et al., Plenum Press, New York and London, 1987, pp. 109–127.
Eissfeldt, O., *Sanchunjaton von Berut und Ilumilku von Ugarit*, Niemeyer, Halle, 1952.
Eliade, M., *The Quest. History and Meaning in Religion,* Chicago University Press, Chicago and London, [1969] 1984.
Fadini, U., "Attraverso il feticismo radicale," *Millepiani*, no. 21, 2002, pp. 63–77.
Febvre, L., "Civilisation: évolution d'un mot et d'un group d'idées" ("Civilisation, le mot, l'idée"), in *I Semaine Internationale de Synthèse*, vol. 2, Alcan, Paris, 1930, now in *Pour une histoire à part entière*, Seupen, Paris, 1962.
Feldman, B. and Richardson, R., *The Rise of Modern Mythology 1680–1860*, Indiana University Press, Bloomington, 1972.
Ferguson, A., *An Essay on the History of Civil Society*, Noulter Grieson, Dublin, 1767, Cambridge University Press, Cambridge, 1995.
Feuerbach, L., *Das Wesen des Christenthums*, Berlin, 1956, 2 volumes.
Finley, M. I., *The World of Odysseus* (1954), New York Review of Books, New York, 2002.
Finzi, R., "The Theory of Historical stages in Turgot and Quesnay," *The Economic Review*, vol. 33, no. 2, April 1982, pp. 109–118.
Von Foerster, H., *Notes pour une épistémologie des objets vivants,* in *L'unité de l'homme*, edited by E. Morin and M. Piattelli Palmarini, Seuil, Paris, 1974, vol. II.
de Fontenelle, B., *Histoire de Oracles (1686)*, in *Oeuvres*, Saillant, Paris, 1767, vol. II.
de Fontenelle, B., *De l'Origine des Fables* (1724), edited by J. R. Carré, Alcan, Paris, 1932.
de Fontenelle, B., *On the Origin of Fables*, in *The Rise of Modern Mythology*, edited by Burton Feldman and Robert D. Richardson. Indiana University Press, Bloomington, Indianapolis, 1972.

Foucault, M., *Le mots et les choses*, Gallimard, Paris, 1966.
Fourmont, E., *Réflexions sur l'Origine, l'Histoire et la Succession des Ancien Peuples*, Paris, 1747 (2nd) (1st edition 1735), 2 volumes.
Freedberg, D., *The Power of Images*, University of Chicago Press, Chicago, 1989.
Freedberg, D. and Gallese, V., "Motion, Emotion and Empathy in Esthetic Experience," *Trends in Cognitive Sciences*, vol. 11, 2007, pp. 197–203.
Freud, S., *Totem and Taboo*, translated by A. A. Brill, Moffat, New York, 1918.
Freud, S., *Drei Abhandlungen zur Sexualtheorie (1905)*, in *Gesammelte Werke*, V Bd., Frankfurt am Main, 1972 (5th edition), pp. 52–54 (translated by A. A. Brill, *Three Contributions to the Theory of Sex*, Nervous and Mental Disease Publishing, New York and Washington, 1920, pp. 1–35).
Freud, S., *Fetischismus* (1927), in *GW*, XIV Bd., pp. 301–317.
Freud,S ., *Die Ichspaltung in Abwehrvorgang*, in *GW*, XVII Bd., pp. 59–62.
Freud, S., "The Schreber Case. Psychoanalytic Remarks on an Autobiographically Described Case of Paranoia (Dementia Paranoides)," in *The Schreber Case*, translated by Andrew Webber, London, Penguin, 2002.
Gallese, V. and Freedberg, D., "Mirror and Canonical Neurons Are Crucial Elements in Esthetic Response," *Trends in Cognitive Sciences*, vol. 11, 2007, p. 411.
Gargani, A. G., *Introduzione a Wittgenstein*, Laterza, Bari, 1973.
Gargani, A. G., *Wittgenstein. Musica, parola, gesto*, Cortina, Milano, 2008.
Garin, E., "Alla scoperta del 'diverso': i selvaggi americani e saggi cinesi," in *Rinascite e rivoluzioni. Movimenti culturali dal XIV al XVIII secolo*, Laterza, Bari, 1976, pp. 327–362.
Gautier, T., "The Dead in Love" (1836), in *Demons of the Night: Tales of the Fantastic, Madness and the Supernatural*, edited by Joan C. Kessler, The University of Chicago Press, Chicago, 1995.
De Gebelin, C., *Monde Primitif*, chez l'auteur, Paris, 1773.
van Gennep, A., *Religions, Moeurs et Légendes. Essais d'ethnographie et de linguistique*, V série, Paris, 1914.
Gerbi, A., *La disputa del Nuovo Mondo. Storia di una polemica 1750–1900*, Ricciardi, Milan-Naples, 1983.
Gliozzi, G., *La scoperta dei selvaggi*, Principato, Milan, 1971.
Gliozzi, G., *Adamo e il Nuovo Mondo*, La Nuova Italia, Florence, 1977.
Gliozzi, G., "Il 'Nuovo Mondo' nella cultura del Seicento," in multiple authors, *L'Europa cristiana nel rapporto con le altre culture nel secolo XVII*. La Nuova Italia, Florence, 1978, pp. 327–362.
Godelier, M., "Objet et méthodes de l'anthropologie économique," *L'Homme*, vol. 5, no. 2, 1965, pp. 31–91.
Godelier, M., *Perspectives in Marxist Anthropology* (1973), translated by Robert Brain, Cambridge University Press, Cambridge, New York, Melbourne, 1977.
Godelier, M., "Primitivo," in *Enciclopedia*, Einaudi, Turin, 1981, vol. X.
Goetz, J., *Lesperienza di Dio nei primitivi*, Morcelliana, Brescia, 1983.
Goguet, A. Y., *De l'Origine des Loix, des Arts et des Sciences; et de leurs progrès chez les anciens Peuples*, Desaint & Saillant, Paris, 1758, 3 volumes.
Gossiaux, P. P., *De Brosses: le fétichisme, de la démonologie à la linguistique*, in *Ch. de Brosses 1777–1977*, Actes du Colloque de Dijon, 3–7 mai 1977, Textes recueillis par J.-C. Garreta, Geneva, 1981, pp. 167–185.

Gregory, R. L., *Eye and Brain, The Psychology of Seeing* (1966), Oxford University Press, Oxford, 1998.
Grendi, E., *Polanyi*, Etas, Milan, 1978.
Guidieri, R., *L'abondance des pauvres*, Seuil, Paris, 1984.
Gusdorf, G., *De l'histoire des sciences à l'histoire de la pensée*, Payot, Paris, 1966.
Gusdorf, G., *Les principes de la pensée au siècle des Lumières*, Payot, Paris, 1971.
Harris, M., *The Rise of Anthropological Theory. A History of Theories of Culture*, Routledge and Kegan Paul, London, 1968.
Harris, M., *Cultural Materialism. The Struggle for a Science of Culture*, Random House, New York, 1979.
Hazard, P., *The Crisis of the European Mind, 1680–1715*, New York Review Books Classics, New York, 2013.
Hegel, G. W. F., *Die Vernunft in der Geschichte,* von J. Hoffmeister, Bd. XVIII/A, Hamburg, 1955 (translated by H. B. Nisbet, Lectures on the Philosophy of World History, Cambridge University Press, Cambridge, 1975).
Hegel, G. W. F., *Vorlesungen über die Philosophie der Religionen*, Dunker u. Humblott, Berlin, 1840, translated by J. C. Sanderson, *Lectures on the Philosophy of Religion*, K. Paul Trench Trübner, London, 1895.
Herder, J. C., *Ideen zur Philosophie der Geschichte der Menschheit*(1784–1791).
Hervé, G., "Débuts de l'Ethnographie au XVIII siècle (1701–1765)," *Revue de l'Ecole d'anthropologie*, November, XIX, 1909, pp. 345–366.
Hobbes, T., *Leviathan* (1651), *English Works*, London, vol. III, John Bohn, London, 1839 (reprint Aalen 1962).
Hobbes, T., *Elements of Law Natural and Politic* (1640), New York, Routledge, 2013.
Hodgen, M. T., *Early Anthropology in the Sixteenth and Seventeenth Century*, University of Pensylvania Press, Philadelphia, 1964.
Hölscher, U., "Eredità di concezioni cosmogoniche in Esiodo," in multiple authors, *Esiodo*, edited by G. Arrighetti, Mursia, Milan, 1975, pp. 127–135.
Home, H. (Lord Kames), *Sketches of the History of Man* (1774), Tournelsen, Basil, 1796, 4 volumes.
Huet, P. D., *Demonstratio Evangelica ad serenissimum Delphini*, Huet Stephanum Michallet, Parisiis, 1679.
Hume, D., *Philosophical Essays Concerning Human Understanding* (1748), Millar, London.
Hume, D., *Natural History of Religion* (1757), with an Introduction by John M. Robertson, London, A. and H. Bradlaugh Bonner, 1889.
Humphreys, S. C., "History, Economics, and Anthropology: The Work of Karl Polanyi," in *History and Theory*, vol. VIII, no. 2, 1969, pp. 165–212.
Iacono, A. M., *Paura e meraviglia. Storie filosofiche del XVIII secolo*, Rubbettino, Catanzaro, 1998.
Iacono, A. M., *Attorno al concetto di rappresentazione perspicua. Spengler e Wittgenstein*, in *Goethe, Schopenhauer, Nietzsche. Saggi in memoria di Sandro Barbera*, ETS, Pisa, 2012.
Iacono, A. M., *L'evento e l'osservatore*, ETS, Pisa, 2013.
Iofrida, M., *La filosofia di J. Toland*, Angeli, Milan, 1983.
Jacobson, R., "Coup d'œil sur le développement de la sémiotique," in *A Semiotic Landscape. Proceedings of the First Congress of the International Association of*

Semiotic Studies, Milan, June 1974, edited by S. Chatman, U. Eco, and J. M. Klinkenberg, Mouton, The Hague, 1979, pp. 3–19.

Kanceff, E., *Notes sur l'histoire des Lettres familières sur l'Italie*, in *Charles de Brosses 1777–1977, Actes du Colloque de Dijon, 3–7 mai 1977*, Textes recueillis par J.-C. Garreta, Geneva, 1981, pp. 35–46.

Kant, I., *Die Religion innerhalb der Grenzen der blossen Vernunft*, in Werke, Berlin, 1907, VIB d., pp. 177–180. *Religion within the Boundaries of Mere Reason and Other Writings*, translated and edited by Allen Wood, Cambridge University Press, Cambridge, 1998.

Koselleck, R., "Il secolo XVIII come inizio dell'età moderna," *Studi Settecenteschi*, no. 3–4, 1982–1983, pp. 9–23.

Krader, L. (ed.) *The Ethnological Notebooks of Karl Marx*, Van Gorcum, Assen, 1974.

Krader, L., "Evoluzione, rivoluzione e Stato: Marx e il pensiero etnologico," in *Storia del marxismo*, I, *Il Marxismo ai tempi di Marx*, Einaudi, Turin, 1978, pp. 221–244.

Krader, L. and Kelley, D. R., "Introduction" to "The Science of Anthropology: An Essay on the Very Old Marx," *Journal of the History of Ideas*, no. 2, 1984, pp. 245–262.

Kuhn, T., *The Structure of Scientific Revolutions*, University of Chicago Press, Chicago, 1962.

Labat, J. B., *Voyage du Chevalier des Marchais en Guinée, Isles voisines et Cayenne*, Aux dépens de la compagnie des Jesuites, Amsterdam, 1731 (1st edition in 1730, Paris, volume I), 4 volumes.

Lacan, J., *Le séminaire de Jacques Lacan, Livre IV: La relation d'objet* (1956–1957), edited by J. A. Miller, Seuil, Paris, 1994.

Lafitau, J. F., *Moeurs des sauvages américains comparées aux moeurs des premiers temps*, Saugrain et Charles-Estienne Hochereau, Paris, 1724, vol. 1.

Lafitau, J. F., *Customs of the American Indians Compared with the Customs of Primitive Times*, edited by W. N. Fenton and E. L. Moore, Champlain Society, Toronto 1974, vol. I, 1977, vol. II.

Landucci, S., *I filosofi e i selvaggi (1580–1780)*, Laterza, Bari, 1972.

Lang, A., *Myth, Ritual and Religion*, Longman, London, 1887, 2 volumes.

Latour, B., *Petite réflexion sur le culte moderne des dieux faitiches*, Synthékabo, Paris, 1996.

Leclerc, J., *Bibliothèque choisie, pour servir de suite à la Bibliothèque universelle*, H. Schelte, Amsterdam, 1704, vol. III.

van der Leeuw, G., *Phänomenologied elR eligion*,M ohr,T übingen,1 956.

Lemay, E., "Histoire de l'Antiquité et Découverte du Nouveau Monde chez le auteurs du XVIII siecle," *Studies on Voltaire*, vol. CLI-CLV, 1976, pp. 1313–1328.

Lemay, E., "Introduction," in Lafitau, *Moeurs des sauvages américains* (textes choisis), Maspero, Paris, 1983, 2 volumes.

Le Rond D'Alembert, J. B. and Diderot, D. *Encyclopédie,* https://encyclopédie.unichicago.edu.

Leroy, Ch. G., *Lettres philosophiques sur l'intelligence et la perfectibilité des animaux, avec quelques lettres sur lhomme*, Paris, 1802.

Lévi Strauss, C., "Introduction," in M. Mauss, *Sociologie et anthropologie*, P.U.F., Paris, 1950 (translated by F. Baker, *Introduction to the Work of Marcel Mauss*, Routledge & Kegan Paul, London, 1987).

LéviStrauss, C., *Totemism*, Beacon Press, Boston, 1963.
Lévi Strauss, C., "L'analyse structurale en linguistique et en anthropologie," "Langage et société," "Linguistique et anthropologie," "La notion de structure en ethnologie," contained in *Anthropologie structurale* I, Plon, Paris, 1974.
Loewenstamm, S. E., *Sanchuniaton, Pauly-Wissowa*, Suppl. XIV, Druckenmüller, München, 1974, pp. 593–598.
Lombardo, M.G., "La filosofia della religione di William Warburton," *Studi Settecenteschi*, cit., pp. 119–127.
Lotman, J. M., *Universe of the Mind. A Semiotic Theory of Culture* (translated by A. Shukman), Tauris, London and New York, [1990] 2001.
Lotman, J. M., "Painting and the Language of Theater: Notes on the Problem of Ironic Rhetoric" (1978), in *Tekstura: Russian Essays on Visual Culture*, translated by Alla Efimov, edited by Lev Manovich and Alla Yefimov, Chicago University Press, Chicago, 1993.
Lovejoy, A. O. and Boas, G., *Primitivism and Related Ideas in Antiquity*, Johns Hopkins University Press, Baltimore, 1955.
Loyer, G., *Relation du Royaume d'Issini, Côte d'Or, païs de Guinée, en Afrique*, Seneuze et Morel, Paris, 1714.
Lubbock, J., *The Origin of Civilization and the Primitive Condition of Man*, Appleton, New York, 1871.
Luhmann, N., *Political Theory in the Welfare State*, de Gruyter, New York, 1990, translated by John Bednarz Jr.
Luporini, C., "Critica della politica e critica dell'economia politica in Marx," *Critica marxista*, no. 1, 1978, pp. 17–50.
Malinowski, B., "The Primitive Economics of the Trobriand Islanders," *The Economic Journal*, vol. 31, March 1921, pp. 1–16.
Malinowski, B., *Argonauts of the Western Pacific*, George Routledge, London, 1922.
Malinowski, B., *Magic, Science and Religion and Other Essays* (1948), Anchor Books, New York, Doubleday, 1954.
de Mandeville, D., *The Fable of the Bees: or, Private Vices, Public Benefits*, edited by F. B. Kaye, Clarendon, Oxford, 1966, 2 volumes.
Manuel, F., *The Eighteenth Century Confronts the Gods*, Harvard University Press, Cambridge, MA, 1959.
Manuel, F. E., *The Prophets of Paris*, Harvard University Press, Cambridge, MA, 1962.
Marramao, G., *Potere e secolarizzazione. Le categorie del tempo*, Editori Riuniti, Rome, 1983.
Marx, K., *Karl Marx and Frederick Engels: Selected Correspondence, 1846–1895*, translated by Donna Torr, International Publishers, New York, 1942.
Marx, K., *Economic and Philosophic Manuscripts* of 1844, translated by Martin Milligan from the German text, revised by Dirk J. Struik, International Publishers, New York, 1964, contained in *Marx/Engels, Gesamtausgabe*, Abt. 1, Bd. 3.
Marx, K., *Grundrisse*, Diez Ferlag, Berlin, 1953; *Foundations of the Critique of Political Economy*, translated by Martin Nicolaus, Penguin, London, 1973.
Marx, K., *Collected Works*, New York, International Publisher, 1975.

Marx, K., *Texts on Method*, translated by T. Carver, Blackwell, Oxford, 1975.
Marx, K., *A Contribution to the Critique of Political Economy*, Progress Publishers, Moscow, 1977.
Marx, K., *Marginal Notes on Adolph Wagners* "Lehrbuch der politischen Ökonomie," in The *Collected Works of Karl Marx and Frederick Engels*, International Publishers, New York, 1989 (1874–1883), vol. 24, 50 volumes.
Marx, K., *Das Kapital. Kritik der politischen Oekonomie (1867)*, I Bd., Dietz Verlag, Berlin, 1977, B. I, K. 1,4, pp. 85–98 (translated by B. Fowkes, *Capital. A Critique of Political Economy*, Vol. 1, Harmondsworth, Penguin, in association with New Left Review, London, [1976] 1990).
Marx, K., *Early Political Writings*, Cambridge Texts in the History of Political Thought, edited by Joseph O'Malley, Cambridge University Press, Cambridge, 1994.
Maturana, H., "Stratégies cognitives," in *L'unité de l'homme*, edited by E. Morin and M. Piattelli Palmarini, Seuil, Paris 1974, vol. II.
Maturana, H. R. and Varela, F. J., *Autopoiesis and Cognition. The Realization of Living*, D. Reidel Publishing Company, Dordrecht, 1980.
Mauss, M., *The Gift*, English edition first published in 1954 by Cohen & West, London.
Mauss, M., *L'art et le mythe d'après M. Wundt (1908)*, in *Oeuvres*, vol. II, Minuit, Paris, 1969, pp. 195–227.
Mauss, M., "Les civilisations: éléments et formes," in *Oeuvres*, vol. II, Minuit, Paris, 1969, pp. 456–447.
Mauss, M., *Essay sur le don*, PUF, Paris, 2007.
Macpherson, C. B., *The Political Theory of Possessive Individualism: Hobbes to Locke*, Oxford University Press, Oxford, 1962.
McLennan, J. F., "The Worship of Animals and Plants" (1869), in *Studies in Ancient History: The Second Series*, Macmillan, London, 1896.
McNiven Hine, E., *A Critical Study of Condillac's Traité des systems*, M. Nijhoff, The Hague–Boston–London, 1979.
Meek, Ronald L. (trans. and ed.) *On Universal History, Turgot on Progress, Sociology and Economics*, Cambridge University Press, Cambridge, 1973.
Meek, R. L., *Social Science and the Ignoble Savage*, Cambridge University Press, Cambridge, 1976.
Meiners, C., *Allgemeine kritische Geschichte der Religionen*, Verlag der Helwingischen Hofs Buchhandlung, Hannover, 1806–1807, I Bd., pp. 142–143.
Métraux, A., "Précurseurs de l'ethnologie en France du XVI au XVIII siècle," *Cahiers d'histoire mondiale*, vol. VII no. 3, 1963, pp. 721–738.
Millar, J., *The Origin of the Distinction of Ranks* (1771), in W. C. Lehmann, *John Millar of Glasgow*, Cambridge University Press, Cambridge, 1960 (reprint of the third 1779 edition).
Minerbi Belgrado, A., *Materialismo e origine della religione nel '700*, Sansoni, Florence, 1977.
Mistura, S. (ed.), *Figure del feticismo*, Einaudi, Turin, 2001.
Momigliano, A., "The Place of Herodotus in the History of Historiography," in *Secondo contributo alla storia degli studi classici,* Edizioni di storia e letteratura, Rome, 1960, pp. 29–44.

Momigliano, A., "Interpretazioni minime VII," in *Annali della Scuola Normale Superiore di Pisa* Pisa, 1980, serie III, vol. X, 4, pp. 1227–1231.

Momigliano, A., *Sui fondamenti della storia antica*, Einaudi, Turin, 1984.

Moravia, S., *La scienza dell'uomo nel Settecento*, Laterza, Bari, 1978.

Moscati, S., *Il mondo dei Fenici*, Mondadori, Milan, 1979.

Moscovici, S., "A propos de quelques travaux d'Adam Smith sur l'histoire et la philosophie des sciences," *Revue d'Histoire des Sciences et de leur applications*, no. 9, 1956, pp. 1–20.

Müller, F. M., *Natural Religion. The Gifford Lectures* 1888, Longmans, London, 1889.

Negri, A., *Marx oltre Marx. Quaderno di lavoro sui Grundrisse*, Feltrinelli, Milan, 1970.

Nisbet, R. A., *Social Change and History. Aspects of the Western Theory of Development*, Oxford University Press, New York, 1969.

Nisbet, R. A., *Lectures on the Philosophy of World History*, Cambridge University Press, Cambridge, 1975.

Parrinder, G., *African Traditional Religion*, Hutchinson, London, 1954.

Pastine, D., *Le origini del poligenismo e Isaac Lapeyrére*, Miscellanea Seicento, I, Le Monnier, Florence, 1971.

Pastine, D., *La nascita dell'idolatria*, La Nuova Italia, Florence, 1979.

Paton, L. B., *Sanchuniaton*, in *Encyclopaedia of Religion and Ethics*, Charles Sgribner's Sons, New York, 1920, vol. XI, pp. 178–181.

De Pauw, C., *Recherches philosophiques sur les Américains*, J. M. Place, Londres, 1774, .t. II.

Peirce, C. S., *Peirce on Signs. Writings on Semiotic*, edited by J. Hoopes, University of North Carolina Press, Chapel Hill, 1991, p. 252 (article originally published in 1906).

Pietz, W., "The problem of the fetish," in *Res*, no. 9, 1985, pp. 5–17; no. 13, 1987, pp. 23–45; no. 16, 1988, pp. 105–123.

Pietz, W., *Lef étiche.G énéalogied 'unp roblème*, Kargo & L'Éclat, Paris, 2005.

Pizzorusso, A.,"Fontenelle e l'idea del progresso," *Belfagor*, no. 2, 1962, pp. 150–180.

Polanyi, K., *The Great Transformation: The Political and Economic Origins of Our Time*, Beacon Press, Boston, 1944.

Polanyi, K., *The Livelihood of Man*, Academic Press, New York, 1977.

Pouillon, J., "Fétiches sans Fétichisme," in *Objects du fétichisme, Nouvelle Revue de Psychanalyse*, no. 2, 1970, pp. 135–147.

Prévost, A. F., *Histoire générale des voyages, ou nouvelle collection de toutes les relations de voyages*, P. de Hondt, La Haye, 1747, vol. IV, Book VIII.

Radcliffe-Brown, A., *Method in Social Anthropology*, University of Chicago Press, London–Chicago, 1958.

Rank, O., *DerD oppelgänger*, Leipzig–Wien, 1914.

Remotti, F., "Lewis H. Morgan e lo studio della società antica," *Sociologia del diritto*, vol. X, 1982/1983, pp. 92–93.

Robertson, W., *History of America* (1777), in *Works*, Cadel, London, 1827, vol. VI.

Rosdolsky, R., *Genesi e struttura del 'Capitale' di Marx*, Laterza, Bari, 1975, vol. I, pp. 161–162.

Rossi, P., *Sterminate antichità. Studi vichiani*, Pisa, 1969.
Rossi, P., *I segni del tempo*, Feltrinelli, Milan, 1979.
Rossi, P., "Cultura' e civiltà come modelli descrittivi," in *Cultura e antropologia*, Einaudi, Turin, 1983, pp. 76–104.
Rousseau, J. J., *Émile ou de l'éducation* (1762), Garnier-Flammarion, Paris, 1966 (translated by B. Foxley, *Emile*, Dent, London, 1974).
Rubin, I. I., *Essays on Marx's Theory of Value*, Aakar Books, Delhi, 2007.
Sachs, I., "Selvaggio, barbaro, civilizzato," in *Enciclopedia*, Einaudi, Turin, 1981, vol. XII.
Sahlins, M., *Stone Age Economics*, Aldine de Gruyter, New York, 1972.
Sahlins, M., *Culture and Practical Reason*, University of Chicago Press, Chicago, 1976.
Sahlins, M., *Stone Age Economics* (1974), Routledge, London, 2004.
Sapir, E., "The Unconscious Patterning of Behaviour in Society," in *Selected Writings of Edward Sapir in Language, Culture and Personality*, edited by D. Mandelbaum, University Press of California, Berkeley, 1949, pp. 544–559.
Sapir, E., *Culture, Language and Personality: Selected Essays*, edited by David Goodman Mandelbaum, University of California Press, Berkeley, 1985.
Schmidt, A., *The Concept of Nature in Marx*, Verso Books, London, 2013.
Schmidt, G., *Manuale di storia comparata delle religioni*, Morcelliana, Brescia, 1934.
Scribano, M. E., *Natura umana e società competitiva. Studio su Mandeville*, Feltrinelli, Milan, 1980.
Sebag, L., *Marxisme et structuralisme*, Payot, Paris, 1964.
Shanin. T. (ed.), *Late Marx and the Russian Road, Marx and the "peripheries of capitalism,"* Monthly Review Press, New York, 1983.
Sismonde de Sismondi, J. C., *New Principles of Political Economy, or, Of Wealth in its Relation to Population* (1819), translated and annotated by Richard Hyse, Transaction Publishers, New Brunswick and London, 1991.
Smith, A., *Lectures on Justice, Police, Revenue and Arms*, edited by E. Cannan, Clarendon, Oxford, 1896 (reprint, Kelley, New York, 1964).
Smith, A., "The Principles which Lead and Direct Philosophical Enquiries," in *The Early Writings of Adam Smith*, edited by J. R. Lindgren, New York, 1967 (published posthumously in 1795).
Smith, A., *Lectures on Jurisprudence* (Report 1762–1763), edited by R. L. Meek, D. D. Raphael, and P. G. Stein, Clarendon, Oxford, 1978, vol. V, *The Glasgow Edition of the Works and Correspondence of Adam Smith*.
Smith, A., *Saggi filosofici*, edited by P. Berlanda, Angeli, Milan, 1984.
Spencer, H., *Principles of Sociology*, London, 1873.
Spinoza, B., *The Chief Works of Benedict de Spinoza*, translated from the Latin with an Introduction by R. H. M. Elwes, *Tractatus Theologico-Politicus*, George Bell and Sons, London, 1891, vol. I, Chapter V.
Stewart, D., "Account of the Life and Writings of Adam Smith," in A. Smith, edited by I. S. Ross, Clarendon, Oxford, 1980, vol. III, The Glasgow Edition.
Tarot, C., *De Durkheim à Mauss. L'invention du symbolique*, La Découverte, Paris, 1999.
Tega, W., *Arbor Scientiarum*, Il Mulino, Bologna, 1984.

Thompson, E. P., "Time, Work-Discipline, and Industrial Capitalism," in *Past and Present*, no. 38 (December, 1967), pp. 56–97.
Thomson, H. F., "Adam Smith's Philosophy of Science," *Quarterly Journal of Economics*, no. 79, 1965, pp. 212–233.
Todorov, T., *La conquête de l'Amerique. La question de l'autre*, Seuil, Paris, 1982.
Toland, J., *Letters to Serena* (1704), Italian translation by E. Lecaldano, Laterza, Bari, 1977.
Troiani, L., *L'opera storiografica di Filone da Byblos*, Goliardica, Pisa, 1974.
Turgot, A. R. J. *Plan de deux discours sur l'histoire universelle (1751)*, in *Oeuvres*, edited. by G. Schelle, Alcan, Paris, 1913, vol. I.
Tylor, E. B. *Primitive Culture* (1871), Brentano, New York, 1924, vol. I.
Valeri, V., "Objets du Fetichisme," *Nouvelle Revue de Psycanalyse*, no. 2, 1970.
Valeri, V., "Feticcio," in *Enciclopedia*, Einaudi, Turin, 1979, vol. VI.
Varela, F. J., *Principles of biological Autonomy*, Elsevier, New York, 1979.
Vernant, J. P., *Mythee ts ociétée nG rècea ncienne*, Maspero, Paris, 1974.
Vernant, J. P., *The Origins of Greek Thought* (1962), Cornell University Press, New York, 1982.
Verra, V., *Mito, rivelazione e filosofia in J.C. Herder e nel suo tempo*, Marzorati, Milan, 1966.
Viano, C. A., "La ragione, l'abbondanza e la credenza," in *Crisi della ragione. Nuovi modelli nel rapporto tra sapere e attività umane*, edited by A. Gargani, Einaudi, Turin, 1979, pp. 305–366.
Vico, G. B., *La Scienza Nuova l'edizione del 1744 con le varianti dell'edizione del 1730 e di due redazioni inedite e corredata di note storiche*, edited by F. Nicolini, Laterza, Bari, 1916, vol. III.
Vico, G. B., *Scienza nuova seconda* (1730/1744), *The New Science of Giambattista Vico*, revised translation of the third edition by Thomas Goddard Bergin and Max Harold Fisch, Cornell University Press, Ithaca, 1948; Cornell Paperbacks, 1976.
Vidal Naquet, P., *Le Cru, l'Enfant grec et le Cuit*, edited by J. Le Goff and P. Nora, *Faire de l'histoire*, Gallimard, Paris, 1974, vol. III, pp. 137–168.
Vieira, D., *Grande Diccionario Portuguez ou Thesouro da Lingua Portugueza*, Chardron, Porto, 1873, vol. III.
Voltaire, *Essai sur les moeurs et l'esprit des nations*, edited by R. Pomeau, Garmer-Flammarion, Paris, 1963, vol. I.
Warburton, W., *The Divine Legation of Moses Demonstrated*, Fletcher Gyles, London, 1738–1741, vols. I–II.
Warburton, W., *Essai sur les hiéroglyphes des Egyptiens*, translated by L. de Malpeines, Hippolyte-Louis Guerin, Paris, 1744.
Wiener, N., *Cybernetics*, MIT Press, Cambridge, MA, 1965.
Wittgenstein, L., *Philosophische Untersuchungen*, Oxford, 1953 (edited and translated by G. E. M. Anscombe, *Philosophical Investigations*, Blackwell, Oxford, 2001).
Wittgenstein, L., "Bemerkungen über Frazers 'The Golden Bough' in *Synthese*," edited by R. Rhees, XVII, 1967 (translated by J. Beversluis, "Remarks on Frazer's *Golden Bough*," in *Wittgensstein: Sources and Pespectives*, edited by C. G. Luckhardt, Cornell University Press and Harvester-Wheatsheaf, 1979,

pp. 61–81, reproduced, with minor corrections, in *Philosophical Occasions 1912–1951*, edited by J. C. Klagge and A. Nordmann, Hackett, Indianapolis and Cambridge, 1993).

Wundt, W., *Völkerpsychologie. Eine Untersuchung der Entwicklungsgesetze von Sprache, Mythus und Sitte*, Engelman, Leipzich, 1904 (translated Edward Leroy Schaub, *Elements of Folk Psychology: Outlines of a Psychological History of the Development of Mankind*, George Allen & Unwin, London, 1916).

Zizek, S., *The Plague of Fantasies*, Verso, London–New York, 1997.

Index

Acosta J. De, 155n14
Adler A., 156n28
Adorno T. W., 7
Alembert J.-B. Le Ronde De, 38, 161n85, 162n100
Althusser L., 179n21, n22
Anscombe G. E. M., 171n19
Antenhofer Ch., 152n12
Apergi F., 176n7
Aristophanes, 165n144
Aristotle, 6
Arrighetti G., 168n25
Atkinson G., 160n70
Auroux S., 166n4

Bachofen J. J., 164n116
Baczko B., 171n17
Badaloni N., 155n14, 162n102, 163n105, 168n43, 175n39
Baker F., 171n12
Balibar E., 179n21, 180n29
Baltus J. F., 155n11
Barros J., 152n1
Bartolomei S., 163n107
Bateson G., 81, 90, 96, 97, 98, 171n14, 172n29, n30
Baudelaire C., 8
Baudrillard J., 7, 122, 133, 151n9, 175n38, 176n9, 177n12, 181n30
Bayle P., 18, 27, 38, 52, 154n10, 155n18, 156n29, 159n56, 162n101
Bednarz J., 174n26

Bekker B., 12, 13, 14, 15, 19, 21, 55, 152n3, 153n5, n6, 155n14, n15
Benjamin W., 7, 174n32
Benveniste E., 153n4
Berlanda P., 165n141
Bernard J., 155n11
Bettelheim B., 152n10
Beversluis J., 170n7
Binet A., 74, 153n3, 170n71
Bloch M., 171n18
Boas G., 161n91
Bochart S., 61, 62, 168n26, n29, n31
Bonafré P., 156n28
Bosman W., 15–21, 24, 55, 154n9, 155n18, 156n19
Bossuet J. B., 78, 170n8
Böttiger C. A., 74, 103, 153n3, 169n67, 173n4
Bourdieu P., 172n38
Bradbury R. E., 155n18
Brain R., 175n41
Brewster B., 179n21
Brill A. A., 151n4, 172n26
Brosses A. De., 73–4, 169n49
Brossess Ch. De, 5, 8, 11, 12, 14–18, 20, 24–7, 48, 53–68, 70–2, 75, 86, 88–90, 103, 104, 107, 111, 119, 122, 152n3, 153n3, n5, 155n18, 158n45, 163n105, 166n3, n4, 167n4, n5, n6, n10, n11, n12, n23, 168n43, 169n49, 170n1
Brumoy P.,165n144
Bukharin N., 131, 176n1

Cagiano E., 166n3
Callander J., 167n5
Campanella T., 155n14
Canetti E., 177n14
Canguilhem G., 48, 164n123, 170n72
Cannan E., 166n160
Cantelli G., 163n111, 164n118
Carandini A., 182n48
Carolinus G., 14, 152n3, 155n16
Carré J. R., 162n104, 164n118
Casini P., 161n85
Cassirer E., 162n101, 182n44
Chardron E., 152n1
Chatman S., 172n28
Chinard G., 26, 158n44, 159n52
Cocchiara G., 160n70
Coleridge S. T., 7
Comte A., 48, 74, 104, 122, 169n66, 170n72
Condillac E. Bonnot De, 35–8, 42, 49, 161n83, n84, n85, n86, 162n96, n99, n103
Condorcet Caritat A. N. De, 171n17
Constant B., 74, 103, 113, 169n67, 173n1, n5, 174n24
Court De Gebelin A., 168n26

D'Alambert J. Le Rond, 38, 161n85, 162n100
Dale A. Van, 13–14, 21, 55, 154n10, n11, 155n11, n13, 161n95, 168n26
Dalton G., 176n7
David M., 167n6, n9, 169n47, n49, n56, n64, 170n72
David M. V., 160n81
De Martino E., 182n45
De Moraes B. H., 152n1
Debord G., 7
Defoe D., 133, 176n8
Della Porta G. B., 155n14
Democritus, 6
Dennett R. E., 75
Descartes R., 36

Destutt De Tracy A. L. C., 74, 169n64
Detienne M., 27, 158n44, 159n54, 164n119
Diderot D., 4, 65–7, 161n85
Diodorus Siculus, 35, 37, 160n81
Doroszewski W., 177n13
Droixhe D., 166n4
Duchet M., 27, 158n44, 159n55, n57, n65, 160n70, 164n117
Dumont L., 135, 139, 169n59, 171n12, 177n15
Dupuis C. F., 74, 169n63, n64
Durkheim E., 35, 160n79, 177n13

Easton D., 173n11, n13
Eco U., 172n28
Eissfeldt O., 167n25
Eliade M., 171n18
Elwes R. H. M., 154n9
Engels F., 106, 108, 110, 112, 115, 173n1, n6, 174n23
Eusebius of Caesarea, 61, 167n25, 168n27

Fadini U., 151n9
Fage J. D., 155n18
Febvre L., 153n4
Feldman B., 163n111, 167n10, 169n51, n61
Fenton W. N., 156n33, 158n44, n45, n48, 159n48, n49, n50, n58
Ferguson A., 26, 39, 158n48, 164n116
Feuerbach L., 107, 112, 173n15, n21
Finzi R., 163n107
Fisch M. H., 161n95
Foerster H. von, 171n21
Fontenelle B. Le Bovier de, 13, 14, 21, 23, 27, 28, 38–41, 44–51, 55, 56, 61, 63, 154n11, 155n11, 161n95, 162n97, n99, n101, n102, n104, 163n105, n107, n111, 164n112, n118, 165n138, n144
Foucault M., 80, 171n11, 179n22
Fourmont E., 61, 168n26, n32

Fowkes B., 172n26, 174n31
Foxley B., 169n62
Frazer J., 26
Freedberg D., 6, 151n5
Freud S., 2, 4, 6–9, 71, 74, 86–95, 151n4, n9, 172n26, n27, n34, 177n14

Galbraith J. K., 181n30
Gallese V., 151n5
Gallino C., 182n45
Gargani A. G., 151n7, 170n7, 177n12
Garin E., 160n70, 161n85
Garnier, 19, 157n41
Garreta J.-C., 166n3
Gautier T., 175n36
Gennep A. van, 26, 158n44, n45, n48, 159n51
Gerbi A., 160n70, 163n105
Gliozzi G., 157n42, 160n70, 163n105, 172n25
Goddard Bergin Th., 161n95
Godelier M., 122, 160n70, 175n41, 177n13
Goetz J., 76, 170n6
Goguet A.-Y., 26, 54, 158n48
Goodman D., 182n44
Gossiaux P. P., 167n4
Gregory R. L., 174n30
Grendi E., 176n7
Guddat K. H., 173n11
Guidieri R., 171n12
Gusdorf G., 166n154, 167n4

Hargreaves R., 151n7
Harris M., 171n21
Harrison F., 170n72
Hazard P., 153n5, 155n11
Hegel G. W. F., 74, 115, 169n68, 174n28, 179n21
Herder J. C., 26, 158n48
Herodotus, 28, 63, 164n116
Herrera A., 173n9

Hervé G., 158n44
Heyne C. G., 73, 169n61
Hobbes Th., 6, 13, 29, 37, 49, 134, 153n9, 154n9, 155n14, 161n94, n95, 177n11
Hodgen M. T., 158n44, 160n70
Hölscher U., 168n25
Hoopes J., 172n36
Huet P.-D., 33, 61, 160n72, 168n26, n28
Hume D., 5, 6, 21, 24, 37, 38, 49–56, 65–70, 73, 74, 111, 122, 151n2, n3, 162n101, 163n105, 165n138, n139, n140, n142, n144, n145, 167n6, n23, 169n49
Humphreys S. C., 176n7
Hyse R., 178n20

Iacono A. M., 151n7, 171n21
Iofrida M., 162n101

Jakobson R., 88, 94, 172n28, 176n52
Jephcott E., 174n32

Kames, Home H., Lord, 26, 54, 158n48
Kanceff E., 166n3
Kant I., 8, 18, 73, 144, 156n31, 169n60
Karady V., 170n1
Kaye F. B., 162n101
Kelley D. R., 179n25
Kessler J. C., 175n36
Kircher A., 155n14
Klagge J. C., 151n7, 170n7
Klinkenberg J. M., 172n28
Koselleck R., 160n70
Krader L., 156n25, 179n25, 180n27
Krampen M., 172n28
Krois J. M., 182n44
Kuhn Th., 82, 171n16, 173n44

Labat J.-B., 20, 157n36
Lacan J., 7, 151n9

Lafitau J.-F., 18, 19, 23, 25–36, 38–47, 49, 52, 55, 57–9, 61, 63–5, 67, 68, 72, 156n25, n32, n33, 157n34, 158n44, n45, n48, 159n48, n55, n58, n61, n65, n66, 160n71, 73, n80, 162n97, n98, 163n105, 164n116, n136, 167n19, 168n43, 169n57
Landucci S., 158n44, n45, n48, 160n70, 163n105, 169n61
Lang A., 163n111
Latour B., 9, 152n14, n15
Lecaldano E., 162n101
Leclerc J., 154n11, 155n11, 162n101, 163n111
Leeuw G. van, 152n3, 170n4
Lehmann W. C., 158n48
Lemay E., 158n44, 159n48
Leopardi G., 7
Leroy Ch. G., 74, 169n65
Lévi-Strauss C., 81, 82, 90, 96, 145, 171n12, n13, n15, n21, 177n13, 181n38
Lindgren J. R., 165n141
Loewenstamm S. E., 168n25
Lombardo M. G., 161n81
Lotman J. M., 95, 172n29, n37, 178n18
Lough W., 174n23
Lovejoy A. O., 161n91
Loyer G., 156n32
Lubbock J., 16, 74, 156n25, 170n70
Luckhardt C. G., 170n7
Lucretius, 37, 161n91, n92, n93
Luhmann N., 174n26, 177n12
Lukács G., 7
Luporini C., 175n42, 180n26

Macpherson C. B., 159n64, 178n16
Maine H. S., 179n26
Malinowski B., 31, 34, 145, 160n68, n77, 181n39
Malpeines L. de., 161n82
Mandel E., 174n31
Mandelbaum G., 177n13, 182n44

Mandeville B. de, 38, 157n36, 162n101
Manovich L., 178n18
Manuel F. E., 56, 153n5, 155n11, 162n102, 163n105, 165n138, 166n2, n4
Marchais Ch. de, 20, 21, 24, 55, 157n36
Marramao G., 158n43
Martineau H., 169n66
Marx K., 4, 7–9, 71, 74, 86–95, 101–29, 131, 139–41, 143–50, 151n8, n9, 156n25, 172n26, n27, 173n1, n2, n6, 174n23, n25, n31, n34, 175n34, n39, n40, n42, 177n13, n16, 178n17, 179n22, n23, n24, n26, 180n26, n27, n28, 181n31, n34, n40, 182n43, n45, n46
Maturana H. R., 98, 163n109, 171n21, 172n43
Mauss M., 19, 25, 34, 73, 75–9, 81, 86, 87, 90, 91, 152n11, 157n35, 160n78, 170n1, n3, 171n10, n12, 172n24
McLellan D., 177n16
McLennan J. F., 16, 74, 156n27, 164n116, 170n69
McNiven Heine E., 161n85
Meek R. L., 158n48, 159n48, 163n106, n107, n110, 166n156, n158, n159, n160, 178n17
Meinecke F., 26, 158n44, 159n53
Meiners C., 74, 103, 153n3, 169n67, 173n3
Métraux A., 158n44
Mill J., 105, 108, 109
Millar J., 26, 54, 158n48, 165n139
Miller J. A., 151n9
Milligan M., 173n19
Minerbi Belgrado A., 162n95
Mistura S., 151n9
Moebius G., 155n11
Momigliano A., 27, 28, 159n54, n59, 163n105, 168n25
Montesquieu Ch. Secondat de, 4, 26, 39

Moore E. L., 156n33, 158n44, n45, n48, 159n48, n49, n50, n58
Moravia S., 158n44, n45, 162n102
Morgan L. H., 26, 85, 159n49
Morin E., 171n21
Moscati S., 168n25
Moscovici S., 165n141
Müller F. M., 170n1
Mutton H. D., 170n72

Negri A., 181n29
Neugroschel J., 177n14
Nicolaus M., 180n26, 182n46
Nicolini F., 161n95, 163n105
Nietzsche F., 7
Nisbet H. B., 169n68
Nisbet R. A., 171n22
Nordmann A., 151n7, 170n7
Nugent Mr., 157n41

Oehler K., 172n28
O'Malley J., 173n1
Orth E. W., 182n44

Parrinder G., 167n11
Pastine D., 155n14, 157n42
Paton L. B., 167n25
Pauw C. de, 26, 39, 158n47
Pearson H. W., 160n69
Pearson R., 151n1
Peirce C. S., 94, 172n36
Pennavaja C., 175n40
Penner H. H., 152n3
Pettazzoni R., 170n4, 171n18
Philip F., 161n84
Philo of Byblos, 61
Piattelli Palmarini M., 171n21
Pietz W., 8, 152n12, n13, n15
Pirandello L., 7
Pizzorusso A., 163n111
Plato, 6
Polanyi K., 31, 160n69, 176n7
Pomeau R., 157n41
Porset C., 167n4

Pouillon J., 156n28, 170n1
Prévost A. F., 157n36
Proudhon C., 150
Pystorius, 173n2

Radcliffe-Brown A., 85, 158n45, 171n22
Rank O., 175n36
Raphael D. D., 158n48, 166n160
Remotti F., 159n49
Rhees R., 151n7, 170n7
Richardson R. D., 163n111, 167n10, 169n51, n61
Robertson J. M., 151n3, 165n138
Robertson W., 26, 158n48, 159n48
Roja R., 174n34
Rosdolsky R., 106, 173n12
Rossi Paolo, 157n36, 160n81, 164n135, 168n26
Rossi Pietro, 153n4, 171n22
Rousseau J.-J., 74, 169n62
Rubin I. I., 175n35

Sabetti A., 162n101
Sachs I., 160n70
Sahlins M., 122, 145, 149, 171n12, 174n27, 175n38, 176n2, 177n12, 181n36, 182n42, n45
Sanchuniaton, 61, 167n25, 168n25
Sanderson J. C., 170n68
Sapir E., 177n13, 182n44
Saussure F. de, 177n13
Schaub E. L., 156n26
Schelle G., 163n106
Schmidt A., 144, 181n35
Schmidt G., 170n4
Schmidt W., 76
Schreber D. P., 135
Scribano M. E., 162n101
Sebag L., 117, 174n33
Shakespeare W., 7
Shanin T., 179n23
Shukman A., 172n29
Sismondi J. C. L. Simonde de, 178n20

Smith A., 6, 26, 39, 51, 54, 74, 108, 158n48, 165n141, 166n154, n157, n158, n160, 178n20, 180n28
Smith P., 152n3
Socrates, 165n144
Spencer H., 74, 169n66
Spinoza B., 6, 13, 153n9, 154n9, 155n14, 162n101
Statius, 161n95
Stein P. G., 158n48, 166n160
Stewart C., 177n14
Stewart D., 53, 166n154
Stirner M., 115
Struik D. J., 173n19

Tarot C., 152n11
Taylor E. B., 26, 89
Tega W., 161n85
Thompson E. P., 131, 176n3
Thomson F., 165n141
Thucydides, 28, 159n60
Todorov T., 179n22
Toland J., 162n101
Torr D., 179n24
Tournemine R. J. de, 163n111
Troiani L., 168n25, n27
Turgot A. R. J., 40–3, 54, 56, 163n106, n107, 166n4, 178n20
Turner Ch., 176n9
Turner J. E., 152n3
Tylor E. B., 6, 151n4

Valeri V., 76, 152n2, 153n3, 156n28, 170n5, 171n10, 172n27

Varela F. J., 98, 163n109, 171n21, 172n43
Velazquez D., 4
Vernant J.-P., 27, 158n45, 159n54
Verra V., 169n61
Viano C. A., 161n83, 177n12
Vico G. B., 6, 26, 37, 38, 161n95, 162n102, 163n105, 168n43
Vidal-Naquet P., 27, 158n44, 159n54, n55, n60
Vieira D., 152n1
Vitruvius, 35, 37, 160n81
Voltaire (Abouet F. M.), 3, 4, 23, 26, 39, 151n1, 157n41, n42, 158n44, n46, 168n26

Wagner A., 146–8
Warburton W., 35, 37, 160n81, 161n81, n82, 168n26
Webber A., 177n14
White R., 151n7
Wiener N., 172n41
Willis J. R., 155n18
Winterbotton Th., 153n3
Wittgenstein L., 6, 83, 85, 89, 151n7, 170n7, 171n19
Wood A., 156n31
Wundt W., 16, 73, 75, 76, 78–80, 156n26, 170n2, 171n9

Yefimov A., 178n18

Zeleny M., 163n109
Zizek S., 151n9

The manufacturer's authorised representative in the EU is Springer Nature Customer Service Centre GmbH, Europaplatz 3, 69115 Heidelberg, Germany. If you have any concerns regarding our products, please contact ProductSafety@springernature.com

Printed and bound by CPI Group (UK) Ltd, Croydon, CR0 4YY
23/03/2026
02076663-0016